Latin Politics,
Global Media

Latin Politics,
Global Media

Elizabeth Fox and Silvio Waisbord, *Editors*

 *UNIVERSITY OF TEXAS PRESS, AUSTIN*

First edition, 2002

Requests for permission to reproduce material from
this work should be sent to Permissions, University
of Texas Press, Box 7819, Austin, TX 78713-7819.

⊚ The paper used in this book meets the minimum
requirements of ANSI/NISO z39.48-1992 (R1997)
(Permanence of Paper).

Library of Congress Cataloging-in-Publication Data

Latin politics, global media / Elizabeth Fox and
Silvio Waisbord, editors.— 1st ed.
    p.   cm.
Includes bibliographical references and index.
ISBN 0-292-72536-1 (alk. paper) —
ISBN 0-292-72537-x (alk. paper)
    1. Mass media—Political aspects—Latin America.
2. Mass media policy—Latin America. 3. Latin
America—Politics and government—1980– I. Fox,
Elizabeth (Fox de Cardona) II. Waisbord, Silvio R.
(Silvio Ricardo), 1961–

P95.82.L29 L38 2002
302.23'098—dc21   2001048064

To Marjorie Ferguson, who demystified globalization, and to José Antonio Mayobre, who lived within its paradoxes, in memoriam

CONTENTS

Elizabeth Fox and Silvio Waisbord

Two parallel forces, local politics and the globalization of media markets, shaped the development of Latin American media in the 1990s. Under various different circumstances technological changes and the emergence of the global market were the key factors in the development of the media in Latin America. Under other circumstances it was local politics that determined the course of ownership and content. At the cusp of a new century and in the aftermath of substantial political and economic change in the 1980s and 1990s, it is time to take a look at how local politics and media globalization shaped the recent evolution of the media in the region. The consolidation of democracy coupled with the adoption of neoliberal economic policies introduced important transformations across the region. Against the backdrop of these transformations we wanted to understand recent changes in media systems and provide in-depth analyses of the interaction of local and global dynamics in media industries.

With these goals in mind we asked a number of country specialists to consider these dynamics in the analysis of media policies. As editors we wanted to convey a sense of the dynamics of change occurring throughout the region and of the continued strengths of local and national cultures and of political interests as a countervailing or parallel force to globalization. The national chapters pick up and echo these themes, adding texture to a rich understanding of contemporary media in Latin America. The authors of the national chapters come from, and employ the tools of, varied academic traditions: politics, law, journalism, communications, and history. All these disciplines continue to be present in the study of Latin American media and are represented in the book.

Our interest was to analyze how globalization affects the historical pattern of the relationship between states and markets. How are local politics and global dynamics articulated at the country level? Has the recent process of media globalization fundamentally altered the close-knit relation between states and markets that historically has prevailed?

Considering that media globalization coincided with remarkable developments in Latin American political history—namely, the stability of
democratic institutions amid deepening social inequalities and political
unrest—what has been the impact of democratization on media policies?
These are the questions the contributors set out to answer.

In Chapter 1, we present an historical overview of the development of
media systems in Latin America. We stress that states as well as private
interests have profoundly shaped the evolution of the region's media. The
relations between them have shifted between accommodation and confrontation during both democratic and authoritarian periods. The media
have been exposed to international flows since the early beginning of
broadcasting. This pattern has intensified during the last decade as media
policies have favored the opening of media markets to global flows of
capital, technology, and programming. The old debate of public vs. private
media, which has characterized Latin American politics, has seemingly
come to an end; the private model rules almost uncontested. Confronta-
tions of the past have substantially diminished, and debates about mixed
models are almost absent from policy debates. Media markets are dominated by a few conglomerates that have tremendously benefited from the
politics of privatization and liberalization implemented during the 1990s,
and, in many cases, from proximity to governments.

In Chapter 2, Hernán Galperín observes a transformation in the relationship between the state and broadcasting in Argentina. In the 1990s
the transition occurred from a system controlled by the state but operated
commercially for profit (or loss) to a mainly privately owned and largely
deregulated broadcasting industry. This change took place under conditions of political strength and economic growth. In less than a decade,
Argentine markets shifted from a situation of limited competition (i.e.,
terrestrial broadcasting) or no competition (i.e., telecommunications) to
an open, fiercely competitive environment. The television industry was
no exception. Until 1990 it was characterized by an oligopolistic structure with tight state control on the number of companies. Advertising
revenues provided most of the funding for the system, and a nationalist
orientation pervaded industry regulation, reflected in national programming quotas and the ban on foreign investments in media industries.
Regulation was neither seriously exercised nor needed since the government of Argentina, unlike those of most other Latin American countries,
directly controlled the major television networks. The TV market thus
remained closed, underfunded, and—as in the case of other public ser-

vice industries—highly vulnerable to the changing winds of Argentine politics.

Today the picture is radically different. The major TV networks are in private hands, multichannel TV (cable or direct broadcast satellite) is found in over 50 percent of TV households, and specialized channels are mushrooming in the pay-TV sector. Competition is fierce among the major networks and between rival delivery platforms, and has sparked the revival of the national programming industry. Both infrastructure and content regulations have waned, resulting in one of the most liberal environments in the world for the television industry. In essence, the broadcasting system of yesterday—a tripartite entente between the political (and notably the military) elite, a handful of programmers, and national advertisers—has been eroded by technological, political, and economic transformations. The nationalist model of TV predominant up to the mid-1980s has given way to a competitive, internationalized market environment. The changes that occurred in Argentina, however, were not the result of public debate or of a new legal framework for broadcasting. In fact, Galperín notes a lack of public accountability in the reform process. The most important changes to broadcasting were part of an omnibus reform law, the Law of State Reform, passed in 1989, that, according to Galperín, "overhauled state-industry relations across all economic sectors." The law required the privatization of state-owned commercial TV stations and eliminated cross-media ownership limitations. However, he observes: "Aside from the privatizations, none of the major changes were introduced through open decision-making procedures, either through parliamentary debate, judicial review, or consultation with intermediate associations representative of society at large. It is telling that after fifteen years of democratic government in Argentina, and despite many failed attempts (see Albornoz, Mastrini, and Mestman 1996), not a single law specific to communication industries was passed by Congress."

Galperín's concerns about the lack of democracy in media policies are echoed in Roberto Amaral's analysis of Brazilian media. In Chapter 3, Amaral worries about the consequences of globalization—namely, runaway media concentration and increasing division between the haves and have-nots. Amaral's pessimistic perspective follows central tenets of media imperialism theory. First, globalization is another phase in the intensification of dependency relations between the North and South. Media globalization favors highly concentrated Western interests in alliance with powerful domestic corporations. There is no stark opposition between global and domestic capital, but as some joint ventures show, they work together to further their goals. Second, the media essentially reproduces larger social inequalities. The widening gap between rich and poor is crystallized in the information society. Rather than helping to ameliorate preexisting divisions, the so-called digital divide represents the deepening of differences in access to information. A central good in today's society, information is available only to those who can afford it, Amaral suggests. New technologies have not ameliorated this problem but, rather, have widened social exclusion. Moreover, the coming of new technologies has not unsettled power structures as "old media" companies have quickly prevailed by incorporating the new media into their business. While elites have more access to information, the vast majority is still limited to the old media. Third, media content often reproduces existing social divisions by perpetuating racial and ethnic stereotypes. Media messages continue to ignore cultural diversity and the needs of the majority of impoverished Brazilians. For Amaral, global content does not serve domestic audiences and results in the weakening of national cultures.

Economic concentration is also a central theme in the transformations that the media in Central America have undergone in recent years. In Chapter 4, Rick Rockwell and Noreene Janus argue that developments in the region benefited conservative elites. The 1990s meant the end of civil wars of the preceding twenty years. As Guatemala, Nicaragua, Honduras, and El Salvador move away from civil strife and into a period marked by a transition to democracy, the authors see larger forces at work to create an era for the media caciques.

Mexican Angel González González and the Central American region present a unique type of emerging relationship between media and politics in the Americas. In Guatemala, González, a former Televisa employee, has a virtual monopoly of commercial television, along with considerable radio holdings. What appears to have facilitated González's rise to power in a highly politicized environment, rather than alliances with the state or a political party, is a studied neutrality or downplaying of local news and controversy. In Guatemala, González simultaneously neutralized television as a source of political plurality or partisanship and ran the government-produced information programs on his stations. His greatest strength, as the authors observe, was his attempt to remain above politics on a day-by-day basis. In Nicaragua, although not the biggest player, González has major holdings in three of the nation's nine television outlets. Rockwell and Janus point out that González has teamed with various Nicaraguan nationals as partners to gain control of three channels, the most important of which was Channel 4, the Sandinista station that was up for sale. Besides the Sandinista channel, he also controls Channels 10 and 12. After the sale of Channel 4, González remained low-key in his programming shifts, planning to steer clear of controversy, although the move was seen as a way to purge Nicaragua's airwaves of the Sandinista message without any of the blame falling on the country's longtime media owners. Rockwell and Janus see González's role in Nicaragua as one of change agent rather than an oppressive force. In El Salvador, the situation is somewhat different. Here González met with a homegrown cacique, Boris Esersky, whose political connections shaped the current Salvadoran broadcast spectrum and kept forces disloyal to the government from buying ad time with most Salvadoran broadcasters. Esersky owns three of the country's five VHF stations and dominates the market with a 90 percent share of the audience. In 1997, however, Mexico's TV Azteca purchased controlling interest in Esersky's only competition, Channel 12. The sale, however, did not represent an opening of the airwaves to political pluralism. In El Salvador, as in Nicaragua, at a time when opposition radio is entering an increasingly commercial mode of operation, Mexican investors played a similar role of helping conservative and long-dominant elites remove political opponents from television broadcasting. Panama also has a single dominant broadcasting organization, MECOM, the fruit of the merger in the 1990s between the Eleta and González Revilla properties. Likewise, one man, Rafael Ferrari, dominates Honduran broadcasting, although competition is greater in that country. In fact, in Honduras, broadcasting has become a route to political power, and running a media enterprise means competing for the leadership in one of the country's political parties. Rockwell and Janus attribute this greater competition to Honduras's unfinished transition from military control. In the other Central American countries, the authors observe, outside forces such as the United States or the United Nations intervened at the end of the wars to impose limitations on the military. In Honduras, where no war occurred, although the military buildup was enormous, the military still maintains considerable power.

In Chapter 5, Valerio Fuenzalida tackles the question of public television in Chile. In Latin America as a whole, as well as in Chile in particular, public television has a long record of failures. Public has often meant state-owned television at the service of the propaganda needs of governments. Within this context, important efforts have been made in Chile toward the establishment and strengthening of a public television system since the return of democracy. The inclusion of legislation to guarantee political pluralism, program diversity, and financial autonomy in the current legislation are major advances, particularly considering the absence of similar initiatives in other countries in the region. In addition to perennial difficulties in making pluralism effective, Fuenzalida's chapter illuminates a number of problems that public television currently faces. Against the backdrop of substantial political changes brought about by the consolidation of democracy, the Chilean media environment has changed remarkably in the last decade with the entrance of foreign companies and the multiplication of channels. As has happened in other countries, public television had to accommodate these changes. It is expected to produce content for mass audiences and to be financially solvent. It receives public funds according to its performance in the ratings. A series of legal considerations, however, relatively isolates public television from broader commercial pressures that private networks regularly face. Subsidies aim to support programming that, particularly given the small size of Chile's market, private companies are not likely to produce. In summary, Fuenzalida argues that Chilean public television exists at the point of convergence of different interests and different demands. Since the return of democracy, it has managed somewhat successfully to strike a balance among competing forces, a balance that perhaps reflects the delicate equilibrium that exists among political interests in the country at large.

In Chapter 6, Fernando Calero Aparicio suggests that in Colombia the movement of constitutional reform toward increasing decentralization of the state, a growing free market economy and globalization, and a deepening political, social, and economic crisis created the conditions to renegotiate the relationship between the state and the media. One of the most important changes was the decentralization of television that began in 1985 with the authorization of three regional channels, which were, like the national channels, set up as public/private hybrids. This decentralization coincided with the gradual reform of the Colombian state itself that included, for the first time, the popular election of mayors. In 1991 the reform process culminated in a new Constitution that included language substantially modifying the relationship between the state and broadcasting. Article 20 guaranteed freedom of expression, meaning the right to inform and be informed truly and impartially, and to establish mass media that will be free and will exercise social responsibility. The right to reply under equality of conditions also was guaranteed; censorship was prohibited.

As a result of the new Constitution and of the legislation that followed, an independent body was set up to regulate television and guarantee equality of access including a prohibition of monopolistic practices. Under this new body (Consejo Nacional de Televisión) Colombian television exploded in a plethora of administrative and legal formulas, including for the first time full ownership of television stations by the private sector. Contemporary Colombian television consists of national, regional, local, and municipal stations as well as subscription cable services.

These reforms, however, did not occur in a political or economic vacuum. Between 1994 and 1998, the administration of President Ernesto Samper, formally accused of ties with the drug mafia, was charged with political manipulation in the nominations of members of the body regulating television. An economic recession dealt an even more serious blow to the new television panorama, originally projected for an economy growing at 4.5 percent annually. The faltering economy cut into the advertising revenue of the new stations, throwing their future into doubt. The shrinking advertising base led to fierce competition and charges of unfair and monopolistic practices among advertisers and broadcasters. And, for the first time, foreign capital entered Colombian media through direct investments from Venezuelan and Spanish media companies in the new national private networks. At the same time, regional and local stations suffering from the recession found it more difficult to produce public service content. The economic turmoil in Colombian television took place in the context of growing civil unrest and narco-terrorism; by the end of the century, the central government had ceded control of over one-third of the national territory to guerrilla forces. While the state no longer controlled broadcasting and many more outlets were now available for the expression of different opinions, the combination of political turmoil, terrorism, civil unrest, and weak economic conditions cast a long shadow over the financial and journalistic viability of the majority of the new private and public broadcast outlets.

The tight relationship between the state and the media has been a dominant feature of Mexican communications. Two chapters deal with this issue in the context of important changes in the country's politics and media. In Chapter 7, Rick Rockwell analyzes continuity and change in the relationship between the government and print and broadcasting media before and during the landmark 2000 presidential election in which, for the first time in its seven-decade history, the PRI lost to the Partido de Acción Nacional's Vicente Fox. Rockwell describes the rise of publications ("the mavericks") that investigated and criticized PRI authorities in the years preceding the historic election. Uninterested in playing the role of a lapdog press to the ruling PRI, a handful of newspapers and newsweeklies pushed the boundaries of a media system characterized by widespread corruption and favoritism. Throughout the PRI's long presidential tenure, the media as a whole did not even make any pretense of impartiality and fairness. The monopoly Televisa repeatedly declared its unflinching support for the PRI, officials dictated the news, newspapers survived on life support provided by government subsidies, and the existence of different forms of corruption was an open secret in Mexican newsrooms. Whenever a newspaper dared to cross the accepted boundaries, PRI officials promptly shut down any form of criticism. In this context, the emergence of investigative reporting was both a symptom and a cause of increasing political opening. Despite changes, old practices persisted during the 2000 election. Both Televisa and TV Azteca slanted election coverage in favor of the PRI, and intimidation and murder of dissident reporters persisted. Questions remain unanswered, Rockwell concludes, about whether the PAN's victory will fundamentally alter the historic pattern of state-media relations. Given the power of the presidency in Mexican politics, he suggests, the future of state-media relations hinges largely on whether the Fox administration has the political will to change old practices.

Similar questions about the future of media systems underlie John Sinclair's analysis in Chapter 8. Sinclair concentrates on the analysis of how dominant monopolies in Brazil and Mexico have adapted to changing political and technological conditions at the same time they are undergoing generational changes in upper management. Historically identified with patriarchs that ran tight ships, Televisa and Grupo Globo, partners in regional satellite business, have been confronting different domestic conditions. The consolidation of TV Azteca means that, for the first time in its history, Mexican television is not synonymous with Televisa. Having been the kingmaker of Mexican politics and an unabashed defender of the PRI since the early days of radio broadcasting, Televisa remains the powerhouse of Mexican media. It is no longer the monopoly that it once was, however. In Brazil, Grupo Globo's dominant position in over-the-air television is not under threat as other networks hardly offer substantial competition. In new media industries such as cable and satellite, Grupo Globo faces limited competition in duopolistic markets. In any case, Sinclair suggests, both Televisa and Grupo Globo could not do business as usual as they had to form alliances with global corporations to remain dominant in new audiovisual markets.

In Chapter 9, Aníbal Orué Pozzo analyzes the changes that the Paraguayan media underwent with the collapse of the thirty-five-year Stroessner dictatorship. Gen. Alfredo Stroessner ruled Paraguay between 1954 and 1989, one of the longest dictatorships in the history of Latin America. Even before Stroessner, the army played a major role in the country. The Paraguayan military were active in broadcasting, beginning with the rise of National Radio under the military in 1940 and continuing throughout Stroessner's long rule with the implementation of a mandatory daily national radio network of all private stations. When private television stations began in 1965, the military did not see a need for a mandatory national network. Orué Pozzo attributes this to the shared political interests of the various actors involved in the process and their satisfaction with the situation. Providing that the media did not question the sociopolitical framework of the dictatorship's scaffolding, they were bound for success. And this was the consensus compromise worked out all through the dictatorship. Orué Pozzo argues that during the last years of the dictatorship the consensus compromise showed some cracks. In the mid-1980s several dailies were closed sporadically—in the case of *ABC Color*, for a longer period, along with the radio station Ñandutí. Despite these incidents, Orué Pozzo writes, "There was no economic conflict that might have caused media entrepreneurs to look for allies in the popular movement to confront the Stroessner government politically. The consensus policy manufactured throughout these years brought benefits to media and communications interests." Orué Pozzo observes little modification of this basic consensus policy with the gradual democratization of the country. He notes that despite the large-scale political changes, the government continues to negotiate with the largest economic groups and hold the key role in the distribution of broadcasting licenses. Significant changes have occurred, however, in the use of the mass media during the electoral process, a process that started with the political transition. Television especially has become an important, central force in the electoral process. Orué Pozzo hints that the 1995 Telecommunications Law potentially created a new framework for developing communication in the country, even without an explicit policy regarding the media. In conclusion he observes that media owners and politicians have reached a new consensus compromise that allows them to continue their activities without any political setbacks. Perhaps more significantly, however, this compromise has been achieved without opening the airwaves to the parts of society that still are not seen or heard on Paraguayan broadcast media.

The proximity between ruling powers and commercial media interests has also been central to recent developments in the Peruvian media. In Chapter 10, Luis Peirano argues that the Peruvian media experienced the combination of open market economics with increased political control during the Fujimori administration. In 1992, the second year of his first presidency, Fujimori dissolved the Peruvian Parliament and the Supreme Court and took over the country in a bloodless coup d'état supported by the military. Fujimori sent soldiers to maintain control in the leading opposition newspapers and the most important radio and television stations. Using executive powers, Fujimori modified the law regulating private investment in the telecommunications sector, allowing for privatization of the state-owned telephone company and of the rapid-growth cellular phone companies and cable television channels. The military success of Fujimori against the Sendero Luminoso and his economic success in combating hyperinflation and in privatizing state-owned industries guaranteed his reelection. During his second presidency, according to Peirano, Fujimori developed a style and concept of management of the mass media that, while respecting their formal rights, resulted in an authoritarian regime of strict control. Helped by a growing recession, Fujimori maintained control of the media through the direct ownership of one television station and the selective distribution of advertising dollars by the government, by far the largest single advertiser in Peru, to private stations. Other means of control included the support of a tabloid press that attacked the opposition media, a tightening of self-censorship on serious television journalism, and court decisions facilitating the takeover of opposition television stations resulting in a significant reduction of hard-hitting television news and discussion. In the case that received the most international attention, Fujimori used the selective application of limitations on foreign ownership of Peruvian media to remove the owner of a vocal opposition TV network (Channel 2), Baruch Ivcher. Israeli-born Ivcher was stripped of his Peruvian citizenship in 1997 and forced to relinquish control of Channel 2. The station had conducted investigations of government officials. The Peruvian government also charged Ivcher with tax and customs violations (Ivcher went into exile in Miami and returned to the country after Fujimori's unexpected resignation in November 2000).

In Chapter 11, Roque Faraone describes the Uruguayan transition to democracy as a unique Uruguayan solution that influenced the future course of state-media relations. A civilian government was elected in March 1985 after a peaceful negotiation with the military, which realized that its time in power was over amidst an unfavorable international climate. This "Uruguayan solution" put many limitations on the actions of the new (and subsequent) civilian administrations. Although all remaining political prisoners were freed, most of the decisions taken during the twelve-year military government were not changed. The climate of political freedom was different from the one that characterized Uruguayan society between the 1920s and 1960s. The fact that the military appropriated the Dirección Nacional de Comunicaciones had not only institutional but also symbolic value. Media owners who had temporary permits understood this decision perfectly well in terms of being careful about the content of future broadcasts. Faraone's description of Uruguayan television under democracy is bleaker than perhaps expected given the early hopes for real change. Although television improved technically, with longer hours, wider audiences, and more interviews and talk shows, it did not carry out investigative reporting on controversial issues or attempt to air information critical of the current or past regime. The habits developed during the dictatorship and the fears of the military presence persisted—"national defense, pension privileges for officers and their families, the excessive number of personnel, and the disappeared were never debated."

The attitude of Uruguayan broadcasters toward the state over the last decade has been pragmatic—offering support for those in power and opportunities for the larger opposition parties, including the left-wing party, as long as these are moderate, colorful, or scandalous. The state-owned channel remains a very minor player, kept low-key by the opposition of the cartel-like three national networks. Even the advent of cable could not change this relationship. Faraone concludes: "The political and television powers maintain relations as associates. Private television seems to say, 'As long as you don't harm my business, you will receive coverage.' The political power seems to say, 'As long as you support power, you will be treated well.' Both seem to say to the military: 'You will not be touched.'"

José Antonio Mayobre analyzes changes in the Venezuelan media in Chapter 12. At the center of his analysis is the role of the media in the rise of Lt. Col. Hugo Chávez from leader of the failed 1992 military putsch against President Carlos Andrés Pérez to being elected president in 1998. A deteriorating economic and political climate during the Caldera administration in the early 1990s served as the backdrop for this process. Oil prices had sunk to new lows on the world market; unemployment and poverty thus had increased. The broadcast media, distancing themselves from the traditional political elite, criticized the political parties and leaders who had allowed the country to reach this state. President Caldera pardoned Chávez after he had served two years in prison. After his release, Mayobre writes, the Chávez populist movement of support for Chávez "caught fire and started to develop and grow. Meanwhile, polls and pollsters kept reassuring the traditional political class that a movement of this sort could never really catch on in Venezuela." Majorities also voted to discard the 1961 Constitution and elect a National Constituent Assembly, charged with revamping the country's institutional framework. Chávez dissolved Congress, and voters gave Chávez followers a resounding majority of the membership in the new assembly.

Mayobre compares Chávez to other Latin American populist leaders. Chávez created his own newspaper and weekly call-in radio and television programs and used "highly symbolic visual and semiological elements such as the creation of the People's Balcony in the Miraflores Presidential Palace as well as military parades and uniforms. The traditional media, caught by surprise by Chávez's swift and total rise, in Mayobre's words, "seemed to turn into paper tigers under the onslaught of the emerging populist movement." The two major television channels, Radio Caracas Channel 2 and Venevision Channel 4—joined by a host of new satellite, cable, and broadcast outlets in the past decade—were at a loss and turned their attention to their more robust international operations. HBO and Sony both established offices in Caracas, taking advantage of low costs and an educated workforce, but with few contacts with local media. By 2000 Chávez was firmly in control of the country without, it appears, the benefit or support of the media. In fact, he seems to have cut the traditional tie between media and politicians. With the exception of the owner of a regional radio station elected as an independent, no member of the National Constitutional Assembly appeared to have ties to the media. Although they campaigned against the Chávez presidency, the major media outlets moderated their voices of opposition, even when Chávez exercised his right to link the national networks to broadcast presidential speeches, military parades, and official ceremonies. Mayobre concludes that the surprising public support for Chávez's use of the media is somehow linked to the public's concomitant lack of affection for the traditional media outlets. By the time Chávez arrived on the scene, Mayobre observes, Venezuelan broadcasters had dropped any pretense of quality or minimal sense of social responsibility. Perhaps as proof of the public's dissatisfaction with the media, in December 1999, Venezuelans overwhelmingly approved a new constitution that changed the structure of government and included a new right for Venezuelan citizens: "the right to timely, truthful, impartial and uncensored information." The Miami-based Inter-American Press Association suggested that the wording could lead to a crackdown on news media.

In summary, several threads run through the chapters. First, media democratization remains a pending task in Latin America. Since the return of civilian rule in the 1980s and 1990s, the media has experienced substantial changes that have largely benefited concentrated private interests at the expense of wider political and social goals. Aided by privatization and liberalization of media markets and often with close ties to ruling political powers, commercial interests were in a position to consolidate their grasp on domestic media. They have been extremely successful in bringing new media technologies into their fold. Dominant interests in the cable, satellite, and Internet industries are largely the same interests that control old media. Early hopes about media democratization that arose after civilian governments replaced military dictatorships did not materialize in concrete policies. The weakness and/or absence of a tradition of antitrust legislation in the region has discouraged any optimism about substantial changes in the near future. One of the most remarkable features of contemporary media policies is that questions of media protectionism and cultural nationalism, which were prominent in the past, have almost entirely disappeared (Waisbord 1998). Similarly, issues of public access and control of the media also have been remarkably absent. The prospects for a vast array of political and social interests to become effective participants in media operations and policymaking remain bleak. Because recent changes have been largely planned and executed without consultation or participation of society at large, it is more difficult to foresee significant changes toward democratization of media institutions.

Another thread is that the centrality of the media in Latin American democracies deserves continuous attention. Improving the quality of the region's democracies requires media organizations that can effectively monitor ruling political and economic powers. The penchant of media owners to court government officials in order to advance multiple business goals hardly suggests a firm commitment to maintaining a proper distance from those whose actions they should scrutinize. When the advancing of their business interests overshadows the public interest, and when the expectations of the powerful are deemed more important than the needs of citizens, the media are hardly a paragon of democratic virtue. The fact that some administrations have resorted to authoritarian means to suppress dissent and criticism adds more reason to worry about the prospects of media democratization. Particularly in countries that have a checkered record with regard to respect of freedom of speech and other constitutional rights, such actions run counter to democratic principles that are fundamental for the existence of a democratic media.

Finally, the dynamics between media and politics in Latin American democracies, the authors also conclude, need to be understood by bringing together local and global developments. The strengths and weaknesses of globalization and national control must be filtered through the lens of local politics. Globalization does not make domestic politics irrelevant. The effects of globalization are varied, depending on internal politics, the structure of media systems, the size of media markets, the conditions for production of media content, the entrance of foreign capital into national markets, and the regionalization of media industries. Consequences are comparable but take different shape across the region. The two forces, local politics and global media, must be analyzed together to arrive at a comprehensive picture of contemporary Latin American media.

Latin Politics,
Global Media

Latin Politics, Global Media

Elizabeth Fox and Silvio Waisbord

HISTORICALLY the political elites in Latin America gravitated to-ward building a model of commercial broadcasting on the sur-face quite similar to that developed by their neighbors to the north in the United States. This model consisted of privately owned radio and tele-vision stations, financed by advertising, operating in competitive mar-kets but with one or more large companies controlling a significant market share. U.S. investment in the region in the early decades of the twentieth century facilitated the adoption of this commercial broad-casting model. Paradoxically, however, the Latin American commercial broadcasting model was in many cases both unregulated and highly con-trolled. Given the often undemocratic nature of national governments, political control of the media was of far greater concern to elites than was the regulation of commercial growth or the establishment of public ser-vice goals. The elites required economic growth and political stability to stay in power, and a docile commercial broadcasting system under their political thumb satisfied both needs (Fox 1997).

Consequently, many decades before globalization became a buzzword in political and academic circles, the region's media were already interna-tionalized. The twin ideas of public service and protectionism were never the organizing principles of broadcasting systems, but intervention by the state and political manipulation of the media held back the expansion of market forces. The results were media systems featuring mixed ele-ments that, according to government policies and historical situations in specific countries, showed influences of either state- or market-centered conceptions.

Alongside the precocious commercial development of Latin Ameri-can broadcasting, in some countries nationalism also played a role in the development of the media, especially regarding ownership and content.

Sporadically, over the course of the first sixty years of broadcasting, factions within governments and progressive social movements pushed for increased state control of domestic radio and television in order to insure national content and the access of different groups to broadcasting outlets. Attempts at nationalist broadcasting policies by Latin American states were largely successful when motivated by the need for increased political control of the media but largely unsuccessful when motivated by considerations of public services or national culture (Waisbord 1995). At times state-directed media policies were couched within broader political and economic reforms, ostensibly focusing on broadcasting's foreign "dependency" and lack of a role in social and economic development. The main concern, however, was usually domestic political control.

Government censorship quickly became the norm in the Latin American version of private commercial broadcasting. The state imposed controls on the political content of the media through censorship, licensing, and later, the use of paid government advertising. State interference in the media began early on, for example in Brazil in the 1930s under Vargas, in Argentina during the "*década infame*," and during the early years of radio in Peru.

When Latin American broadcasting began in the 1920s, most countries had enjoyed their independence from colonial power for over a hundred years. Although political elites did not see broadcasting as a nation-building instrument, like their counterparts in other Third World regions did, the media became a catalyst for national unification as new technologies disseminated the same content (films and radio programs) in a given territory (Martín-Barbero 1993).

In some countries, during certain periods, state or public broadcasting was seen as a way to integrate new populations into the culture or economy of the country, as was the case of Mexico and Uruguay. In 1924 the Mexican government set up a radio station within the Ministry of Education. Ten years later, President Lázaro Cárdenas (1934–40) donated radio receivers to all agricultural and workers' communities to enable them to listen to the courses, book reviews, and concerts transmitted by the state radio station (which was itself sold to private entrepreneurs within ten years). Uruguay was a prosperous, politically stable country in the 1930s, and the state could afford to finance media and the arts as well as other public services for its small, urban middle class. In 1929 the Uruguayan state set up a noncommercial public broadcasting service, SODRE (Servicio Oficial de Difusión Radio Eléctrica), with one state-financed shortwave and two medium frequencies. The government did not limit the growth of private commercial media, however, and by the 1950s the Uruguayan commercial broadcasting sector was sufficiently powerful to block the further expansion of state-owned cultural media. In Colombia, radio and later television first began as public-private hybrids. The Colombian government originally put up for bid the time slots on state-owned radio stations to private companies who exploited them commercially by selling advertising time. Without limitations on commercial stations, private radio soon overpowered these public-private hybrids.

In the late 1950s and early 1960s, within the general thinking on economic and political development in the region, some of the earlier ideas about national or public service broadcasting resurfaced. Development communication focused on the use of broadcasting to provide education, information, and modern values to the "traditional masses." Development programs of international agencies and organizations such as UNESCO, the Alliance for Progress, and the Organization of American States made funds available for communication equipment and programs to use the mass media to promote health, education, rural improvements, and family planning. Recipients of assistance included educational radio and television systems and vast agricultural extension programs.

In 1966, using foreign aid, Colombian president Carlos Lleras set up an educational television program in coordination with the Ministry of Education as a complement to regular classroom programs. He also established a program of grassroots integration and rural development using television to reach lower-income adults. In 1968 the Mexican government began an open-circuit educational television system for secondary school called Telesecundaria. These efforts at public service broadcasting flourished as long as foreign financing or domestic political support was forthcoming. When funds and support dried up, public service broadcasting languished in the backwaters of official bureaucracies.

Accommodation and Confrontation

The endorsement of free market economics by the military dictatorships that swept Latin America in the 1970s spurred broadcasting's commercial growth, usually under ironclad political control. The evolving nature of state and media relations influenced the way the broadcasting industries developed. When the state was able to forge a mutually beneficial relationship with national broadcasting industries, strong media monopolies developed. This was the case of Mexico and Brazil, where monopolistic domestic broadcasters grew strong under the protection of authoritarian states. The mutual benefits of this relationship and the enormous size of domestic markets explain why Mexico and Brazil today have the two largest, most monopolistic, and politically powerful broadcasting industries in the Western Hemisphere. Brazil's authoritarian rulers worked closely first with private radio stations that they censored and in part directly controlled and later with commercial television networks, notably TV Globo, that they helped create and had no need to control. In Brazil, the state's coming to terms with television took place later than it did in Mexico. In Mexico this accommodation was the natural outgrowth of the radio broadcasters' ongoing relationship with the country's political leaders, dating from the 1940s. In Brazil, a mutually beneficial working arrangement between television broadcasters and the government was reached after 1964 under the military dictatorship, well into the development of commercial broadcasting. U.S. investors were active in the establishment of commercial radio in Brazil as well as in the rise of TV Globo. Although U.S. influence strengthened commercial broadcasting, the manner in which the Brazilian industry evolved was first and foremost the result of the good relationship between broadcasters and Brazil's authoritarian rulers. The Brazilian media eventually proved the stronger partner in this relationship, outlasting the military and successfully transferring their loyalties to the civilian governments that followed (Sinclair 1999).

Where a cozy relationship between the state and broadcasters was not possible, the broadcasting industry remained politically weaker and generally more fragmented as it has been in the rest of the region. Peru, Argentina, Chile, and Uruguay have been paradigmatic cases of fragmented broadcasting industries. In Peru, major swings in policy between laissez-faire and government intervention made the consolidation of media monopolies impossible. The most radical of these swings occurred under a progressive, nationalist military government between 1968 and 1980. As part of broader, more ambitious goals of reform inspired along nationalistic lines, the government decreed the expropriation of media companies. The ultimate result, however, was government censorship and stronger private broadcasters. In 1980 the newly elected civilian administration of Fernando Belaunde gave the expropriated radio and TV stations back to their original owners, in some cases compensating them with tax breaks and reduced tariffs on imported equipment and programming. Peru returned to an almost wholly private commercial broadcasting system with two large national networks, hardened against government intervention and operating largely without competition.

In Argentina, fragmentation of media ownership resulted from the fact that the military, which came to power in 1976, was unwilling to privatize television stations that the Peronist administration had expropriated in 1974. Despite its strong privatizing rhetoric, the military dictatorship distrusted the formation of private networks, and instead preferred to divide television and radio stations among the armed forces. This situation remained unchanged during the Alfonsín government in the 1980s. For a variety of reasons, no fundamental changes in the structure of media ownership were instituted until the Menem government quickly moved to privatize broadcasting stations soon after taking power in 1989.

In Chile, the fragmentation of the broadcasting industry largely resulted from the compromise decision of the political parties to place television channels under the administration of state- and church-run universities rather than under the government or private owners. In Uruguay media industry fragmentation was the result of competition among different radio and television station owners, none of which were linked directly to the state or to a particular government or political party, operating within a democratic system. In both countries, domestic broadcasting policies before the dictatorships were a basic part of the democratic give and take of the societies, with different interests competing for control of broadcasting and no single monopolistic media industry developing. In both Uruguay and Chile, the competition among different interests in broadcasting ended with the gradual breakdown of democracy and, in 1973, with brutal military takeovers of the respective governments. For over a decade in Uruguay and for even longer in Chile, the military kept the media under strict control and censorship while, at the same time, allowing for commercial growth of the media in commercially competitive domestic markets. Neither dictatorship, however, was able to forge a close political relationship with a private domestic broadcaster, as was the case in Brazil and Mexico, leading to the formation of monopolistic domestic broadcasting industries in these countries.

This was the situation in the early to mid-1980s when military dictatorships started showing cracks and the transition to democracy gained momentum. Back then, few could have imagined the Latin American media would undergo phenomenal modifications in the following years. As civilian administrations replaced military dictatorships, the region's media have experienced perhaps the biggest transformations in the past half century. Transformations ranged from technological to legal, from political to policy, from production to distribution of media content, and from economic to financial.

Globalization, a process that profoundly reshaped media structures and dynamics worldwide in the 1990s, did not spare Latin America. Regional transformations need to be understood as part of the global implementation of market-centered policies and free-trade economics in media industries. The trinity of privatization, liberalization, and deregulation has been the mantra of the makers of media policies. In a way, such policies were not completely new in Latin America, as they were in media systems elsewhere that had been historically organized around the notion of public service. Because Latin American media had long been open to international capital and programming flows and dominated by private and commercial principles, globalization has not been a completely novel development that radically transformed the foundations of media systems. What the globalizing push of the 1990s has done is to tip the balance further in the direction of the market but without downplaying, let alone eliminating, the role of the state and domestic politics. Globalization and market forces have not made the state and domestic politics less relevant but have actually brought them once again to the forefront. The Latin American cases suggest that it would be misleading to see globalization as the imposition of foreign processes onto domestic media systems. The historical evolution of the region's media already put in evidence that neither globalizing and domestic dynamics nor state and market forces are antithetical. Recent developments confirm this historical pattern: these dynamics and forces are not in straight opposition but are articulated in a process of perpetual negotiation. National politics filter and mediate globalization, outlining its limits and possibilities. States and market forces continue to be locked in constant battles in which accommodation and mutual benefits, rather than one-sided victories, are the norm.

New Technologies and Changes in Media Consumption

The widespread introduction and adoption of technological innovations is a necessary starting point in analyzing how globalization relates to sweeping changes in Latin American media. Little can be understood about structural and policy changes without keeping in mind that such changes were in large part responses to technological changes.

Whereas some media technologies (and industries) declined, others exploded. At the same time the region was experiencing one of its worst economic and social crises in contemporary history, more people gained access to television and radio sets than ever before, reflecting the substantial increases in the total number of sets, as shown in table 1.1.

Table 1.1
Television and Radio Receivers in Latin America and the Caribbean
(Total per 1,000 inhabitants)

	1980	1985	1990	1996
Television	97	138	164	204
Radio	259	316	349	413

Source: UNESCO Yearbook 1998

Cable television also underwent significant development. From a small and marginal industry in the early 1980s, cable had become by the late 1990s one of the most dynamic media industries. As table 1.2 indicates, recent estimations conclude that there are more than 15 million cable-TV subscribers in the region, a small number compared to the wealthy industrialized countries, but 20 percent of the regional total of 81 million television households.

Table 1.2 / Cable TV Households in Latin America and the Caribbean, 1998

Country	Households
Argentina	5,096,000
Mexico	2,351,000
Colombia	2,235,000
Brazil	1,745,000
Central America/Caribbean	1,218,000
Chile	906,000
Venezuela	536,000
Others	1,064,000
Total	15,151,000

Source: Los medios y mercados de latinoamérica, 1998

Cable television did not develop evenly across the region. It reaches over 50 percent of television households in Argentina, 25 percent in Chile and Mexico, and less than 10 percent in Brazil. Predictably, distribution patterns are socially stratified. In a region with persistent and deepening socioeconomic inequalities, cable audiences are concentrated for the most part among the upper and middle classes. There has been modest growth of cable subscription in poorer districts, but the growth has been observed mainly among well-to-do households. Coupled with the explosion in the number of radio and television households, the existence of 35 million VCRs and 2 million satellite television subscribers suggests a media landscape substantially different than that which existed in the early 1980s.

Whereas these figures indicate dynamic and expansive media industries, other numbers offer a more complex picture of simultaneous growth and decline across industries. For example, the number of daily newspapers as well as overall newspaper circulation declined (UNESCO 1998). Also, the number of movie theaters experienced a substantial decrease. As presented in table 1.3, latest estimations conclude that fewer

Table 1.3
Movie Theaters in Latin America and the Caribbean, Selected Countries

Country	1985	1995
Argentina	900	400
Bolivia	120	55
Brazil	1,900	1,200
Chile	130	90
Colombia	400	270
Cuba	530	350
Mexico	2,400	1,600
Peru	400	100
Venezuela	470	220
Uruguay	110	40

Source: Getino 1998

than half the number of theaters that existed in 1985 were still open by 1995.

Trends in the general evolution of media technologies and industries in Latin America can be summarized as follows: the explosive growth of radio and television, the rise of new forms of distribution of TV programming (cable and satellite), the decline in newspaper readership, and the concomitant decrease in the number of movie theaters and audiences and consolidation of new channels for the exhibition of filmed entertainment.

The Politics of Privatization

These developments underpinned the policymaking decisions that shaped the fundamental transformations in the organization and operation of media industries in the 1990s. The main trends in Latin American media have been the formation of multimedia corporations; the decline of family-owned companies; the articulation between local, regional, and international capital; the intensification of cross-regional trade of investment and content; and the increase in the production and export of television programming.

The adoption of market-oriented policies put an end to the longstanding tug-of-war between state and market models of media organization. During the 1990s, media policies shrunk the participation of state and public interests and helped consolidate market principles. Such policies were part of a wider change in the region's political zeitgeist. The ascent of market-oriented policies in media industries happened simultaneously with the implementation of neoliberal programs of stabilization and state reform that deeply transformed Latin American economies. As in other industrial sectors, privatization, liberalization, and deregulation were responsible for dismantling the old media order and strengthening market forces.

It is important to note that neither NAFTA nor Mercosur, the two major trade agreements passed in the 1990s, had major impact on these trends. Market-driven policies of privatization and liberalization were already in motion before the agreements came into effect. Neither agreement introduced new laws that radically changed structures and dynamics. NAFTA left untouched ownership and programming regulations that concerned Mexican interests. Mercosur virtually ignored cultural industries (Galperín 1999; Recondo 1997).

As in other media systems worldwide, privatization became the policy du jour in the television industry. In Argentina and Mexico, administrations decided to auction major state-owned television stations that had been nationalized in the early 1970s. In 1984 the Bolivian government allowed private companies to own television licenses. In Chile, private capital was authorized to bid for television licenses that had been historically in the hands of universities. Private ownership was also permitted in Colombia, where the state had controlled television and where private companies were limited to producing a restricted amount of hours of programming. Private companies also benefited from the transition from an era of scarcity to an era of abundance of electromagnetic spectrum. The vast majority of the new radio and television frequencies were awarded to private bidders, and only a few to public organizations and governments.

These changes have not fundamentally altered old dynamics in the interaction between states and markets in media policies, most notably the lack of wide participation of civil society in the decision-making process and, ultimately, in the lack of public access to media organizations. Political democratization has not brought genuine democratization of media ownership, content, and control. Nor has public accountability been an integral part of the process by which media licenses have changed hands. Public officials approached the politics of privatization as a way to gain personal advantages, both politically and economically, by accepting the demands of powerful media interests. The old system in which the state had an all-pervasive role in media matters, particularly in terms of ownership, has certainly been changed, but the quid pro quo dynamics of personal favors and clientelism remain. Consider the case of Brazil as an example of "electronic clientelism": of the 302 licensed commercial TV stations in 1995, 94 were owned by politicians or ex-politicians, and 1,169 of the 2,908 radio stations were owned by the same crowd, about one-third (De Lima 1999). Of the 594 members of the Brazilian Parliament, 130 owned either a radio or a TV station or both; the same is true for twelve of the twenty-seven state governors as well. Moreover, of the 1,848 TV transmitting stations authorized under the presidency of Fernando Henrique Cardoso, 268 were given to politicians, among which were included nineteen federal representatives, eleven state representatives, six senators, two governors, seven mayors, three former governors, nine former federal representatives, eight former mayors, and twenty-two others.

The Consolidation of Conglomerates

Together with privatization, the removal of cross-media ownership restrictions and the liberalization of new media industries were the catalysts for a process of rapid concentration of information resources and the consolidation of media corporations. Certainly, the existence of highly concentrated companies is not new in the region. Televisa and Grupo Globo were already horizontally and vertically integrated companies that held almost monopolistic positions in Mexico and Brazil respectively, the two largest media markets in the region.

In flagrant contradiction to constitutional rules in some countries that ban the formation of monopolies and oligopolies in media industries, recent policy decisions accelerated the process of concentration (Mastrini 1999). Policies opened new media sectors and strengthened the position of already dominant local groups. Domestic corporations such as Argentina's Grupo Clarín and Colombia's RCN and Caracol, for example, received the plums of the privatization of television stations. This decision allowed them to control important resources in the television industry and build a backbone for their media business. Privatization also made it possible for companies with diverse industrial interests to move quickly and aggressively into television; for example, Mexico's Elektra Group formed Azteca in its successful bid for state-owned Channel 13. For media companies with ambitious domestic and global goals, having a solid position in the television industry is crucial: over-the-air television receives the lion's share of advertising dollars and is indispensable as the launching pad for producing programs and conquering global markets.

Cable and satellite television also entered the fold of dominant companies. Firms that already controlled over-the-air television branched into cable, as happened in Uruguay. In countries such as Argentina and Brazil, where cable development was originally fragmented in numerous mom-and-pop companies, leading companies swallowed local companies and subscribers, leading to an intense and rapid process of concentration. The result was the formation of duopolies in cable markets: Grupo Clarín and the CEI group have 80 percent of Argentine subscribers, and Grupo Globo (70 percent) and TVA (30 percent) dominate the Brazilian market.

Regional media powerhouses took the lead in the development of satellite television. Approximately thirty satellites currently cover Latin America, including BrasilSat, Mexico's Morelos, Intelsat, PanAmSat, and Argentina's NahuelSat. Optimistic prospects about growing numbers of subscribers stimulated the launch of two regional satellite services in the mid-1990s. Galaxy Latin America includes as partners Hughes Electronics, Venezuela's Grupo Cisneros, Brazil's Grupo Abril, Mexico's Multivisión, and Argentina's Grupo Clarín. Sky Latin America brings together News Corporation, TCI, Televisa, and Grupo Globo. Both feature an alliance between global technology and media behemoths with the largest producers and owners of television hours in Latin America. Each party brings to the table indispensable resources: Western media groups provide satellite connections, large international operations, and extensive film and television archives; regional partners offer domestic experience and popular local programming.

Privatization and liberalization in the telecommunications industry also contributed to the formation of conglomerates. It is impossible to analyze the evolution and structure of contemporary media industries without addressing developments in telecommunications. Technological and industrial convergence has blurred clear-cut distinctions, making it necessary to analyze the linkages between traditional media and the telecommunications industry. As in broadcasting, market-oriented policies substantially changed old telecommunications structures and dynamics. Initially, the breakup of state monopolies meant the entrance of foreign companies, namely Telefónica (Spain), Telecom (France), and Bell South (U.S.), into formerly closed markets. Subsequently, local media companies took advantage of liberalization to enter into different telecommunications sectors. The parent companies of traditional newspapers such as *O Estado de São Paulo, Jornal do Brasil,* and *Folha de São Paulo* in Brazil, for example, acquired interests in cellular telephone and cable television companies.

Meanwhile, established media companies rushed ahead in Internet developments. According to a recent estimate, there are 7 million Internet users in Latin America, less than 2 percent of total world users (International Telecommunication Union 1999). The high cost of phone services is one factor that holds off further growth. These obstacles have not deterred media companies from establishing a beachhead in Internet business. Old media companies such as Folha and Grupo Abril's Universo Online in Brazil and Grupo Cisneros in Venezuela control major Internet portals and access providers in the region.

As a result of the formation of conglomerates, a handful of companies controls the majority of media interests in Latin American countries. Most media markets are increasingly dominated by duopolies: the CEI group and Grupo Clarín in Argentina, Grupo Globo and SBT in Brazil, Televisa and TV Azteca in Mexico, Venevision and TVC in Venezuela. These media behemoths control the main television stations/networks, receive the largest share of advertising revenues, and draw the largest audiences.

What Has Globalization Wrought?

Privatization and liberalization also accelerated the internationalization of media industries. In Latin America, as happened elsewhere, media were not immune to globalizing dynamics that were revolutionizing media structures around the world. The recent wave of transnationalization has brought in a new phase in the history of the region's media. New developments include the expansion of regional companies beyond their home countries; new relations between local, regional, and global companies; and strong competition among groups domestically and regionally.

First, Latin American companies expanded into neighboring television markets. Whereas media internationalization historically meant the expansion of U.S. companies southward, today's media landscape shows a different pattern, one in which media companies from larger national markets have made inroads in medium-size and small countries. Mexico's Televisa and TV Azteca, Grupo Cisneros, and Angel González, a Mexican citizen with extensive media interests in Central America, purchased interests in television stations throughout the region. They have expanded mainly to small or medium-size markets with little indigenous production (Waisbord 1998).

Liberalization and deregulation of cable television facilitated the expansion of global interests. U.S. cable powerhouses such as TCI and Liberty Media have been particularly interested in expanding into countries with high (actual or potential) numbers of subscribers and television households. Given its substantial number of cable subscribers (comparable to some of the most-cabled countries worldwide), Argentina became a regional launching pad for the pay-TV business. The 1994 Argentina–United States trade agreement of reciprocal investments paved the way for the entrance of U.S. investors into the media industry. The agreement ushered in profound transformations in the ownership structure of Argentine media. Also, the 1995 Cable Law initiated important changes in Brazilian pay television. By increasing foreign ownership to 49 percent the law shook off Brazil's tradition of media protectionism and attracted the interest of global companies. Despite its small number of subscribers, trade analysts have repeatedly forecast a bright future for pay-TV in Brazil. The size of the population and amount of advertising investment make it the biggest and potentially most profitable market in the region.

Latin America also has been affected by the worldwide phenomenon of global financial companies entering into media markets. Goldman Sachs, Citibank, and buyout firm Hicks, Muse, Tate & Furs own substantial media interests and programming sources. In need of capital to bankroll acquisitions, maintain expansion, and keep ahead of competitors, domestic groups reached out for capital from financial firms. For these firms, the decision to enter media industries responded to the interest to secure dominant positions in newly privatized economies and particularly in the dynamic and highly profitable media markets. Citibank's dominant position in the Argentine media (through Citibank Equity Investment, or CEI) followed the decision of the Menem administration to privatize major state-owned companies in the early 1990s. One of the major creditors of Argentina's public debt, Citibank was able to trade public debt titles for public active interests. Hicks, Muse, Tate & Furs aggressively expanded in key media sectors. Besides its participation in the CEI group and ownership of cable interests and Internet portal, it also owns 49 percent of the companies that have the rights to soccer broadcasting in Argentina and Brazil.

Global companies also expanded as programming distributors for cable and satellite services. U.S. cable programmers such as Discovery, ESPN, FOX, HBO, MTV, and TNT launched operations in the region. CNN and CBS created Latin American divisions and offer 24-hour news services (NBC's Canal de Noticias was canceled). A number of partnerships were formed. Telenoticias teamed up the U.S. Spanish-language network Telemundo, Reuters, Spain's Antena 3, Argentina's Grupo Clarín, and Productora y Comercializadora de México. USA network entered into a joint-venture with three regional operators to provide cable services. Cine Canal, a regional movie channel, is the result of the alliance of Hollywood studios and cable companies with interests in Brazil, Chile, Mexico, and Venezuela. Additionally, cable programming in most countries includes the international services of RTVE, RAI, BBC, and Deutsche Welle from Europe. Programming is distributed through Intelsat, PanAmSat, and domestic satellites from Argentina, Brazil, and Mexico. Two-thirds of PanAmSat's Latin American revenues come from leasing transponders for broadcasting.

Cable and satellite networks also allowed further expansion of regional firms. Although the vast majority of cable and satellite systems in each country offer foreign programming, Spanish-language networks are the majority. Services include the international signals of the largest regional producers such as Telefe (Argentina), Manchete (Brazil), Universidad Nacional (Chile), Televisa's Eco (Mexico), and a large number of small, low-budget operations that have local or national reach. Despite modest audiences, the opening of cable outlets encouraged the mushrooming of local programming.

The formation of conglomerates coupled with media globalization has accelerated the transition from family to corporate ownership of media companies. The transition is far from complete, but it has become increasingly evident that traditional family-owned companies are unlikely to continue as such. This ownership structure that remained relatively stable until the 1990s in all countries is now an anachronism. The removal of protectionist legislation, the easing of the circulation of global capital, higher barriers to entry in media markets, and the need for large amounts of capital to finance conglomerates make it impossible for family ownership to survive.

Local Production, Regional Exports, Unequal Markets

The multiplication of distribution windows created the need for more television content. Some estimates conclude that the number of annual television hours has tripled during the 1990s (Catalán 1999). This situation, in theory, should have favored mainly Hollywood producers. No other audiovisual industry worldwide can successfully compete with Hollywood in terms of output, well-established distribution networks, product familiarity, and extensive libraries. Actual results, however, suggest a more complex picture. Far from having reinforced Hollywood's historical preeminent position as *the* lingua franca of Latin American television, more demand for television programming has resulted in new developments.

The number of domestic and regional television hours has increased markedly throughout the region. The increase resulted from several factors. First, the decrease in costs of video technologies and production inputs removed important obstacles that, particularly in the early days of television, discouraged local productions and overwhelmingly favored cheaper U.S. imports. Television stations and networks, particularly in metropolitan areas and large markets, own state-of-the-art studios. Strong audiovisual companies such as Televisa and Grupo Globo own enormous studios equipped with the latest technological innovations. Local productions are not cheaper than Hollywood fare (or other imports, for that matter); still, these up-to-date technologies provide the basic infrastructure for local production.

Second, networks and stations' preference for scheduling local shows encourages local production. Local content is attractive for a very simple reason: it consistently performs better than regional or U.S. productions in audience ratings. *Telenovelas* (soap operas) and locally produced sitcoms, dramas, sports, and news programs consistently top popular preferences, confirming that when available, local television outperforms imports (Waisbord 1998). For an industry organized around commercial principles, ratings determine programming decisions. The prices for foreign shows are lower than the production costs of drama or comedy. Local productions, however, regularly garner higher ratings and, consequently, bring higher advertising revenues. Only in countries where the market is too small to cover costs, and where one-hour episodes of foreign productions cost as little as $500 to $800, do imported shows tend to predominate. Cultural proximity accounts for why imported programming (particularly in prime time) tends to be regional productions, particularly from neighboring countries. Imported programming tends to be Mexican in Central America, Colombian and Venezuelan in Ecuador, and Argentine in Paraguay and Uruguay. Programming crosses borders more easily and suffers less "cultural discount" (Hoskins, McFayden, and Finn 1997) when audiences have already been accustomed to stories, actors, and accents.

Third, local productions offer the opportunity to reap gains in ancillary markets. The opening of international markets in the 1990s and the expansion of demand for Latin American content (mainly *telenovelas*) were important incentives for local production. The exportability of content has been a constant concern for Televisa, Grupo Globo, and Venevision, companies that were trailblazers for regional producers around the world in the late 1970s and in the 1980s. Lately, however, other companies based in medium-size audiovisual markets have successfully exported productions (and coproductions) worldwide. Although international markets are an afterthought in many cases, they offer the possibility of greater earnings. Still, most programs are largely expected to cover their costs domestically before going on the international circuit.

Only rarely is programming produced directly with international audiences in mind, such as Grupo Globo's high-production novelas, spin-offs of Argentine novelas that were hits in global markets, or coproductions with other regional companies or with Hollywood and European partners. In these cases, budgets may be higher than average. *La Extraña Dama*, for example, an Argentine-Italian soap opera, cost $160,000 per episode, a figure that exceeded the cost for typical domestic productions. The prospects of international revenues have become more important, however, particularly for programs (e.g., high-cost *telenovelas*, dramas, and documentaries) where production costs are unlikely to be recovered domestically.

Finally, protectionist policies account for the increase in local productions in some countries. Governments rarely monitor and enforce quotas and other measures intended to nurture local production and protect domestic companies (Getino 1998). But, in some countries quotas and the regulations banning the airing of foreign content in prime time have contributed to a strengthening of local production.

Audience preference for local productions coupled with the need to meet quotas often means that low-budget productions fill up large portions of television schedules. Talk shows, game shows, variety shows, and sports programming do not require extravagant production investments and offer many opportunities for in-program advertising that adds further revenue. Borrowing a page from Rupert Murdoch's programming strategy, many Latin American media companies went on a shopping spree for popular sports teams to guarantee a source of programming that usually delivers huge audiences and revenues.

Networks' preference for low-budget genres is more evident during economic crises when the advertising dollars shrink. Executives opt for shows that do not require large casts, stars, writers, outdoor scenes, large crews, and twenty-hour shooting days. Such genres have no potential to cross boundaries and bring extra revenues but are preferred to the more expensive programming alternatives. It is no coincidence that, urged to fill schedules in times of economic recession, television executives have opted to purchase foreign formats. Filling schedules with domestic or imported game shows and talk shows is cheaper than airing drama and telenovelas. The import of regional programming is another cost-cutting alternative. After the mid-1990s financial crisis that hit the region's advertising and, consequently, television industries, imports became a favorite option. Even in countries with strong production capacity such as Brazil, networks that regularly broadcast local content relied on Mexican telenovelas. The cost for local production was higher than $30,000 per hour, whereas Mexican telenovelas were sold for $10,000.

As a consequence of the growth of local production, television schedules in most countries offer fewer hours of U.S. programming than in past decades, particularly during prime time. Domestic shows monopolize or dominate prime time in Argentina, Brazil, Chile, Colombia, Mexico, Peru, and Venezuela. Daily schedules in small national markets (Bolivia, Ecuador, Central America, Paraguay, and Uruguay), however, commonly feature regional and, to a lesser extent, local shows. Hollywood productions are commonly used as filler in fringe slots, or broadcast during low-audience weekends. In some cases, regional imports have replaced Hollywood content as a quick, low-cost alternative to local production. Angel González's stations in Chile, Costa Rica, the Dominican Republic, Ecuador, Honduras, and Peru are filled with Mexican programming.

As a region, Latin America confirms the conclusion that markets with a substantial number of television households coupled with large advertising investments and GNPs offer better conditions for the development and consolidation of a domestic audiovisual industry. As some authors have concluded, these factors are the comparative advantages that account for dissimilar development of media industries across markets. Brazil, for example, offers more propitious conditions for the consolidation of an indigenous audiovisual industry than do Panama or Nicaragua. Considering 1998 numbers, Brazil's $3.8 billion television advertising market provides advantages that Panama's $30 million and Nicaragua's $17.5 million markets, for example, cannot match. Moreover, Mexico's Televisa and Brazil's Grupo Globo are able to produce approximately 3,000 hours of programming annually, largely because they have long maintained a quasi-monopolistic position in the television industry that allowed them to capture the largest share of television audience and advertising in the biggest and richest Spanish- and Portuguese-speaking markets, respectively (Sinclair 1999).

Conclusion

In scaling back the role of the state in broadcasting and removing restrictions that prevented or limited foreign participation, globalizing policies have deepened disparities among media markets in the region. Globalization contributed to the consolidation of a three-tier structure formed by large producers and exporters of audiovisual content based in Brazil, Mexico, and Venezuela; medium-size producers and exporters in Argentina, Chile, Colombia, and Peru; and modest-size producers with virtually no exports in Bolivia, Central America, Ecuador, Paraguay, and Uruguay.

What does the case of Latin American media say about larger developments and debates concerning media globalization? Revisionist views of traditional "one-way street" models rightly have drawn attention to the complexity of contemporary flows that resulted from technological changes and the maturation of television industries in different countries and regions. The new revisionism has forced us to rethink theoretical paradigms that dominated debates about international media in the 1960s and 1970s. It has done so by sketching the formation of geolinguistic markets and outlining the major producers/exporters in each market (e.g., Brazil and Mexico/Latin America, Hong Kong/Greater China, Egypt/Middle East).

When revisionist studies first appeared (Straubhaar 1991), Brazilian and Mexican programming was flooding television screens in Latin

America, Spanish-language networks in the United States, and newly opened markets in Europe. This phenomenon provided impetus to reexamine central tenets of the "media imperialism" theory. The situation of contemporary television in Latin America suggests even more complex patterns. Perhaps it is necessary to take this revisionism a step further, and analyze television programming flows inside one region. If global patterns of such flows need to be understood as a "patchwork quilt" (Sinclair, Jacka, and Cunningham 1996), television in Latin America suggests that analysis of flows inside regional/geolinguistic markets also needs to discriminate among complex inflows and outflows. There is no single, dominating center that exports content to the rest of the region but a Latin American "patchwork quilt," formed by multilayered flows of capital and programming. Intraregional trade of television shows and formats, and ownership and production partnerships among regional and global companies suggest that globalization is not unified in terms of such flows. Instead, it is a highly uneven process that affects media markets differently.

These developments raise questions about the oft-made argument that media globalization in the post–Cold War era chiefly worked for the benefit of Hollywood and at the expense of indigenous cultural industries. Privatization, liberalization, and deregulation of media industries removed obstacles that had halted Hollywood's ambitions and thus primed its global engine. Certainly, both television and film are audiovisual industries, and boundaries between them are hard to draw given technological and industrial convergence. Latin American television, however, suggests that globalization does not have identical effects on both industries, and that the analysis needs to be attentive to particular issues and dynamics in each.

Like their counterparts worldwide, regional film industries continue to experience tremendous difficulties. State protectionism in the form of subsidies and credits, the ambitions of television-based companies to expand into film, and coproduction and distribution arrangements with European companies were responsible for keeping local productions afloat and, occasionally, increasing the number of releases. Generally, local films can barely compete with mighty Hollywood productions. Some local productions have done extremely well at the box office, but they are few and far between, lost in a sea of blockbusters sustained by Hollywood's deep advertising pockets, huge output, and global stars.

The situation in the television industry is somewhat different. Domestic television has a better chance to survive and expand than film. As paradoxical as it may sound to gloom-and-doom views of globalization, some Latin American media companies actually benefit from structural reforms in television industries that have opened systems to foreign programming and investment. Because Latin American television production is cheaper than film, output is larger. Because television companies do not compete head-to-head with Hollywood television divisions, they are in a stronger position than film companies.

Globalization does not affect all television markets in the same way. The strength of local companies, the size of the audience and advertising revenues, and the existence of protectionist policies mitigate or favor the entry of regional and global interests. Global capital and programming moves easily into weaker, smaller markets with low production, and aggressively in partnerships with local powerhouses into advertising-rich countries with large, actual or potential, audiences. Nor are all regional media companies on equal footing vis-à-vis globalization. To some, it has been a boost to their business; to others, globalization has facilitated the entry of powerful competitors and thereby introduced major challenges to domestic companies. The trajectories of Grupo Globo and Televisa show that securing a dominant position at home through extensive horizontal and vertical integration and close contacts with political elites is fundamental for plans of regional and global expansion.

Globalization has exacerbated preexisting characteristics and accentuated differences in the region. It has facilitated the expansion of already dominant media companies in domestic, regional, and international markets. It has increased the differences among media markets: while large countries produce a substantial amount of televisual content, smaller countries continue to experience enormous difficulties. Due to rising demand for more television hours created by the explosion in the number of cable and satellite channels, globalization has augmented regional programming traffic. After decades of governments promoting state-owned media, threatening private owners with nationalization, and toying with projects for media reform, globalization signals the consolidation of commercial media systems and the end of alternative models. But states and governments are hardly the losers in the process. They are still able to keep the media on a short leash by negotiating the terms of business practices and defining the workings of media markets. Governments may no longer control broadcasting stations or overtly try to restrict media content, as in past decades of authoritarianism and state-owned media, but they are still able to pull levers that define the conditions under which businesses operate. Globalization has not shaken off old relations but has, in a way, perfected them. In a region where markets historically dominated media systems, it would be a mistake, and even trivial, to affirm that globalization has ushered in a new order in which business interests rule. Markets and states, local and international forces have long been intertwined, locked in a relationship more confrontational or peaceful depending on the specific political and economic conditions of the times. Domestic politics are not accessory to global dynamics but, as has been the case since the early beginnings of Latin American broadcasting, continue to be fundamental in mediating and articulating the interaction between national and supranational forces.

CHAPTER TWO

Transforming Television in Argentina

Market Development and Policy Reform in the 1990s

Hernán Galperín

O F THE sweeping changes in the organization and regulation of Argentine industries in the 1990s, those in the communication sector have been among the most dramatic. In less than a decade, Argentine markets have shifted from a situation of limited competition (i.e., terrestrial broadcasting) or no competition (i.e., telecommunications) to an open, fiercely competitive environment. The TV industry is no exception. Until 1990, it was characterized by an oligopolistic structure with tight state control on the number of players. Advertising revenues provided most of the funding for the system, and a nationalist orientation pervaded industry regulation, reflected in national programming quotas and the ban on foreign investments in media industries. Regulation was neither seriously exercised nor needed since the government, unlike most other Latin American countries, directly controlled the major TV networks. The TV market thus remained closed, underfunded, and—as in the case of other public service industries—highly vulnerable to the changing winds of Argentine politics.

Today the picture is radically different. The major TV networks are in private hands, multichannel TV (cable or direct broadcast satellite, or DBS) is found in over 50 percent of households with televisions, and specialized channels are mushrooming in the pay-TV sector (see table 2.1). Competition is fierce among the major networks and between rival delivery platforms, and has sparked the revival of the national programming industry. Both infrastructure and content regulations have waned, resulting in one of the most liberal TV business environments in the world. In essence, the broadcasting system of yesterday, a tripartite entente between the political (and notably the military) elite, a handful of programmers, and national advertisers, has been eroded by technological, political, and economic transformations. The nationalist model of television predominant up to the mid-1980s has given way to a competitive, internationalized market environment.

Table 2.1 / Facts on Argentina, 1999

Population: 35.8 million	*TV households:* 10.4 million
GDP per capita: US $7,770	*Cable-TV subscribers:* 5.7 million
Fixed telephone lines: 7.4 million	*Cable-TV penetration:* 54%
Teledensity: 20.8%	
Cellular telephone subscribers: 2.4 million	
Internet users: 250,000	

Source: Latincom

This chapter intends to provide an account of these transformations. It assumes that the changes in the organization and dynamics of the Argentine TV industry in the 1990s can be accounted for by analyzing three transformation vectors: deregulation, internationalization, and technological innovation. The first refers to the changes in the regulatory framework of communication industries, and in particular to the attempt to minimize government intervention in the TV industry by selling off publicly owned networks and loosening ownership and content regulations. The second vector, internationalization, refers to the opening of the Argentine media industry to foreign investors, as well as the growing presence of local players in international markets. The third vector, technological innovation, refers to the development of new delivery platforms in the Argentine market (most importantly cable TV) and the increasing convergence among different industry sectors in terms of infrastructure (e.g., joint provision of cable TV and Internet services) and market structure (multimedia corporations). These three vectors, although pushing changes in different (yet not opposed) directions, are certainly interrelated. For example, there would be no (or at least limited) internationalization had the regulations on foreign investments not been lifted; and the rapid development of cable TV certainly prompted numerous changes in media legislation. In addition, larger trends come to bear in the analysis such as the new economic policy orientation of the governing Peronist coalition during the 1990s (Gerchunoff and Torre 1996), the changing political climate in Latin America (Przeworski 1991), and the global expansion of media industries (Herman and McChesney 1997). Although not developed explicitly in this chapter, these larger factors will be acknowledged within the analysis of the aforementioned vectors.

Though the main purpose of this chapter is to provide a road map of the key changes in the Argentine TV industry in the 1990s, I will nonetheless advance a working hypothesis. I will contend that, from an industrial policy perspective, Argentina has successfully developed its TV industry in the last decade. Revenues have grown exponentially, the cable-TV sector is by far the most developed in Latin America, its content industry is strong and has regained an important position in the international market, and this momentum has now spilled over to the film sector. However, from a media policy perspective, a major problem remains unchanged: the lack of an independent, well-financed system of regulation to guarantee basic democratic tenets such as media pluralism, journalistic freedom, affordable access to new communications technologies, and healthy market competition among providers. In other words, in the last decade the old regulatory system has simply been loosened, without much public debate, and without being replaced by a new regulatory regime better suited to ensure achievement of economic and democratic goals under the new industry structure. This is the remaining task for Argentina's modernization of its TV industry, and communications industries in general.

The chapter is organized as follows: the first section outlines a theoretical model for understanding the recent changes in the Argentine TV industry within the larger context of transformations in the dynamics of TV markets worldwide. In the second section a brief historical review of the Argentine TV industry is presented as a background for the third, in which the three vectors of transformation are discussed separately. In the conclusion, I resume the discussion about the need for renewing public control mechanisms—and the potential dangers of not doing so—in the current Argentine TV market.

From Fordism to Post-Fordism in the Television Industry

Changes in the TV industry worldwide in the last two decades have paralleled those in other industries. Scholars have described these as a transition from a Fordist model of serialized production, highly regulated competition, and broad social alliances between labor, industry, and the state toward a post-Fordist model of segmented output, market-driven regulation, and loose arrangements between industry, labor, and the state (Castells 1996). The broadcasting industry was certainly one of the last to be brought under this current of changes, and there is still controversy, particularly in Europe, about how to renew the old public service broadcasting regime (Burgelman 1997). Despite the surprising resilience of some old regime players such as the BBC or the three major American networks, there is little doubt that today's international TV industry bears little resemblance to that of a decade or two ago. In general terms, the structure of the Fordist TV industry can be described as an entente between the local political elite, a handful of broadcasters with close ties to this elite, large advertisers, and national equipment manufacturers (Richeri 1994). Each participant in this entente had a different role. The state typically provided most of the funding for the development of the communications infrastructure (satellite links, relay stations, etc.) needed to create a national broadcasting market. The development of such a market was the main goal under which all participants coalesced: the political elite, to foster national cohesion, maintain military security, and use the media for political mobilization; broadcasters, to package audiences to national advertisers; equipment manufacturers, to widen markets, as the TV industry evolved into one of the key engines of growth during the post–World War II economic boom in the United States and Western Europe (Garnham 1990).

In the case of Latin America, the Fordist TV industry combined the American model of commercial TV with the authoritarian character of politics in the region during much of the 1960s and 1970s (Fox 1988b). TV markets had an oligopolistic structure, in which a few networks competed, with generalist programming, for the advertising revenues that were the main source of funding for the system. The orientation of the regulatory regime was heavily nationalistic, with pervasive limits on foreign investments as well as local programming quotas. Licensing followed strict political criteria, while public interest mandates and other performance requirements were loosely enforced, in return for which broadcasters guaranteed public officials favorable news coverage and broad political support (Martín-Barbero 1987). Horizontal integration caps, cross-media ownership limitations, and restrictions on the functioning of broadcasting networks were also common, as a means for governments to keep the power of broadcasters—and media corporations in general—at bay.

The reasons for the demise of the Fordist TV industry structure are manifold, and ought to be understood within the context of the economic and political reforms started in Latin America and elsewhere in the 1970s. Schematically, there are two main perspectives: the first contends that market developments undermined the structure of the old broadcasting industry, rendering existing regulatory instruments either too costly or simply obsolete (Neuman, McKnight, and Solomon 1997). This perspective stresses the impact of technological change in communications industries, arguing that digitization, innovations in satellite transmission, and the new delivery platforms (cable TV and DBS) came to question the well-established distribution of economic and political resources among the old entente. The second perspective interprets the demise of the Fordist TV model as a triumph of private interests over governments and the public interest at large (Mosco 1996). The very industries that benefited from regulation in the past, it is argued, successfully lobbied for change because the Fordist regime, for a variety of reasons (including technological and market changes as described by the first perspective), no longer served their interests. Whatever the relative merit of these two perspectives, it is clear that changes in the dynamics of media markets on the one hand and the formation of new coalitions of political and economic interests on the other brought into question an industry structure that had lasted for almost four decades.

The new industrial organization, labeled post-Fordist TV (Richeri 1994) or segmented TV (Noam 1996), is characterized, first and foremost, by the explosion in the number of channels made possible by the new delivery platforms (cable TV, DBS, and MMDS, or multipoint multichannel distribution service). The second characteristic is the growth of pay-TV systems, which changed the underlying economics of the industry. This combination of increased channel capacity and subscription TV has resulted in the segmentation of audiences, thus eroding the once dominant position of generalist, over-the-air networks. In the new context, content regulation becomes virtually impossible, thereby weakening the value of television as a tool for cultural socialization or political mobilization. A third and more recent characteristic of post-Fordist TV is the digitization of broadcasting networks, which is currently weakening the traditional separation between telecommunications, TV, and the computer industry (Neuman, McKnight, and Solomon 1997). In terms of the regulatory regime, the nationalist orientation that once justified foreign ownership restrictions and local programming quotas in the Fordist model has largely waned, allowing for a gradual but steady opening of national TV markets, in terms of both ownership and programming. Cross-media ownership restrictions have also been loosened in most media markets, clearing the way for the consolidation of multimedia firms with interests across sectors and national borders. This new regulatory orientation has also weakened the link between political and industrial elites, as broadcasting policies increasingly follow economic rather than political goals.

The analysis above broadly outlined the transformations in the TV industry worldwide in the last two decades, as well as those of its accompanying regulatory regime. It serves as a general framework for understanding the changes in the broadcasting industry of Argentina in the 1990s. However, in every country the transition to a post-Fordist TV market structure has taken a different path, owing to the peculiar historical development of the industry in each case. Thus, a brief historical review of the Argentine broadcasting industry is presented below, as a background to the discussion of the 1990s transition that follows.

History of Argentine Television

As in most Latin American countries, the emerging TV industry of Argentina followed the American model of commercial broadcasting (Fox 1988b). The first station, inaugurated by Perón in 1951, was owned and operated by the government, but the industry did not develop until the early 1960s, after the military government that toppled Perón in 1955 granted the first commercial TV licenses. Presidential decree 15.460, issued in 1957, established the legal framework for TV broadcasting, with all the characteristics of the Fordist regulatory model described above (presidential control over licensing, numerous ownership limitations, ban on foreign capital, limits on the operation of networks, etc.). In 1973, when the broadcasting licenses issued in 1958 expired, the recently elected Peronist government, informed by a strong nationalistic orientation, proceeded to nationalize the three main private networks and their affiliated programming companies. This expropriation of the major Buenos Aires–based networks seemed short-lived since the military regime that toppled the Peronist government shortly after (in 1976) promised to reintegrate the stations into the private sector (Noguer 1985). However, the stations were never (re)privatized by the military regime, most likely because public ownership of commercial stations seemed to serve many interested parties well. While a handful of programmers and national advertisers were guaranteed cheap access to audiences through shady deals with government officials, the military elite was guaranteed favorable news coverage and strict censorship control (Muraro 1988).

The Broadcasting Law of 1980, sanctioned during the military regime, is still the basic legislation under which the TV industry operates. This law, in its original form, falls squarely under the Fordist regulatory regime discussed above, with an added authoritarian twist. It establishes caps on station ownership (maximum of four), prevents newspaper-TV cross-ownership, prohibits the formation of TV broadcasting networks, bans foreign investment in the industry, and imposes numerous content regulations such as a 50 percent national programming quota. Licensing is kept under the sole responsibility of the executive, in the case of terrestrial broadcasting, and of the Comité Federal de Radiodifusión (COMFER), in the case of the so-called complementary services (notably, cable TV). The regulatory agency created in 1972 to oversee the broadcasting industry functioned as a simple branch of the executive, with its staffing and policy guidelines under direct presidential (and often military junta) control.

It is interesting to note that, by defining cable TV as a "complementary service," the 1980 Broadcasting Law relieved this sector from the heavy regulatory burden and the scarcity in licenses that characterized terrestrial TV. Cable service grew steadily during the early 1980s, fueled by the lack of regulation and the freeze in TV broadcasting licenses. The final leap for the cable sector came in 1986, when satellite transmissions were opened to private cable operators. This allowed for a large increase in the number of channels available. First, cable operators were able to down-link regional and international cable networks.[1] Second, the economies of scale created by satellite delivery of programming permitted the creation of several segmented local channels.[2] Seemingly minor, the presidential decree (1613/86) that ended state monopoly in satellite transmissions in 1986 was the first step toward a new industry structure, ushering Argentine TV into the post-Fordist era.

The 1990s: Deregulation

Argentina's TV industry was on the verge of collapse when the country regained democracy in 1983. Public ownership of commercial stations had left the system in virtual bankruptcy, and regulation was exercised by three different agencies (the COMFER, the Secretaría de Comunicaciones, and the Secretaría de Información Pública) with overlapping mandates, dated legislation, and scarce resources (Landi 1987). The system was crying out for reform, but disagreements over the direction of such reforms and more pressing concerns pushed the issue onto the back burner for a number of years. Despite failed attempts at revising the 1980 Broadcasting Law, the only significant change during President Alfonsín's tenure (1983–89) was the aforementioned decree liberalizing satellite transmissions. It was not until 1989, with the sweeping changes brought about by President Menem's election, that the industry underwent significant transformations.

Three elements define the character of regulatory reform in the TV industry of Argentina since 1989: a strong market orientation, the loosening of ownership and content regulations, and the lack of public accountability in the reform process. The most important changes were contained in the Law of State Reform (23.696/89), an all-encompassing bill passed in 1989 that overhauled state-industry relations across all economic sectors. With one eye on curbing public deficits and the other on gaining the support of established media corporations, this law thoroughly transformed the structure of ownership in the TV industry. First, it mandated the privatization of all state-owned commercial TV stations, of which the most important were the privatization of two national networks, Channels 11 and 13, which was carried out shortly after the bill passed. Second, it eliminated a number of ownership limitations, most notably lifting the restriction on newspaper publishers from entry into broadcasting (a restriction long questioned, and often violated, by the publishers). Finally, it changed the legal status of Argentina Televisora Color (the original public station founded by Perón), clearing the way for its privatization (not carried out to date).

Content regulations were loosened through a number of steps. Presidential decree 1771/91, issued in 1991, lifted the ban on the formation of national networks, although restricting network time to 50 percent of affiliates' programming and prohibiting networks from selling spots directly to advertisers. This decree also eliminated two restrictions that were long questioned, and frequently violated, by broadcasters: the twelve-minute-per-hour cap on advertising and the ban on product placement during regular programming. The national programming quota was reduced from 50 to 40 percent, though the decree introduced a new in-house production requirement of 5–10 percent of total programming (depending on the total broadcasting time of the station) and extended the 40 percent national quota to cable TV and other "complementary services" operators. Regulations on advertising were further loosened in Resolution 1226/93, which lifted the ban on foreign-produced spots.

These presidential decrees and ministerial resolutions highlight the way in which regulatory reform was carried out in Argentina. Aside from the privatizations, none of the major changes were introduced through open decision-making procedures, either through parliamentary debate,

judicial review, or consultation with intermediate associations representative of society at large. It is telling that after fifteen years of democratic
government in Argentina, and despite many failed attempts (see Albornoz, Mastrini, and Mestman 1996), not a single law specific to communication industries was passed by Congress.[3] The lack of public accountability in communication policy is also illustrated by the negligible role
that the COMFER and other regulatory agencies, as well as the courts,
have had in the restructuring of the industry.

In essence, regulatory reform in Argentina has been tightly controlled
by the old entente between the political elite and established media corporations, whose distinct objectives coalesced under a common reform
plan. As part of a major state reform program, the Menem administration
(re)privatized the major TV networks and loosened ownership restrictions, aiming at curbing public deficits (to which most publicly owned
commercial stations contributed), and at gaining political support from
the established media organizations. These media organizations, for their
part, were eager to develop new businesses and alliances in the new, relaxed regulatory environment. Regulatory reform in Argentina thereby
proceeded through the dismantling of a legal apparatus that no longer
served the old coalition of interests. However, few attempts were made to
modernize the legislation and renew state regulatory capabilities under
the new industry structure.

The 1990s: Internationalization

Despite local programming quotas and the ban on foreign investments
in media industries until 1994, the internationalization of the Argentine
TV industry is hardly new. In fact, in some respects (e.g., network programming) the industry is today less internationalized than before (see
Falkenheim 1998). It is therefore important to separate the discussion
about internationalization into two dimensions: that of the structure of
ownership of the industry, and that of the programming flows—the relation between the two being far from obvious. The transformations in
the last decade have pushed the industry in different directions. On one
side, foreign investment in Argentine media industries skyrocketed after
1994, when the ban on foreign ownership was lifted. On the other, market liberalization and the increase in the industry's revenues have allowed greater spending on national programming, now exported to several Spanish-speaking markets. In this section these two dimensions are
analyzed separately.

With respect to the structure of ownership of the industry, Argentina is one of the most internationalized TV markets in Latin America, thanks to its complete opening of media markets to foreign investment in 1994. Following the pattern of communications policymaking, the ban on foreign ownership established by the 1980 Broadcasting Law was lifted not through congressional legislation but via the signing of an investment treaty with the United States (which, according to the reforms made to the Argentine Constitution in 1995, takes precedence over national law), and met with surprisingly little opposition. Soon after, investments were pouring into Argentine media industries, attracted by a relatively wealthy and stable economy (compared to other Latin American countries), a mature multichannel TV market, and a relaxed regulatory environment. It is virtually impossible to follow the pace of acquisitions, joint ventures, and stock trading within the Argentine media industry. For our purposes, it will suffice to outline the case of CEI Holdings, which represents well the new ownership structure in the Argentine TV market.

The CEI group began in 1989 as a vehicle for Citibank to exchange its seemingly worthless $1 billion in Argentine debt bonds for stakes in the public companies being privatized by the Menem administration. The company took stakes in a broad range of sectors, from telecommunications to paper and steel mills, but gradually focused on communications industries.[4] CEI's foray into the TV industry came in 1995 with a minority stake in Multicanal, then the leading multiple system operator (MSO). When competing MSO Cablevisión (which had been acquired by TCI in 1994) was put up for sale in 1997, the CEI group and Telefónica de España jointly bought 66 percent of the company. Subsequently, the CEI group would buy interests in Torneos y Competencias (the leading sports programmer, which holds rights to the Argentine soccer Premier League until 2014), ATCO (a publishing company that also controls Telefe, the leading TV network, as well as several radio networks), Canal 9 (the fourth-ranked TV network, now renamed Canal Azul, in a 50–50 joint venture with Australian media group Prime Television), and Advance (the leading Argentine Internet service provider). The case of the CEI group is interesting not only because in less than five years, and thanks to the lifting of virtually all ownership restrictions, the group has come to control the leading firm in almost every media sector, but also because, unlike the traditional, family-controlled media corporations of Latin America (such as its rival Grupo Clarín in Argentina, Organizações

Globo in Brazil, or Grupo Televisa in Mexico), the CEI group is controlled exclusively by financial investors.

The other dimension of internationalization, that of programming, falls under the decades-old debate about the international flow of films and TV programs (Varis 1974), to some extent now repackaged under the label of globalization. In the case of Argentina, two different trends are observable. As a result of the high penetration of cable-TV services, there is little doubt that in terms of sheer volume there is more foreign programming being offered today than was ever the case, particularly through specialized-interest channels (news, music, feature films, etc.). However, the availability of regional or international cable networks has had only limited impact on terrestrial networks, as audience shares for such channels remain low.[5] In addition, the expansion in channel capacity has fostered the development of local segmented channels, which in many cases compete head-to-head at the national and regional level with the better-known international brands. As far as terrestrial TV is concerned, Argentina is increasingly self-sufficient in programming. A recent survey found a drop in imported programming from 49 percent in 1983 to 22 percent in 1996 (Falkenheim 1998). As several scholars have noted, TV markets, for cultural and linguistic reasons, are still organized along national (Straubhaar 1991) or at best regional (Collins 1994; Sinclair, Jacka, and Cunningham 1996) borders.

The second observable trend is the growing presence of Argentine programming in the international TV market, and in particular in the neighboring Mercosur countries. The Mercosur agreement in itself has had little impact since, thus far, media industries have not been included in the trade liberalization schedule, and a regional media policy like that of the European Union has not been implemented (Galperín 1999). Nonetheless, given the similarities in language, viewing patterns, and genre preferences among Mercosur audiences, Telefe and Artear, the two Argentine networks privatized in 1989, have successfully expanded into these neighboring markets. Telefe exports to several other Latin American countries, and some of its most successful shows are picked up by panregional networks such as Gems Television, available in numerous U.S. markets. Interestingly, a handful of these shows are produced in wholly localized versions for the Argentine, Brazilian, and Mexican markets (Television Business International 1999). Likewise, Artear has been active in the international market, although its trade volume remains small compared to the major players in the Spanish-speaking programming market like TV Globo and Televisa. Foreign revenues for Artear (part of Grupo Clarín) in 1995 amounted to $5 million, whereas Televisa exported $84 million during the same period.

An interesting side effect of the new structure in the TV market has been a relative revitalization of the Argentine film industry. Until 1996 local film production in Argentina remained weak, with imported fare accounting for over 85 percent of the films shown in theaters and over 90 percent on TV (*Boletín Industrias Culturales* 1996). The local industry started regaining momentum after passage of the new Film Law in 1994, but significant growth only came in 1997 thanks to a new relationship between the film and TV industries. Three of the four highest box-office takers in 1997 were local productions. Of those, two were spin-offs from TV shows, while the other was funded by Artear (*Variety* 1998). Although these examples do not override some of the perennial problems of film production in Argentina (inadequate financing and distribution, small volume of complementary "windows," etc.), they reveal a positive trend based on a new film/TV industry partnership. The case of Argentina, though certainly unique in some respects, emphasizes the need to nuance some of the tenets in the media globalization debate (cf. Herman and McChesney 1997). It is apparent that, to date, technological innovation and the liberalization of market entry have had a much greater impact on the structure of ownership than on the content of national TV programming. While foreign investment in media industries is ever increasing, and more international programming is available than ever before, locally produced *telenovelas*, variety shows, and soccer games still command, by far, the largest audiences. As technological innovation renders programming flows cheaper, easier, and faster, and regulatory barriers for such flows decrease, foreign programming meets with little audience interest and a saturated TV market. The Argentine case illustrates well the inertia of cultural patterns in comparison to the swift internationalization of investment and the rapid pace of technological innovation in the media sector.

The 1990s: Technological Innovation

Technological innovation has been a major factor in changing the structure and dynamics of the TV industry worldwide (Noam 1996). Of particular importance has been the development of alternative delivery platforms for TV programming, such as cable TV and DBS, which have increased multifold the channel capacity offered by terrestrial TV. Digitization, introduced in the late 1990s, promises a new leap forward by allowing more efficient use of bandwidth capacity across all platforms (including terrestrial TV), and by permitting the integration of TV with a plethora of interactive services. Although in Latin America the impact of such innovation is still incipient (as terrestrial TV still dominates in most countries), Argentina is a case apart. The early deployment of cable networks has had a profound impact on the structure of the TV industry, in terms of both financing and programming. Thus, it is worth recounting a brief history of cable TV in Argentina.

This history has many parallels with that in the United States. Unlike in Western European countries, where development of cable TV was part of a public industrial project, in Argentina cable systems started as a typical community antenna set up by small entrepreneurs (many of them TV-set retailers), particularly in the outskirts of Buenos Aires and the provinces with poor reception of terrestrial channels (Lovino 1998). Given the prohibition on the formation of TV networks, for a large number of viewers cable TV was the only means to access the more attractive Buenos Aires–based programming. The lack of regulation was also a major incentive for the development of cable TV. Initially, obtaining a municipal permit was the only requirement to install cable operations, as these did not utilize the radio spectrum. This sector was brought under federal auspices with the passage of the 1980 Broadcasting Law. As noted above, by defining it as a "complementary service," the 1980 law placed cable TV under a light regulatory regime. But a significant onus that remained was the prohibition on the use of satellite transmissions by cable operators, which limited channel supply and hindered the growth of cable services in the affluent urban areas well served by terrestrial TV.

With the lifting of this restriction in 1986, cable TV experienced a boom. And with growth came the consolidation of the industry, with small cable operators being bought out by the large MSOs. By 1996, three operators controlled 40 percent of cable subscribers. Today two operators, Grupo Clarín's Multicanal and Cablevisión (jointly owned by the CEI group, Telefónica de España, and TCI), control about 60 percent of Argentina's 5.7 million cable subscribers (Latincom 1999). With a 54 percent penetration rate and generation of over 66 percent of the overall TV industry revenues, the sector is by far the most developed in Latin America (Television Business International 1998). Argentina is thus well poised for the technological convergence era: cable operators already offer high-speed Internet access, and with the liberalization of basic telephony scheduled for the end of 1999, many cable operators expect to enter this profitable market.[6]

Digital DBS debuted as recently as June 1998 in Argentina, although given the high penetration of cable TV many consider it a failed proposition (Hudson 1998). The first entrant in the DBS market was Televisión Directa al Hogar (TDH), a small subsidiary of Supercanal, the third-largest MSO and part of the Grupo Vila media corporation. TDH transmits via NahuelSat, which until recently held monopoly rights to DBS transmissions in Argentina. TDH launched analog DBS services in June 1996 but met with little success. With the signing of a bilateral satellite accord with the United States in June 1998, NahuelSat's monopoly was formally ended. Soon after, Galaxy Entertainment Argentina—a subsidiary of Galaxy Latin America controlled by Grupo Clarín, Grupo Cisneros, and Hughes Electronics—launched its digital DBS service, and rival operator Sky Latin America (backed by News Corporation and Telecom Argentina, the other fixed telephony operator) was set to start services in mid-1999.

Lastly, Argentina has taken the first steps in the transition from analog to digital terrestrial television (DTT). In early 1998 a resolution by the Secretaría de Comunicaciones (433/98) assigned current broadcasters frequencies for experimental DTT transmissions, and in October 1998 Resolution 2357/98 was adopted defining several technical aspects of the transition. Although licensing procedures for DTT are yet to be defined, the existing networks have already carried out the first experimental broadcasts (Albornoz, Hernández, and Postolski 1999). Following the pattern of Argentine communications policymaking in the last decade, Resolution 2357/98 defined critical issues in the transition toward DTT—such as the selection of the American ATSC transmission standard over its rival European DVB-T standard—in a closed policymaking process involving existing market actors and compliant regulators.

Technological innovation has been a major force in reshaping the Argentine TV industry in the 1990s, in terms of both programming and financing. Undoubtedly, the light regulatory touch on the new delivery platforms has been a major incentive for technological upgrading. Nonetheless, by the same token, the deployment of new technologies has followed a strict commercial logic. Unlike other mature multichannel markets such as the United States, or even emerging ones like neighboring Brazil, there are no leased access obligations or coverage requirements for Argentine pay-TV operators.

Competition policies to discipline market actors and guarantee afford-able access are equally absent, even though most cable operators enjoy a de facto monopoly in their service areas. The lack of such public interest safeguards, or of any real public policy for new communications tech-nologies, has left virtually all decisions in the hands of shortsighted mar-ket actors. In the long run, such policy void might hinder the develop-ment of a truly open information society in Argentina.

Conclusion: What's Old, What's New?

This chapter has presented the major changes in the Argentine TV indus-try in the 1990s around three dimensions: deregulation, internationaliza-tion, and technological innovation. A hasty reviewer of such changes may conclude that the industry, at the outset of the twenty-first century, bears little resemblance to that of a decade ago. And to a certain extent, this is a valid conclusion. However, there is also evidence that many of the old industry dynamics and the established state-industry relations, have changed little under the new market structure. The reason is that indus-try developments and technological innovation have far outpaced insti-tutional reform, resulting in an environment of de facto deregulation, for lack of regulation.

Licensing decisions, regulatory agency staffing, and other key instru-ments of media policy remain centralized under the executive branch, and thus sheltered from mechanisms of public accountability. This inevi-tably reproduces political clientelism as a central dynamic in the commu-nications policymaking process. Despite the recent institutional restruc-turing with the creation of the Comisión Nacional de Comunicaciones in 1997 (which merged part of the COMFER with the telecommunica-tions and postal regulatory organs), lack of funding, dated legislation, and political pressures render the role of regulatory agencies almost purely administrative.[7] In other words, a hybrid system in which a post-Fordist TV industry structure is developing under the institutional legacy of the old Fordist regime is what best characterizes the changes in the TV indus-try of Argentina in the past decade. Renewing state capabilities in com-munications policy and updating the existing regulatory framework are among the challenges ahead for the yet unfinished modernization of the Argentine television industry.

Notes

1. The first two international cable networks offered were ESPN and CNN, in March 1989.

2. The first such channel was Premier, launched by cable operator VCC in 1987.

3. The only legislation passed since 1983 that indirectly bears on the broadcasting sector is the new film funding law passed in 1994.

4. CEI's most valuable asset is a 50 percent stake in Telefónica de Argentina, the largest of the country's two fixed telephony companies.

5. In 1998 the top-ranked cable network was HBO Olé, with less than 1 rating point (Latincom 1999).

6. Multicanal is already part of the cellular telephony operator CTI, and entered the telephony market in partnership with GTE in November 1999 (Latincom 1999).

7. A similar situation exists in the regulation of other public utilities (see Murillo 1998).

Mass Media in Brazil

Modernization to Prevent Change

Roberto Amaral

E, dopo, tutto sarà lo stesso mentre tutto sarà cambiato.
Tomasi di Lampedusa, Il gattopardo

Introduction

The mass media reflect and help shape whatever society in which they exist. The Brazilian media, like Brazil itself, are monopolistic and elitist. Although significant changes occurred in the Brazilian media and political system over the last decades, these changes in truth helped preserve rather than alter the larger media and political system. The media do not reflect society passively. The Brazilian media are political actors who intervene in the political order, have an active voice in the electoral process, and take sides, almost like a political party. The media help maintain the status quo because state and media interests coalesce.

The monopolistic and elitist characteristics of Brazilian society, which includes the media, also reflect the way Brazil is inserted in the global economy as a source of cheap labor for multinational corporations. Economics, culture, information, and politics in Brazil have become tied to broader global interests. All this adds up to a bitterly divided society—and world—of haves and have-nots.

A new phase of the organization of civil society has emerged within this situation with the goal of replacing the traditional mediations between citizenship and the state. In this phase political parties and popular representation are reduced in importance.

The new actors of this politics (*without* politics and parties) lead popular movements of collective and mass mobilization, leaving to political parties the function of simply conferring institutional legitimacy. In this way the essential role of political parties is transferred to other institutions, and popular mobilization becomes dependent on the monopoly of the mass media, which determine the direction of the social process on the basis of their own interests.

In setting the political agenda the media act independently of the demands and needs of society. Mostly they help dictate those demands and create those needs. Beginning in the 1980s, the combined effects of deregulation and privatization together with the proliferation of new technologies accelerated the globalization of communications. Even when the nation-state maintains regulatory power, today its effects are secondary in the face of satellite, pay-TV, and the Internet.

Technology and Exclusion

Business concentration is the first characteristic of the Brazilian system of mass media. Three national networks control over-the-air television. One of those networks is the largest conglomerate in the country with activities in all cultural industries. Concentration also exists in radio and print media. Two big networks, NET (owned by Organizações Globo) and DirectTV-TVA (owned by Grupo *Abril*, the largest print conglomerate), control cable television. Grupo Globo and Abril–Folha de São Paulo control the largest Internet portals. In partnership with Grupo Globo, Folha de São Paulo launched the national newspaper *Valor Econômico*. The concentration in the Brazilian media industry is part of a wider phenomenon throughout the political economy that includes the concentration of federal powers at the expense of states and municipalities, and of executive power at the expense of that of other branches of government. Concentration of income in Brazil is the highest in the world. This is what some Brazilians call *macrocefalia*, a monopolistic system that has the power to add or suppress facts.

A consequence of *macrocefalia* is vertical and horizontal monopoly—that is, the process through which economic domination in the cultural industry (i.e., radio, print, recording, video, film, show business) expands vertically to control creation, production, marketing, and distribution leading to the development of an independent, national industry. Organizações Globo has a national monopoly of communication and information and controls television, radio, and print media. The control of regional broadcasting and print media also is concentrated: television is in the hands of the Grupo Globo affiliate, and this company also owns a newspaper that consistently has the highest circulation in states where generally there are no more than two dailies. The local system repeats the national model of domination. The distribution of regional broadcasting licenses is of secondary importance because they simply reproduce the content of the big networks.

Concentration, like capitalism, is a global phenomenon. Fewer than ten companies dominate the global media market. Half of their revenues come from outside the country in which they are headquartered (Biernazki 2000; McChesney 1997). Only some fifty companies are responsible for the majority of the global production of films and television programming, own most cable and satellite systems and publishing companies, and control the recording industry. As early as the beginning of the 1980s, foreign programs (mostly from the United States) made up a third of television hours broadcast in the world (Gershon 1997; Sinclair, Jacka, and Cunningham 1996). Today U.S. television is present in Brazil mainly through CNN and other cable channels in Spanish and English; CNN rebroadcasts news programs on national channels, and CNN's formats as well as its production, aesthetic, and ideological models appear on Brazilian stations.

The economic model of concentration and exclusion that results from market freedom and globalization influences classic media (print and broadcast television) as well as newer media (pay-TV). Brazil has 32 million television households—that is, 87 percent of total homes. The national audience of over-the-air television is estimated at 100 million. In contrast, only 3 percent (2.7 million) have access to pay-TV: of which 10 percent have access through MMDS; 32 percent through satellite; and 58 percent through cable, which reaches only 7 percent of Brazilian homes (*Folha de São Paulo* 2000). This is not surprising considering that pay-TV subscriptions cost about $94 up front (with a $39 monthly fee) at a time when the minimum wage in Brazil is $84 per month. Consequently, 97 percent of subscribers to pay-TV are among the wealthiest 1 percent of the population, while among these subscribers 42 percent earn $5,600 monthly, or sixty-seven times the minimum wage (*Jornal do Brasil* 1996).

The Brazilian pay-TV audience has access not only to CNN (in English and Spanish) but also to other channels, even though its array of options has not increased in recent years. The NET subscriber, for example, could choose MTV, Deutsche Welle (journalistic and variety programs in German, English, and Spanish), TV5 (public channel owned by a consortium of the governments of France, Canada, Belgium, and Switzerland that airs journalistic and cultural programs in French), Cartoon Network, Fox Kids, Nickelodeon, BBC World, MGM (films and serials), RAI (Italian television), Animal Planet, GNT (documentaries and interviews),

Multishow, People and Arts, AXN (films and extreme sports), USA, TNT, Warner, Discovery Channel, Superstation (shows and news programs), Fox, Bloomberg Television, ESPN, TVE (Spanish television), or one of the five film channels. Playboy and SexyHot for erotic films are also available. The Brazilian audience does not lack programming related to its culture, although changing channels does not mean changes in programming as there is little real difference between stations. National pay channels include Rede SENAC (Serviço Nacional de Aprendizagem Comercial), Rede Globo's Canal Rural, Globo News (a mix of programming of over-the-air Globo television), Canal Futura (Globo's educational channel), and Canal Brasil (national films, music videos, and interviews) (Guia de Programação Net 2000). Brazil also has channels that carry the proceedings of the House of Representatives and the Senate.

The Brazilian audience could choose TVA, which offers access to CNN International, Cartoon Network, E! Entertainment Television, Discovery Kids, Fox, Fox Kids, Nickelodeon, People and Arts, TNT—all these signals are broadcast live—RTPi (a European cultural newscast), AXN, ESPN International, ESPN Brasil,[1] Eurochannel, F&A, HBO/HB2, Sony (films), and Warner Brothers (films). In October 2000, TVA offered 800 films, by countries of origin (TVA 2000).

Table 3.1 / TVA's Film Offerings

Country of Origin	Number of films	Country of Origin	Number of films
United States	614	Denmark	2
England	56	Argentina	2
France	43	Poland	1
Italy	26	Portugal	1
Spain	15	Russia	1
Australia	9	China	1
Canada	8	Korea	1
Germany	6	Ireland	1
Switzerland	5	Brazil	1

It is no different on the Internet. If an alien were to land in any Latin American country today, and knew that country only through the Internet, it would face an anglophone, westernized, white, consumer world. The great promise of information democracy remains an illusion.

Users cannot surf the Internet if they do not have a computer, a modem, adequate software, a good phone line, access to an ISP, a certain educational background and training, and a reasonable knowledge of English—which language is not just a means of communication but a way of thinking. By accumulating and concentrating information and offering subscribers a high number of portals, Internet access is conditioned by paid subscription. But who has access? An overwhelming 93 percent of Internet sites are in English, 4 percent are in French, and only 3 percent are in other languages (Zappa 1996). The non-English-speaking Internet user in Brazil has little to surf besides Brazilian sites.[2]

In Brazil, a country of 150 million people in 2000, there are 2.5 million Internet users, less than 2 percent of the population, including private, public, government, and business connections.[3] More availability of information and the possibility of high-speed connectivity thus has no meaning, and better information has not contributed genuinely to improved access to information. Quite the opposite: we are witnessing the construction of a new form of inequality among people. The world, already divided between rich and poor, powerful and exploited nations, has also built a division between information-rich and information-poor citizens.

Old Communications Technologies, Old Models of Domination

Despite commonalities with other Latin American countries, the Brazilian case offers some unique characteristics. The incorporation of Brazil into contemporary patterns of cultural production and consumption happened against a background of scandalous social inequality, the most notable and permanent characteristic of Latin America. In 1999, almost 57 million Brazilians (38 percent of the population) lived in extreme poverty with incomes lower than their counterparts in Mexico and Argentina.[4] While ranked eighth, ninth, or tenth in economic power globally (depending on which criterion is used), Brazil shows the most perverse concentration of wealth in the world. A fraction of the population (approximately a third of the country's total) with consumption patterns similar to the First World shares its habitat with a population that is on the threshold of misery, and absolutely marginalized socially, economically, and politically (United Nations 1999). A characteristic of Latin American societies, this feature has become more pronounced amid globalization. Its unfavorable consequences are seen as inevitable by national governments; the prospects are of fewer jobs and lower wages in a context of inefficient, insufficient, or altogether absent social policies—the shrinking of the welfare state. Such social inequality has historically defined the main boundaries of a political culture of exclusion, deepening the gaps between first-, second-, and third-class citizens.

Investment and Concentration in the Television of the Elites

The development of pay television and the still restricted use of computers and the Internet in Brazil signal the increasing reduction of democratic spaces (even formal ones), and the domination of the culture of exclusion as policy. It is not just a consequence (though relevant) of economic dysfunction, but a political project.

Pay television officially began in Brazil in 1991.[5] Today it is an expanding market, whose model of development is not different from the traditional trend toward media monopoly that prevails in over-the-air television, a market unequally divided among three networks. The growth of pay-TV fits the international model of big media monopolies that stretch through many countries in association with local business. Those relations, previously secret, are now explicit, legal, and legitimized by neoliberal discourse. In this highly concentrated context, the pay-TV market has grown, led by two companies: Organizações Globo's NET (associated with Sky Latin America), which controls 64 percent of the market; and Grupo Abril's TVA (associated with DirecTV), which has 25 percent. Independent companies have 7 percent of the market. Those groups received their licenses in 1989, four months after the 1988 Constitution was approved, and began operations in 1991. Regulations were not implemented until 1995 after the companies had acquired important technical advantages and the control of the main markets in the country. The law refrained from enacting any protection against the formation of monopolies, oligopolies, and vertical and horizontal concentration of production and ownership. Nor did it consider the protection of citizens against information monopolies.

To exploit satellite television, starting in 1996, businessman Roberto Marinho's Globo and megabusinessman Rupert Murdoch's News Corporation agreed to expand Direct Home TV in Latin America.[6] Similarly, Grupo Abril teamed up with Hughes Electronics to launch the service in the region with 144 channels in either Spanish or Portuguese and 60 music channels via the U.S. satellite Galaxy Latin America (GLA). Such partnerships of national oligopolies and large foreign concerns make explicit the contribution of foreign capital to national media, although the national cable legislation establishes that 51 percent of the market should be controlled by national business.[7] In the context of globalization, no regulatory mechanisms restrict cross-media ownership, nationally or internationally. Therefore, ownership concentration exceeds national borders on an unprecedented scale. National media monopolies become stronger thanks to foreign capital, thereby weakening any social, competitive, or nongovernmental initiatives. Given the financial and technical competence of these groups, the result is national fragility and lack of protection of citizens/users. This is also observed in the politics of privatization and the denationalization of the national system of telecommunications.[8]

Satellite television followed the same course as cable television. Grupo Globo and Abril distributed among themselves the best market segments as well as technical and marketing knowledge to exploit the new technology. The state took care of legal regulations, and legitimized a market structure that cannot now be changed. Any prospects of competition are unthinkable.

By restricting the market by charging access and monthly fees, pay television excludes the majority of the population, which is relegated to watching over-the-air television. The latter receives less investment because it is aimed at low-income audiences. This segmentation determines the migration of advertising to pay television.

The expansion of pay television does not mean a substantial increase in local production. There is little local journalism. In general, pay television airs a repetition or mix of over-the-air television programming. There are almost no economic and cultural incentives for national television or film production. Newscasts are essentially U.S.- and European-centered, and films are, overwhelmingly, U.S. productions. In pay-TV, English is the dominant language of international channels, and the cultural, political, and aesthetic model is an essentially U.S. one.

The Internet: The Technological Community of the Novices

Despite its potential to enlarge information flow, the Internet is not a mass medium. More expensive than pay-TV, it requires more monetary resources, which, presently, are affordable only by a small segment of the population. The apparent feeling of equality among Internet users is real if we consider the limitations of the network, that is, if we ignore the nonusers, those who are not participants of that transnational, elitist, technological community.

The reality of the Internet's growing commercial use flies in the face of the theoretical possibility of a free and unrestricted flow of information. The Internet has become just another large market that is being appropriated by the same conglomerates that dominate television, radio, film, and print media, which flood it with their seemingly unlimited quantity of self-generated information and news. For 24-hour news providers, the 'net is appropriated as another profitable channel of communication. We are witnessing the conquest of the "new" media by the "old" media. In other words, new technology is being absorbed by the old technology companies, the content of the new media is mixed with the content of the old, and the promise of democratization is replaced by the deepening of concentration and monopoly.

In the Brazilian case, where the use of the Internet is more advanced than in other Latin American countries, practically all newspapers, not only the big dailies but also local papers and magazines, and all television and radio stations are available online. Although other alternative newspapers also are published online, the power lies in those consolidated companies that have found another space for expansion of their empires and promotion of their worldviews. The biggest Brazilian portal is Universo Online (UOL), which resulted from the merger of Grupo Abril's website Brasil Online (BOL) with Folha de São Paulo's Universo Online. With 500,000 subscribers in Brazil, its goal is to have operations throughout Latin America. Recently, Grupo Globo launched its own online service inspired by America Online, Compuserve, and Prodigy. The expansion of this service depends on the increase in the number of providers and the growth of the telecommunications infrastructure. The Internet is also being used, though still somewhat timidly, by television stations to publicize and offer archives of programs and news.

The same economic-financial groups, both national and international, that control the companies that produce and sell information are responsible for the advertising investments that the media depend on for their survival. The unending search for advertising revenues makes many media organizations dependent on sponsors who are often the clandestine owners of many media outlets (Romanet 1996).

Most of the time, globalization represents the intensification of privatizing processes and neoliberal oligopolies, justified by new discourses on a global scale. Countries of the South respond weakly to the requirements of the new world order. Their economic agreements are subtreaties in the service of an order dominated by countries of the North, mainly the United States, in their quest of extraterritorial expansion. More than a natural rupture with the modern world, the new media in Latin America intensify historical relations of domination within countries. Irrelevant information, fragmented information, third-level information will be offered to the Brazilian population that has the television on, but the important information, information as instrument of power, is limited to those who have access to pay television or the Internet.

In a country with such characteristics, it is not possible to talk about public opinion and democracy. Satellites, informatics, digital communications systems, the promise of interactivity and interconnectivity—the interactive Internet-television and real-time Internet—seem to lead to domination and control, to feed the threat of Orwell's Big Brother rather than decentralization. What we have is communications concentrated and directed in a North-South, core-periphery direction. The free flow of international information does not exist, but instead, in Brazil there is an increasingly globalized and antinational system, dependent on ideological sources and technologies developed in the center of power that rule over unequally developed societies, unequally connected to the new media.

Notes

1. Globosat bought 25 percent of ESPN Brasil.

2. According to Media Metrix, a U.S. company that measures Internet use, from the top twenty-five websites in Brazil, fifteen are U.S., six are Brazilian (including the Ministry of Economics), two are Spanish, and two are Portuguese. Only a third of Brazilians who have Internet access at home visit websites (the rest use it only for e-mail).

3. Instituto Brasileiro de Opinião Pública e Estatística Ltda. (IBOPE) states there were 4.8 million Internet users in October 2000, slightly more than 3 percent of the population. Rafael Tonelli says that "almost 58 percent of those who access the Internet daily do not have access at home" (*Ícaro Brasil* 2000).

4. A 2000 official report defines poor as those whose family income per capita is below the minimum wage of $83 monthly.

5. Brazil was one of the last countries in Latin America to have pay television.

6. The partnership of Grupo Globo (54%), News Corporation (36%), and TCI (10%) intends to control the Latin American market of 30 million users.

7. The Ministry of Communications recognizes that the main difficulty is to identify the stockholders of each company.

8. At the time of this writing, there is a proposal in the Brazilian Congress to amend the banning of foreign capital in control of national media companies as decreed by the 1998 Constitution.

CHAPTER FOUR

The Triumph of the Media Elite
in Postwar Central America

Rick Rockwell and Noreene Janus

DURING the 1990s in Central America, as most of the nations in the region moved out of wars and into an era supposedly marked by a transition to democracy, in broadcasting, large forces were assembling to create a decade for the media caciques. In this analysis of the consolidation of media power in the region, we will focus on five countries, all of which were touched by wars. In Guatemala, the region's longest-running guerrilla war ended in 1996. El Salvador's bloody civil war came to a close early in 1992, two years after the Contra War concluded in nearby Nicaragua. Although Honduras was not the scene of any official war, it served as a staging area for the U.S.-funded Contras. The stepped-up U.S. military presence in Honduras and high levels of U.S. military aid certainly contributed to the militarization of that nation and a little-known "dirty war" against opposition forces during the 1980s and early 1990s (Ruhl 1997).[1] This militarization marks Honduras as one of the nations touched by the region's war years. Finally, Panama, as it moves beyond the Noriega era and the scars of the U.S. invasion known as Operation Just Cause, also is experiencing its own media changes.

These five nations experienced unique development of certain aspects of their media systems in the preconflict era and during their war years. However, in the 1990s, two similar forces loomed over the region to affect decision making by Central America's major broadcasters. The first is simply an outgrowth of long-term U.S. foreign policy and commercial interests in the area: preparation for the entrance into the market of U.S. broadcast and cable companies, which already provide large amounts of program content for the region. Those U.S. firms, much like the broadcasters in the Central American region, have seen their own consolidation into massive marketing and cross-platform operations in the 1990s.

Although the U.S. presence in Latin American broadcasting is a constant, many Latin American broadcast companies are also furnishing programming for the region, and direct U.S. investment in the region is stymied both by protectionist laws that prevent outside ownership or simply by U.S. corporate indifference to the region. Thus, this analysis will focus on the owners, trends, and immediate conditions that shape Central American broadcasting, beyond the influence of U.S.-based broadcasting multinationals.

The second force that most broadcasters in the region say has inexorably conquered large swaths of the broadcast spectrum in both radio and television is simply one man: Angel González González, who has a virtual monopoly of the commercial television spectrum in Guatemala, along with considerable radio holdings. Known for consorting with leaders of Nicaragua's counterinsurgency in Miami where he lives, González began investing in broadcasting operations in Managua after the Contra War. González now has major holdings in three of Nicaragua's nine television outlets. He also has holdings in the Costa Rican Broadcast System (Villalobos 1997, 108).[2] González not only exhibits some of the monopolistic tendencies so typical of owners in the region, but he is a significant figure because he has moved his operations into what could be the next phase for a few of the region's broadcasters: controlling media beyond the borders of the one country in which they are the dominant broadcast force. Moving like an amoeba, using investment contacts in his homeland, González has bought enough regional broadcast properties to become a multinational presence.

In media circles throughout Central America, González is referred to simply as "the Mexican," not only because of his country of origin, but because of his connections with Mexico's TV giant, Televisa, one of the top content providers for Latin American television. González sidesteps laws in Guatemala preventing media ownership by foreign nationals because he is married to a Guatemalan woman and the media holdings are technically in her name (Vanden Heuvel and Dennis 1995). In Guatemala, González controls the four main commercial television outlets (the only public television outlet in the country is converting from control by the army to a general state ownership as part of the country's postwar transition) and ten radio stations.[3] He also owns the majority of the country's cinemas, which provide González with a source of films for his television channels (Vanden Heuvel and Dennis 1995). In addition, his cinemas also generate advertising revenue.[4]

What González represents to Central American broadcasters is the threat of a larger production and programming force in Latin America that is aimed at erasing the unique national character of each of these small nations. Members of the media in these nations resent being subsumed by a Mexican investor who broadcasts programs from Mexican television that do not speak to the same history or cultural development as the other nations on the Isthmus. More importantly, González has seized upon the political structures of the region that were not swept away by the region's wars: structures that maintain a consolidation of political and mercantile power in the hands of a few conservative elements in each country. Also, the hemispheric trend toward open markets and a free flow of commerce not only has worked to this Mexican investor's advantage but also has improved the position of leading broadcast forces already in place in these nations during the turbulent war years. What makes González's success in the region so different is that he is a relatively new force, looked upon as an intruder by the region's media. Unlike his competitors, he has not been content with dominating broadcasting in one nation.

Before he dominated Central America's airwaves, González represented Televisa selling programs to broadcasters in the region and selling advertising for one Guatemalan station. In 1981, with Televisa as a partner, he took over his first Guatemalan television station. Televisa still holds a minority stake in two of Guatemala's television outlets. In the 1990s González also found it convenient to team up with Mexico's new commercial broadcast company, TV Azteca, to gain control of Guatemala's Canal 13 (Virtue 1998, 225).

These investment deals have resulted in Guatemalan television being flooded with Mexican programming. For instance, during the morning hours, two of Guatemala's television outlets run the live morning programs from Televisa and TV Azteca. These programs may mention Guatemala only in passing and seem geared toward the elite and middle class of Mexico City rather than a Central American audience. As for the other Guatemalan stations in the morning hours, they run low-quality talk programs, and reruns of local news from the night before. As they look for material, these stations often strip news stories from U.S. sources (CBS and CNN particularly) and overdub Spanish translations or take news broadcasts originating in Mexico or Spain. Using this compendium of source material, the Guatemalan stations piece together a newscast with a local anchor. Or they simply abandon news and talk in the morning hours in favor of music videos.

Some observers maintain that by downplaying local news and controversy, González maintains his monopoly grip on television in Guatemala (Vanden Heuvel and Dennis 1995). Political experts in Guatemala credit González with surfing the shifting and often treacherous political tide for almost two decades. Instead of running overtly favorable stories about those in power, Guatemalan television attempts to filter the news and information by concentrating coverage on what management might determine to be safe topics or stories on the agenda of whichever party may be in power.

"TV doesn't have a function now really," admitted Marco Tulio Barrios Reina, the managing editor of the popular news program *Notisiete* on one of the channels owned by González. "If you want reality, TV isn't the place," he said.[5] Not only has González neutralized television as a source of political plurality; he courts government favor by having popular Canal 7 run the controversial government-produced information program *Avances*. The program has been condemned by international media groups as a propaganda machine for the government of Guatemala's president Alvaro Arzú Irigoyen (Chasan 1998, 195). The program was initiated under the administration of President Ramiro de León Carpio to inform the public about new government programs. However, Arzú's administration has changed *Avances* into a platform for Guatemala's ruling party, the PAN (National Advancement Party, by its Spanish acronym). On the program, government officials often launch attacks against their enemies. Also, many of the stories on the program are aimed at rebutting media accounts from the nation's radio or newspaper outlets.

Journalists also charge González with allowing the Arzú administration to review the editorial content of television newscasts. In 1996, after publicly protesting government review of the content of *Notisiete*, several of the program's reporters were fired. The reporters claimed the Arzú administration was also behind the firings (Alamilla, Pérez, and Taylor 1996, 5–6).

Beyond bowing to such pressure, the key to González's success in Guatemala may be his attempts at remaining scrupulously nonpartisan, while in fact staying cozy with those in power. To do this, the media mogul's strategy includes making substantial campaign contributions. For instance, in 1986, González donated 4 million quetzales (about U.S. $650,000 under current exchange rates) to the election campaign of former president Vinicio Cerezo, the leader of Guatemala's Christian Democrats (Inforpress CentroAmericana 1998). As a way to maintain his good relations with Guatemala's political infrastructure, González's stations give away free airtime to politicians who wish to run campaign advertisements (Vanden Heuvel and Dennis 1995).

"The real threat to advances in our system is this television monopoly," said José Eduardo Zarco, the anchor for *Temas de Noche*, a twice-weekly independent TV newsmagazine program on Canal 13.[6] Zarco is one of the few independent media voices with a major presence in Guatemala. His independent production company rents airtime in the fashion of the popular radio revistas, which allow journalists to become entrepreneurs and sell advertising around program content that they also provide. However, Zarco's views are far from radical, and unlike other journalists he does not fear reprisals if he speaks out. He is the former editor of *Prensa Libre*, Guatemala's most popular newspaper. He is the scion of one of the paper's founding families, a former Guatemalan representative of the Inter-American Press Association (IAPA), and a leader in the Cámara de Periodistas, one of many journalism groups in the country. Because Guatemalan television is devoid of controversy, Zarco's program stands out. On it, he is willing to discuss human rights abuses, the military, and the ongoing peace process. *Temas de Noche* provides one of the few intelligent alternatives in Guatemala to the avalanche of programs originating from across the border in Mexico.

Zarco is just one of many in the media who denigrate the quality of Guatemalan television. Without any local competition and with González's penchant for using Mexican programs to fill time on most of his stations, Zarco said, television is not pushed to improve, especially when the elite class would prefer to squelch criticism from the media. "It is a small country commercially," said Miguel Angel Juárez, a professor at Guatemala's University of San Carlos. "Conflicts of interest are everywhere."[7] Juárez remembers a time when newspapers did not publish film reviews, fearing that cinema owners, like González, would cancel their advertising. "If you want debate and coverage of the national agenda you have to move away from television with a few exceptions," said Zarco. "Radio has the major penetration in this country. It is the way to talk to the indigenous and the campesinos."

Radio may be popular because of Guatemala's low literacy rate. Advertising experts note only 65 percent of Guatemalans can read Spanish.[8] However, most Guatemalans understand spoken Spanish and have access to a radio.

Although radio remains the dominant medium in Guatemala, television's impact is growing due to the size of its audience and its large slice of the nation's advertising pie. Also, for such a small country, the radio audience is ultrafragmented. Guatemala has 296 radio stations, with 80 stations based in the capital. However, many of the stations outside the capital are merely repeaters for stations originating in Guatemala City. Also, many popular stations are simulcast on both AM and FM. Advertising survey information from 1996 showed at least half the population owned a radio (compared to just 12 percent with a phone), and in the ratings from June 1998, radio had a 98 percent penetration of the population. That compares with estimates from 1996 that 43 percent of the population owned a television and that in 1998, 60 percent of the population could view television regularly. However, in Guatemala City, television's penetration equals radio's, with 98 percent of the population tuned in regularly. In 1996 radio pulled in 21 percent of the nation's ad revenue compared to the 28 percent earned by television sources.

So although ownership in the radio spectrum remains diverse, and this medium is still the best way to address all Guatemalans, González's control of the commercial television spectrum grants him almost total access to the population of the capital and the largest base of advertising revenue of any of the country's media owners. (In 1996 Guatemala's newspapers accounted for 40 percent of the nation's advertising revenue, but that is split among four distinct ownership groups.) However, Guatemala's broadcasting baron has not let his dominance of the television spectrum stem his appetite for acquisitions.

To extend his empire beyond the capital, González began buying radio properties in the mid-1990s. By 1998 he had acquired ten stations, including Radio Sonora, a longtime leader in news. After González took control of Radio Sonora, the station adopted a more tabloid style and developed a quick-hitting format, more common to all-news radio in the United States. Radio Sonora also began simulcasting television news programs like *Notisiete*, the most popular television program in Guatemala, from González's Canal 7. By 1998 the result was a major ratings upset for Radio Sonora, which averaged a 9.2 rating, meaning slightly more than 9 percent of Guatemala's population listened to this station on an average day.[9]

However, even with this incursion into radio, González's stations reach less than 20 percent of the radio audience. Until he entered the radio fray, Guatemala's Archila family were the owners with a grip on the most listeners. The family's Emisoras Unidas, which was dethroned by Radio Sonora in 1998, is still considered by many media observers to be the quality outlet for radio news and information.[10] Traditionally, Emisoras Unidas was the radio station that had the most access to government sources, while presenting a mix of news and information that represented conservative and centrist portions of Guatemalan society and politics (Alamilla, Pérez, and Taylor 1996). Besides Emisoras Unidas, the Archila family has a dozen other stations, all based at their modern, computer-driven radio production center in Guatemala City.

The largest radio chain in the country does not compete in the area of news, information, or music. Radio Grupo Alius is a 30-station group of outlets that broadcast Christian religious programs. The stations steer clear of Guatemala's religious divisions and devote their broadcasts to nondenominational evangelical programs that appeal to Catholic and Protestant audiences alike. The group is owned by Alfonso Liu, the head of a successful family of Chinese-Guatemalan entrepreneurs.[11]

What emerges from this pattern of ownership and ratings data is a system where three families—the Archilas, the Lius, and González—control most of Guatemala's radio audience of 11 million people. In a country where just 12 percent of the population makes enough money to exist above the official poverty level, and 60 percent of the population is listed as living in abject poverty, these media barons control powerful communication instruments that have swayed the Guatemalan masses in the past. Yet what chance do the masses have to gain access to these communication tools to send their own messages? In a truly democratic system, alternative voices and opposition voices would have an easier time finding a path for communication. Yet in Guatemala, if the message does not conform with evangelical Christian businessmen, longtime elite families with conservative views, or a multinational broadcaster with Mexican roots who follows government dictates, then that message usually does not find a way onto the country's airwaves. "The people have no access to the system," *Notisiete* news manager Barrios agreed. "They have no way to get their viewpoints on the air, even if they demand it. But it is taboo to talk about this."

Despite what appears to be a relatively closed system, a few alternatives exist. Besides *Temas de Noche*, on television, other independent voices rent time on the various radio stations. One of the most popular programs, *Guatemala Flash*, is broadcast twice daily. This program has stitched together an independent network of stations and reaches as many as 1.5 million listeners per program.[12] Part of the program's popularity is its history of fifty-three years of broadcasting nationwide, plus the willingness of its producers to rebroadcast in K'iche', one of the major Mayan dialects spoken in the country.

Likewise, ninety minutes of daily Mayan news and cultural and religious programming can be heard on Radio Nuevo Mundo. This programming has helped raise the station's profile and made it the third-highest rated in the country, although it only has a third of the audience of González's top-ranked Radio Sonora. Also the program's producers were assaulted in the war years for producing Mayan programs, which angered conservative elements in Guatemala. Threats against the station and the producers have continued in the postwar years.[13]

Nicaragua

In Nicaragua González's entry into the market has been viewed as a means of friendly competition, and also perhaps as a way to push more radical views off the airwaves. In 1998 the Mexican broadcaster added Nicaragua's Canal 4 to his portfolio of Nicaraguan investments. Canal 4 has been the voice of the Sandinista party in Nicaragua, and although programming content was expected to change under González's ownership, the station did not experience a sudden or immediate turn in its partisan line, nor did González inflict massive firings on the staff.

In Nicaragua González has teamed up with various Nicaraguan nationals as partners to gain control of three channels. Besides the Sandinista channel, he also controls Canales 10 and 12. So far, unlike his practices in Guatemala, González has not imported large amounts of Mexican programming. However, following his model of expansion in Guatemala, González has pledged loyalty to the current Liberal government in Managua, and he has decidedly chosen to remain low-key in his programming shifts, planning to steer clear of controversy.[14]

During the years of the Contra War, González struck up a friendship and ultimately a business partnership with Nicaragua's leading broadcast family, the Sacasas, as they tended to their broadcast properties from the safe haven of Miami.[15] The Sacasa family's Canal 2 has dominated Nicaraguan television for the past twenty years. Currently, the station averages control of an amazing 75 percent of the Nicaraguan audience.[16] González's stations fall into the next tier of popularity behind Canal 2; the three stations combine to appeal to almost 20 percent of the market. The remaining five stations in Nicaragua trail both these broadcasting powerhouses by considerable margins, fighting over the remaining 5 percent of the audience.

Media observers in Nicaragua credit the Sacasas with building the most professional operation in the country that includes some of the best news and information programming in the region. Unlike many broadcasters in the region, the family has purchased advanced equipment and fought to keep its best talent. Their station also carries programming from various international sources, including CNN. However, some observers also say the Sacasas maintain their operation through special access to the Liberal government in Managua, built through years of friendships, political favors, and obligations.[17]

Besides the similar political orientation of the leading television ownership family in Nicaragua, what has drawn González to the market is a richer (when compared to Guatemala) advertising climate. In 1996, 70 percent of Nicaragua's $25 million advertising budget went to television (Bodán 1998). In the postwar years, television has supplanted radio as the dominant medium in Nicaragua. Although in the broadcast ratings from 1998 radio listenership and television viewing were even (both at 67 percent on the survey), Nicaraguans ranked television as their primary source of information and entertainment.

Radio's shrinking influence in Nicaragua can be seen through its small percentage of the advertising pool: just 10 percent in the 1996 survey. Immediately following the war, radio's popularity in Nicaragua caused a boom in the number of stations: numbers shot up from thirty stations during the Sandinista era to more than 160 during the peak of the administration of President Violeta Chamorro. Currently 137 stations operate in the country. Media ratings surveys report 94 percent of Nicaraguans own a radio, compared to 92 percent of those living in Managua who own a television, and 76 percent who own a television in rural areas.[18]

Radio is typically reflective of the polarization in Nicaraguan society during the war years, and afterward. Radio Corporación is the top station in the country and it is a strong backer of the right-wing elements in the current Liberal government. Radio Ya and Radio Sandino, two outlets with pro-Sandinista followings, trail right behind Radio Corporación as the country's next most popular stations. As a means of competition and of showing its political stripes, Radio Corporación organized an advertising boycott of stations that are not totally loyal to the Liberal government.

This follows a line of attack against pro-Sandinista media by the administration of Nicaragua's president Arnoldo Alemán Lacayo. The Alemán administration suspended government advertising in media that do not support the government's policies. In addition, Alemán asked private firms to follow this example. This parallels similar ad boycotts organized by the Arzú administration in Guatemala. In Nicaragua Alemán also closed the government's television operation, Canal 6, which produced news and public affairs programming, and which was staffed mainly by former Sandinistas.

It is no surprise that in this atmosphere, González was urged to invest in Canal 4, the Sandinista station that was up for sale, mainly because it could no longer depend on government or party subsidies to stay afloat. Such a move allows the Mexican media baron to slowly purge Nicaragua's television airwaves of the Sandinista message, without any of the blame falling on Nicaragua's longtime media owners. For now, the major editorial change at Canal 4 has been some dilution of the Sandinista message and a move toward greater objectivity in its news and information programming.[19] In Nicaragua González's role seems to be one of change agent, rather than suppressive force. However, this role is in keeping with his model of following the lead of conservative elements in the political and business communities in the Central American countries where he wields some control of the major media outlets. In the end, this is similar to the position his stations play in the Guatemalan media matrix, where left-wing thought or controversial issues are thoroughly strained from the content of most media outlets.

El Salvador

The wave of Mexican broadcasting investment hit El Salvador in 1997. But in El Salvador, the Mexican investors faced competition that looked eerily like the empire González had built in Guatemala. Anyone who wants a part of the broadcast spectrum in El Salvador must deal with Telecorporación Salvadoreño (TCS) and the man who founded it, Boris Esersky. Esersky is a media *caudillo*, whose government connections shaped the current Salvadoran broadcast spectrum and kept forces disloyal to the government from buying ad space with most Salvadoran broadcasters.

Through TCS, Esersky controls three of El Salvador's five VHF television outlets.[20] However, Esersky's stations dominate the market and have captured 90 percent of the audience. Government-owned Canal 10 and independent Canal 12 must cope with single-digit ratings and a minuscule share in the national market.[21] Esersky programs his stations together intelligently, much like U.S. cablecasters have discussed television multiplexing. The result is that Canal 2 specializes in telenovelas, Canal 4 relies primarily on sports, and Canal 6 is where the audience can find movies and music events. Each channel has its own unique news programming, but TCS network news is also simulcast on each channel. Beyond television, Esersky's TCS holdings include cable companies and magazines as well as advertising and public relations firms.

Esersky is not passive about exerting his considerable media power. He has given free advertising to the campaigns of El Salvador's right-wing ARENA party politicians, and the news and information programs on his station have generally been supportive of the conservative politicians in power. In return, when Mexican broadcasters made a bid to the government to buy control of an unused state television frequency, Esersky asked his political friends to block the sale. Although El Salvador's former president Armando Calderón Sol promised to bring the station online as a state educational channel after the controversy over the blocked sale, so far no new state programming has emerged.

The only real competition for Esersky surfaced amidst the civil war, in 1984, with the start-up of Canal 12 by Jorge Zedan. Against the odds, Zedan kept control of his alternative station for thirteen years until finally Esersky wore him down. Esersky's TCS empire openly blocked advertisers from placing their ads with Canal 12, both for competitive and political reasons. TCS, the owner of the cable franchise in San Salvador, also refuses to carry Canal 12 or the new all-news UHF station, Canal 33.

Zedan responded to this competitive challenge by creating a strong objective and critical news presence in the country. Modeled on the U.S. and international journalists covering the war in El Salvador, Zedan's station took on controversy. It created a hard-hitting news operation that proved to be an annoyance to the country's right wing, which was unaccustomed to being challenged on the nation's airwaves. Canal 12 pioneered the extended, early morning interview–talk show concept for Salvadoran television, often pitting sworn political enemies together on television for the first time. Canal 12's morning interview program, hosted by Mauricio Funes, is still one of the most popular programs on Salvadoran television.

Zedan also courted advertisers that the TCS advertising firms would not place. Opposition groups and those out of political favor with the nation's right wing found Canal 12 to be the one spot on the television spectrum they could use to communicate. This drive to find alternative sources of ad revenue helped the station survive a government-organized ad boycott (this preceded similar government control efforts in Guatemala and Nicaragua by a decade) during the civil war in 1987, when the Salvadoran government assessed Canal 12's news coverage as too independent.

Given this government pressure, and in the face of the TCS empire, Canal 12 was never very profitable. Zedan sold control of the station in 1997, retaining a 10 percent stake for himself. Salvadoran Armando Bukele also has a 10 percent share. Controlling interest of Canal 12 was bought by Mexico's TV Azteca. Although the new owners retained the station's balanced news coverage, many of Canal 12's other programming innovations were dismantled. Now the station is the main outlet for Mexican telenovelas and other entertainment originating in Mexico City.

In this way, Mexican investors played a role similar to what is expected to happen in Nicaragua: they were the mitigating force to remove political opponents from the nation's airwaves. In both El Salvador and Nicaragua, many years after the wars, conservative and long-dominant elites seemed to be achieving a cleansing of the opposition from the airwaves by allowing limited intervention by Mexican broadcasters interested in multinational expansion. This development was part of the economic evolution of El Salvador, and not the direct design of Esersky or the government. However, Televisa and TV Azteca have both proved to be supportive of Mexico's longtime ruling party, and thus of Mexico's power structure, for many years—in the case of Televisa, for decades.[22] Although Esersky saw increased Mexican investment in the system as unacceptable from a competitive standpoint, he was unwilling or unable to block the sale of his one real competitor to Mexican investors. In some ways, the sale of Zedan's Canal 12 to Mexican broadcasters worked in favor of El Salvador's elites. In both El Salvador and Nicaragua, Mexican investors seemed willing to protect the status quo and did not seem overly dangerous in a competitive sense, as long as their investments merely wiped out small, alternative voices in the system. Although Mexican broadcasters may only control a sliver of the audience in these nations now, this is not an insignificant change: the door has opened in these nearly monopolistic television systems for multinational competition.

Alternative voices do still exist in the Salvadoran broadcast system, but increasingly they can only be found on the radio, and even then the space for intelligent news and information coverage may be shrinking as all-music formats gain precedence. As in Nicaragua, radio's popularity and reach in El Salvador seemed to peak about the time peace was settling over the country.

In 1998 there were 168 radio stations operating in El Salvador. Those stations had to compete for the 8 percent of national advertising revenues that went to radio.[23] The evolution of rebel radio in El Salvador has provided the largest change in the radio spectrum in the postwar years. During the civil war, Radio Venceremos and Radio Farabundo Martí were the two most popular rebel stations operated by the FMLN (the Farabundo Martí Front for National Liberation). Since the peace accords, the stations were legalized and began accepting advertising, and eventually their protest music was replaced with mainstream rock. By the end of the 1990s it was hard to distinguish these alternative voices from any of the other stations in the country.

Radio Sonora, a popular national radio network during the war that gave voice to university students, labor activists, and other left-wing views remains one of the nation's most popular stations. Radio Sonora's owner, Roberto Castañeda Alas, was forced out of El Salvador during the war years after he was branded a leftist for opening his station to the alternative voices of the country. Today the station has adopted more mainstream programming elements to stay one of the top three radio outlets in the country, behind the popular stations YSKL and YSU.

The brightest star on the radio dial in El Salvador, RCS, appeared in the spring of 1998. RCS became the darling of the intelligentsia almost as soon as it appeared. The station's programming concentrates on quality news and information, and is often fueled by heated debates and in-depth interviews, besides including some comedy programs. RCS also tried to maintain an interactive position with listeners: taking calls and making contributions from the audience a staple of its programming. RCS is owned by a group of investors, headed by Abelardo Torres, José Alfredo Dutriz, and Alex Dutriz. The Dutriz family owned *La Prensa Gráfica*, one of El Salvador's major newspapers, until 1996. Although *La Prensa Gráfica* was renowned as one of the conservative voices in the country, so far the Dutriz presence with RCS has allowed the station's objective format and open exchange of political ideas.

The appearance of RCS on the radio scene proved that substantive information programming could find a place in the broadcast spectrum and that radio had not been abandoned in El Salvador as a medium for the exchange of important ideas and political thought. The days of radio being a sounding board for revolutionary rhetoric might be over, but with the right-wing dominance of the television airwaves, a few frequencies on the radio like RCS showed that Salvadorans had decided radio was not merely for music entertainment, although the trend in radio at the end of the 1990s was away from providing quality news and information.

Panama

In Panama, the postwar period has been marked not by the invasion of Mexican investors, as in other parts of Central America, but rather by consolidation in anticipation of their arrival. Some media critics, however, felt the consolidation by Panama's most powerful, conservative, and elite broadcasters was due mainly to their desire to strengthen their own bottom line rather than respond to any perceived threat. Like other countries of the region, Panama is dominated by a single broadcasting entity. During the 1990s the Eleta family merged its broadcast holdings with the properties of Nicolás González Revilla to form the MEDCOM group. The resulting media company owned Panama's two most popular television outlets and some of its most popular radio stations. MEDCOM's television holdings are where it has the most clout. Canales 4 and 13 belong to MEDCOM, and the company estimated that between the two they control on average 72 percent of·the audience.[24] TVN Canal 2, MEDCOM's main competitor, averages control of 18 percent of the audience.[25] The remaining 10 percent of the audience is split among three stations: FETV, run by the Catholic Church; an educational station operated by the University of Panama; and the U.S. military's English-language station.

In radio MEDCOM owns the top news and information outlet in the country, RPC Radio. RPC's dominance in the news and information area comes partially through its decades-long tradition of providing a strong news product. But the AM-FM combo under the RPC flag are not the top stations in the country. In a survey conducted in 1996, the top Panamanian radio station, Super Q, had a music format that specialized in American pop music and used the familiar Top 40 hit rotation.[26] Media owners confirmed that Super Q retained its dominance in the market after that survey, and the other top radio stations in the country had music formats. Perhaps because of this reason, in 1998, González Revilla revealed MEDCOM was shopping for another FM station to complement its news and information outlets on radio.[27]

Radio is still the dominant medium with the most penetration in Panama, with 92 percent of the population listening on an average day.[28] Radio surveys claim it remains the most popular news and entertainment medium. But Panama's radio airwaves, as in the rest of Central America, are oversaturated, and many stations have dissolved since the beginning of the decade. In 1992, 206 stations were operating in Panama compared to 120 stations currently. More than half of those stations (63) are clustered in the capital, and many of the outlying stations are merely repeater signals for the more popular outlets.

Television is increasingly the most important and profitable medium in Panama. Television executives claim the medium has an 80 percent overall penetration, although that may fall to as low as 15 percent in some rural areas outside the capital. In the years following Operation Just Cause, television was taking in $30 million in advertising and growing at a rate of 56 percent annually, compared to radio's shrinking ad base of $5 million (Correa Jolly 1992).[29]

The main difference between the operations of MEDCOM and González Revilla in Panama compared to their counterparts in other nations in the region is that the elite connections between González Revilla and the government are more obvious, while control of the information coming from the MEDCOM stations is much more subtle. González Revilla is the cousin of Panamanian president Ernesto Pérez Balladares, the leader of the Democratic Revolutionary Party (PRD, by its Spanish initials), the party that supported dictator Gen. Manuel Noriega. The Eletas also are PRD supporters.

Another PRD supporter, Diana Martáns, the publisher of *Pauta*, Panama's glossy business magazine, has written about the Panamanian media wars. She explained why some quibble with the presentation of the government on MEDCOM's broadcast outlets: "If you know what to look for in the news it isn't hard to see some of the subtle biases. Many of the questions aimed at people in the government . . . are rather soft. Look at who gets interviewed in stories that are neutral. . . . You'll see our party represented and others in the opposition ignored."[30] And the administration of President Pérez Balladares has not been beyond protecting its special connections to the media. When Gustavo Gorriti, the Peruvian associate editor of *La Prensa*, Panama's most successful paper, criticized the consolidation of the country's electronic media by MEDCOM, along with directing pointed investigations of the government, the administration moved to have Gorriti expelled from the country by refusing to renew his work permit and visa. Gorriti faced government persecution, perhaps even physical harm, if he returned to Peru, because of his investigative work there. Only international media pressure caused the Pérez

Balladares government to relent. Pointing to the personal connections between powerful media executives and the government, Gorriti noted, "Vertical integration of the media is much more dangerous here than in the States."[31]

With the ouster of the PRD from the executive branch in Panama during the 1999 elections, some of that concern seemed to lessen.[32] But the one challenge that loomed on the horizon with the change of control of the Panama Canal at the end of 1999 and the departure of U.S. troops as the Canal Zone officially disappeared was what would happen to the radio and television frequencies used by the U.S. military.

In 1998 González Revilla of MEDCOM was already worried about the prospects of foreign competition grabbing the opportunity to enter the market via the over-the-air television channel: Venezuelan investors, Televisa, and the ever-present Angel González González topped González Revilla's list of feared potential competitors. González Revilla said he sees the combined operations of MEDCOM as fortification against such international competition. "We have very complex reasons for our business plan. We must perfect our joint operations before someone from the outside can come into Panama and take advantage," he said. The general manager of *La Prensa,* Juan Luis Correa, scoffed at González Revilla's explanation. "That's a convenient excuse," Correa said for a strategy that calls for buying up more broadcast properties, manipulating ad rates to MEDCOM's advantage, and bumping more of the political opposition off of the airwaves.[33]

Honduras

Members of the Honduran media seemed less concerned about international competition, especially from Mexico, after several of the country's media owners turned back bids from TV Azteca to gain controlling interest of some of the nation's major television channels.

In Honduras, as in other countries in the region, one man, Rafael Ferrari, has become a dominant force in the electronic media. And like in Panama, many of the special connections between the media, government, and politics are more than a bit transparent. But unlike in other nations, the lines between government, the media, and politics are blurred. In Honduras, Ferrari's power is often checked by other media owners. The competition among owners of newspapers, radio stations, and television channels in the Honduran system has spilled over into the political arena and become one method for competing for power inside the nation's dominant Liberal Party. Along with partner Manuel Villeda, Ferrari runs Emisoras Unidas, a radio station group that includes the nation's highest rated news and information station, HRN Radio. HRN maintains a national reach through the use of the Emisoras Unidas transmitter in Tegucigalpa and seven repeater stations.

Ferrari's main competitor in radio is Manuel Andonie Fernández, who owns a chain of stations under the control of his company Audio Video. Andonie's Radio América is usually considered Honduras's second-leading news and information source. Andonie is also one of the leaders of one of the country's small minority political parties, the Unity Party.[34]

Due to the country's poor economic conditions, mountainous geography, and relatively high illiteracy rate of 32 percent (Virtue 1996), radio has maintained its position as the most important medium, with 80 percent penetration of the populace.[35] Honduras has 185 licensed stations, but many are repeater stations for the most popular outlets in Tegucigalpa and San Pedro Sula. In Honduras, television may reach only 10 percent of the population on a regular basis, because the populace cannot afford the price of a set. However, television may provide the main source of information and entertainment for the top tier of Honduran society.[36]

The Ferrari-Villeda partnership owns a series of Honduran television companies that control three regional channels based in Tegucigalpa, one regional channel based in San Pedro Sula, and national Canal 5. Their major competitors are the Sikaffy family, who own national Canal 9, and two regional channels based in San Pedro Sula. The Sikaffys also own an AM-FM combo called La Voz de Centroamérica based there. San Pedro Sula is also home to a little-viewed UHF operation and national Canal 6, owned by Cuban immigrant Rafael Nodarse.

Ferrari has flexed his considerable political muscle inside the ruling Liberal party by trying to limit the number of television stations that are licensed to operate in Honduras. Ferrari opposed the licensing of a new national Canal 11 to Jaime Rosenthal, the owner of one of the nation's leading newspapers, Tiempo of San Pedro Sula. Rosenthal was eventually granted the license in 1993, but has not begun a broadcast operation yet.

Presidential politics may have played a hand in some of the intense cross-media competition in Honduras. Rosenthal made an unsuccessful bid for the Liberal Party spot on the presidential ballot in 1996, losing to the current Honduran president, Carlos Flores Facussé, whose family runs the newspaper La Tribuna. Some members of the media felt Ferrari's support of Flores was one of the crucial political moves that put Flores in office.[37] However, Ferrari's support may have come with a price. Since Flores's election, Ferrari has pushed for the closure of Nodarse's Canal 6. Nodarse opened his broadcast and cable operations in Honduras with the blessing of the Honduran military, at a time when the military was in charge of broadcast frequencies.

With the Flores administration came a transition to civilian control of broadcasting through CONATEL, the Honduran Communications Commission.[38] Acting on complaints of broadcast interference by Canal 6 with Ferrari's stations, along with allegations Canal 6 was rebroadcasting copyrighted material without paying licensing fees, CONATEL moved to take legal action to pressure Nodarse to change his operating procedures.

In Tegucigalpa, where Ferrari also controls the cable system, the system dropped Canal 6. In San Pedro Sula, where Nodarse runs the cable system, Ferrari's stations have been removed. As the military's power behind the scenes wanes slowly in these postwar years (before the end of his term, Flores may be the first president since the Cold War ended to appoint the head of the Honduran military), Nodarse's position opposing the civilian elite becomes more and more tenuous. With his Cuban roots, Nodarse is truly an outsider in a system where most of the media owners belong to successful Arab-Honduran families, called *turcos*. The Sikaffys, the Facussés (the president's family), the Rosenthals, Ferrari, and other leading media owners are all *turcos* with clout in the Liberal Party. The Ferrari-Villeda partnership also owns banks and a chain of supermarkets in Honduras. Nodarse, with his perceived ties to the still-powerful military establishment, is not just considered an interloper, but many inside the country's media circles call this immigrant media owner "the pirate."

Conclusion

Honduras seems a throwback to an era of media development where the owners of newspapers nominated presidents. The Hondurans seem to have taken that powerbroker role one step further: in the current system running a media enterprise means competing for the leadership of one of the country's political parties. In Honduras, powerful elites realized they must seize control of not only the political and economic system but also the country's media system if they are to truly realize a transition of power away from the military. Perhaps this was necessary in Honduras, the only nation among the five studied here that did not experience a conventional or guerrilla war. In Guatemala, El Salvador, Nicaragua, and Panama, outside forces (either the United States, the United Nations, or a combination of international interests) intervened at the end of wars in attempts to impose limitations on each nation's military. In the case of Panama, the military was abolished, as a way of equalizing the political forces in the country. However, in Honduras, U.S. pressure after the region's wars has mainly been a result of the vast reduction of military aid for the country. In the Honduran system, where the military maintains more power than in any other nation in the region, perhaps other forces in control of the nation's communications system were inevitably meant to ascend into leadership positions in this information age. But the larger picture regionally seems to place Honduras as an aberration rather than a trendsetter. Another conclusion is that as demonstrated by their failed attempts at investment in Honduras, along with their successes in El Salvador and Guatemala, Mexico's media giants have cast their eyes southward. Televisa and TV Azteca both consider Central America as ripe not only as a target for the export of programming but as a subsidiary of their larger Mexican operations.

Likewise, Angel González González, the Mexican who forged a media empire based in Guatemala, has found teaming up with the Mexican networks is a viable way to gain market dominance. He too has found markets in Central America open to his brand of broadcasting, which includes becoming a friend of the government and each nation's elite establishment. If there is an inevitable trend for the entire region it is toward a future with more broadcast outlets co-owned by González and the Mexican networks, perhaps with minority investors from the Isthmus.

This Mexican broadcasting invasion, of sorts, has worked to bolster the conservative, elite elements in societies regionally. In Panama, the potential of such a Mexican incursion became the excuse for further consolidation of elite media holdings. Beyond their symbiotic relationship with powerful owners, governments across the region have found it necessary to control the media through economic tactics, like advertising boycotts, to neutralize broadcasters and keep them from playing a countervailing role against the weight of the overly strong presidencies that have been set up in many of these pseudo-democracies. In Panama and Honduras, where the media systems are openly allied with powerful presidential systems, there has been no need to employ such tactics.

Honduras and Guatemala also raise concerns about the development and direction of the electronic media in Central America. In such countries where powerful elites rule through the political, economic, and media systems, seemingly without checks, and without a real plurality, how are the myriad voices that are the foundation of a democratic system supposed to develop? Although Nicaragua seemed to take a few steps forward in its postwar period, the Alemán administration has retrenched. In Panama, despite the control of that nation's media system by mostly conservative elites, the 1999 national elections point toward the possibility that the postwar triumph of the region's media caciques will not mean a return to authoritarian rule in the next century, at least in that country. However, if any system points toward a likely regional future, it may be that of El Salvador, where the right wing consolidated gains in the 1999 presidential elections while appointing a new generation of leaders; this handing over of power to younger elites seems to signal the final triumph in that nation's transition out of its civil war period.[39] In the end, the elections were merely a reflection of a broadcasting system dominated by the views of one powerful right-wing owner. And thus the Central American media systems slip back into old patterns: reinforcing elite control and suppressing media access for those without status, instead of presenting a true democratic vision for the future.

Notes

1. Also see the award-winning journalistic work of Serapio Umanzor, a series of reports under the title "La Guerra Secreta," published in Honduras's *La Prensa* during 1996.

2. Villalobos reports that González masks his ownership of two stations in Costa Rica through a holding company. Villalobos claims the media owner has investments in twenty-two television stations throughout Latin America.

3. In 1998 González's stations attracted 96 percent of Guatemala's television audience. His core stations, Canales 3 and 7, which he has owned the longest, share 77 percent of the audience. There are four UHF stations based in Guatemala City with other owners, which along with the government's public station compete for the remaining 4 percent of the viewing audience, according to 1998 figures released by APCU Thompson Asociados, an advertising and polling firm. One of the UHF stations, Canal 32, is owned by Mexico's TV Azteca.

4. Blancanivea Bendfeltd, media director, APCU Thompson Asociados, interview with Rick Rockwell, July 1998, Guatemala City, Guatemala. However, the percentage of ad revenue from cinemas is quite small — less than 1 percent in the Guatemalan system. That total, according to 1995 figures shared during the interview, can be measured in the hundreds of dollars.

5. Marco Tulio Barrios Reina, managing editor for *Notisiete*, interview with Rick Rockwell, July 1998, Guatemala City.

6. José Eduardo Zarco, anchor for *Temas de Noche*, interview with Rick Rockwell, July 1998, Guatemala City.

7. Miguel Angel Juárez, journalism professor, University of San Carlos, interview with Rick Rockwell, July 1998, Guatemala City.

8. Bendfeltd interview. Guatemalans speak at least twenty-four other languages, mostly

Mayan dialects. Some of the Mayan dialects, though similar, share only a few words in common. This diverse linguistic landscape makes mass communication difficult in the country.

9. Radio Sonora's closest competitor, Emisoras Unidas, registered a 6.9 rating during the same ratings period. Most stations registered less than one rating point in Guatemala's oversaturated radio market.

10. Ileana Alamilla, editor for Asociación de la Prensa Guatemalteca (APG), and director of press agency Cerigua, interview with Rick Rockwell, July 1998, Guatemala City, Guatemala.

11. For some time Guatemala has been the scene of intense religious competition among various Christian groups to convert members of the country's large Catholic population. Guatemala's state television channel still shows evangelical Christian programs, a holdover from the 1980s when Gen. Efraín Ríos-Montt, one of the country's dictators, urged massive conversions to evangelical Christian sects.

12. Ramiro McDonald Jr., principal anchor and news director of *Guatemala Flash*, interview with Rick Rockwell, July 1998, Guatemala City, Guatemala.

13. Florencio Simón Chuy, director of Mayan-language programs for Radio Nuevo Mundo, interview with Rick Rockwell, July 1998, Guatemala City, Guatemala.

14. Historically, in Central America the political elites have tended to divide into two camps: liberals and conservatives. Although this traditional division of parties exists in nations like Honduras, in some spots the change of parties in the past 150 years has also changed the true meaning behind the labels. In Nicaragua for instance, the years of the Somocista dictatorships and the subsequent Sandinista rebellion worked to erase some of the old political divisions. The Sandinistas with their Communist ideology certainly represent the left wing in Nicaragua now. The Liberal Party is a revival of a popular name for a party, but today this party represents the country's right-wing political forces (see Skidmore and Smith 1992).

15. Carlos Briceño, owner and general manager of TeleNica 8, interview with Noreene Janus, July 1998, Managua, Nicaragua.

16. Oliver Bodán, "Publicistas Deben Reevaluar sus Estrategias," in *Confidencial*, 5 July 1998, 16. *Confidencial* is the weekly newsletter of the Organización Nicaragüense de Agencias de Publicidad (ONAP).

17. Briceño interview.

18. Adolfo Pastrán, independent news producer, Radio Católica, interview with Noreene Janus, July 1998, Managua. During the interview Pastrán quoted from "Encuesta Sobre Preferencia de Medios," prepared by Universidad CentroAmericana.

19. Osvaldo Zúñiga, independent news producer, Radio Católica, interview with Noreene Janus, July 1998, Managua, Nicaragua.

20. El Salvador also has six UHF stations, which compete for less than 5 percent of the viewing audience and can only be seen in San Salvador and the city's suburbs.

21. Marco Antonio Rivera, producer, Canal 12, interview with Noreene Janus, May 1998, San Salvador, El Salvador.

22. Raymundo Riva Palacio, columnist with Mexico's *Crónica*, interview with Rick Rockwell, August 1997, Mexico City, Mexico. Although Riva Palacio has written and com-

mented on Mexican television and its use as a political tool, he is far from the singular source on this topic. For a more complete review, see Orme 1996.

23. Ignacio Castillo, general manager of all-news Canal 33 and RCS Radio, interview with Noreene Janus, May 1998, San Salvador; throughout the interview, Castillo quoted from "Encuesta Sobre Preferencia de Medios," prepared by the Universidad CentroAmericana.

24. Nicolás González Revilla, Executive vice president of MEDCOM Holdings, interview with Rick Rockwell, August 1998, Panama City, Panama.

25. TVN Canal 2 is owned by a consortium of Panamanian businessmen, who are usually sympathetic with the country's opposition parties.

26. Fernando Correa Jolly, executive vice president of Radio Continente, interview with Rick Rockwell, August 1998, Panama City.

27. González Revilla interview. In the 1996 survey, Super Q averaged a 9.9 national rating, compared to MEDCOM's 5.8, in fourth place behind several other music stations.

28. Correa interview. However, that is tempered by the fact that among the capital's 1 million residents, in the same surveys, 65 percent say they never listen to radio outside their cars, which mirrors the trend in the United States.

29. At the beginning of the decade, radio's share of the advertising in Panama was shrinking by half a percentage point annually.

30. Diana Martáns, director of *Pauta*, interview with Rick Rockwell, August 1998, Panama City.

31. Gustavo Gorriti, associate editor of *La Prensa*, interview with Rick Rockwell, August 1998, Panama City.

32. Mireya Moscoso, the leader of Panama's Arnulfista Party, assumed the presidency in September 1999. She was married to the late Dr. Arnulfo Arias, a three-time president of Panama, who was often unseated by coups. Moscoso comes from a poor family, although her marriage to Arias certainly connects her with Panama's opposition elites (see Nordwall 1999; Navarro 1999b).

33. Juan Luis Correa, general manager of *La Prensa*, interview with Rick Rockwell, August 1998, Panama City.

34. Francisco Umanzor, Radio América news director, interview with Rick Rockwell, March 1998, Tegucigalpa, Honduras.

35. Raul Valladares, news director of HRN Radio, interview with Rick Rockwell, March 1998, Tegucigalpa.

36. Patricia Murillo, professor at Centro Universidad Región Norte–Universidad Nacional Autónoma á Honduras, interview with Rick Rockwell, March 1998, San Pedro Sula, Honduras.

37. Farah Robles, *Tiempo* section editor, interview with Rick Rockwell, March 1998, San Pedro Sula.

38. Norman Roy Hernández, administrator of CONATEL, interview with Rick Rockwell, March 1998, Tegucigalpa.

39. President Francisco Flores Pérez, a member of the ARENA Party, took office in El Salvador in June 1999. The 39-year-old president also assembled a cabinet made up of young members of the party (see Mireya Navarro 1999a).

The Reform of National Television in Chile

Valerio Fuenzalida

The Latin American and Chilean Context

The Latin American Context

After the Second World War public service broadcasting in Europe was associated with the growth of the welfare state. The legal frameworks for public broadcasting stations gave them considerable autonomy in relation to the government. In Latin America, on the other hand, the vast majority of public television channels have been managed directly by governments, and assigned functions of political persuasion with greater or lesser degrees of openness or brutality. In the most blatant cases television was put directly at the service of the reigning political caudillo.

A recent review of public broadcasting stations in Latin America, representing one-fifth of the broadcasting capacity in the region, showed average audience shares under 5 percent. Two exceptions to this last-place position for public broadcasting stations were the National Television Network (TVN) in Chile and the government-managed stations in Colombia (Fuenzalida 2000). In today's more information-rich and diverse media environment, the government news channels usually have low ratings. Government news programs lack credibility, and their entertainment shows, in general, are not as attractive to audiences as are those of commercial stations.

Elizabeth Fox (1997) explained how some Latin American governments, faced with low credibility and small audiences for their official channels, established complicit and often corrupt relationships with privately owned television channels. Stations were compensated for their political complicity with tax breaks on earnings and on imports of equip-

The author wishes to thank the publisher Fondo de Cultura Económica for authorizing the use of parts of the book *La Televisión Pública en América Latina: Reforma o Privatización* (Santiago, 2000). The opinions in this chapter are those of the author and do not represent those of any organization with which he is affiliated.

ment, beneficial labor contracts, and other measures. When these measures proved insufficient, governments often resorted to cruder forms of influence such as what occurred with Baruch Ivcher, the owner of the Peruvian station Frecuencia Latina, whom the Alberto Fujimori government stripped of his citizenship in 1997 in order to force the sale of his station.

Historically, the Latin American experience with government-owned stations demonstrates a downward spiral of inconsistent direction, lack of credibility in news, loss of legitimacy with audiences, declining ratings, economic crisis, and corruption (Fox 1997; Fuenzalida 2000). In the long run, the situation is untenable. The stations have no credibility or social legitimacy; nor do they behave as responsible businesses, failing to show returns on the public's investment. With the return to democracy, the historical failure of government-owned television both as effective means of persuasion and propaganda and as news and entertainment led many countries to explore new concepts and forms of organization to achieve a more socially useful public television.

One form this search has taken is the creation of public television stations to cover sessions of parliaments and other elected bodies along the lines of C-SPAN in the United States. This use is consistent with the newly elected governments' move toward more transparency and social legitimacy. In the 1990s, TV channels covering the national congresses of Brazil (Chacón 2000), Mexico (Corral 2000), Colombia, Chile, and other countries appeared. These channels began as simple witnesses to the legislative sessions. With the passing of time they developed more elaborate programming with broader information and news shows, including programs of debate and history, providing a context for the parliamentary discussions. Today public service channels of this type have become specialized channels providing pluralistic political information for better-informed public opinion, quite a difference from their former incarnations as organs of government propaganda.[1]

In another form the crisis of the government-owned broadcasting channels in Mexico, Argentina, Venezuela, Colombia, Chile, and Panama led to public discussions and opened the door to the possibility of true public broadcasting in the region.

The Chilean Context

The Christian Democrat government that preceded the administration of President Salvador Allende set up TVN in 1969. The new channel was designed to compete with the three university-owned channels that had been established almost ten years earlier. Chilean law only allowed for television channels owned by the government or by universities. Despite the limit on commercial ownership, all the university-owned channels had commercial operations and accepted commercial advertising, including government-paid announcements and other forms of support from the state and the universities themselves. TVN's initial mandate was to cover the entire national territory, a task it achieved rapidly. The university stations, on the other hand, for many years were limited to regional or citywide coverage, although during the 1970s TV 13 (Channel 13) of the Catholic University, and to a lesser extent Channel 11 of the University of Chile, expanded considerably.

The 1992 reform of TVN was part of the general economic and credibility crisis of public television in Latin America. The reform fits squarely within the new conditions Chile was experiencing in the 1990s, the most important of which was the country's return to democracy following a seventeen-year military dictatorship. The new administration inherited a highly monopolistic and politically biased press and broadcasting system. TVN was administratively and financially weak, not to mention its low credibility with the populace. In 1989, the last year of the military dictatorship, ratings for TVN's news programming were 13.7 percent, compared with 30 percent for Channel 13 (Navarrete 1990). To make things worse for TVN, the Chilean television market had become more competitive following the introduction of privately owned stations led by Megavisión.

The government traditionally appointed the director of TVN. Upon taking office in March 1990, the newly elected president, Patricio Aylwin (1990–94), named Jorge Navarrete executive director of TVN and charged him with the reform of the system. Navarrete, a well-known expert in business administration, had created TVN in 1969 and was its director until 1970. To carry out the reform, Navarrete set up a team made up of people who had been working on television policy for many years. The team included the author of this chapter.

President Aylwin sent legislation to parliament aimed at setting up the necessary mechanisms to establish a pluralistic public television network independent of political interests. The network would have sound financial management, allowing it to compete with the other stations.[2] Parliament unanimously approved the Aylwin-Navarrete Law for the Reform of TVN (Law 19.132, 20 March 1992).

The Triple Autonomy of TVN

Table 5.1 summarizes the triple autonomy proposed under the reform law, covering the three basic operations of the company.

Table 5.1 / Autonomy of TVN

1. Legal and Political Autonomy

Public enterprise whose director is coappointed by the president and the Senate.

2. Economic Autonomy

Nonprofit

Self-financing

Competitive (arts. 2, 25)

No government funding

No credit from the government (art. 25)

No donations to the state or to individuals (arts. 27–28)

3. Administrative Autonomy and Management Stability

Not under the administrative norms of state-owned companies but under the norms of private enterprise (arts. 24, 35)

Ability to set up associated companies (art. 22)

Under the labor regulations of private enterprise (art. 29)

Competitively and openly bid (art. 31)

Responsible and transparent operations

Externally audited (art. 24)

Under the fiscal review of the superintendent of the SEC (art. 33) and not the Government Accounting Office (art. 34)

Legal and Political Autonomy

The reform law set up the TVN Corporation, a legally incorporated entity (arts. 1, 4) administered by a board of directors coappointed by the president and the National Senate (art. 4).

As table 5.2 indicates, the president of the board of directors is named by the president of the republic and remains in this position during the term of the president and for thirty days following the end of the presidential term (art. 4a and b). The full-term employees elect the representative of the TVN employees for a two-year period. The six other members of the board are appointed in a special agreement between the president and the Senate. The president presents the Senate with a closed list with six names that are approved by the Senate by absolute majority. (A vote

Table 5.2 / Board of Directors of TVN

Position	Means of Selection	Length of Term
President of the board of directors	Named by president	Same as presidential term
Director representing TVN employees	Elected by full-time TVN employees	Two years
Six directors	Coappointed by the president and the Senate	Eight years

by simple majority on each name was ruled out in order to avoid control by the majority party or the omission of the minority party.[3]) The intent of the law is to include the minority party on the board of directors in order to ensure representation by all interests and not just those of the majority.

The law stipulates that the president as well as the members of the board must have the necessary skills and experience to carry out their functions. The law allows for the rejection of candidates for the board on the basis of their lack of skills and experience but not on the basis of their political or cultural points of view. Each of the six members of the board serves an eight-year term with half the board named every four years, thereby ensuring long-term stability in the management of TVN. The Senate cannot remove the six members. The protection provided by the eight-year terms is a guarantee of legal and political stability and a guard against short-term political pressure.

In order to protect the internal operations of the TVN Corporation, the board carries on its deliberations behind closed doors in a collective manner (art. 7). Members cannot divulge their deliberations (art. 9). Any violation of this secrecy is cause for removal from the board (art. 12). The board was set up to guarantee:

- Autonomy from the executive and legislative powers and the agreement of the two political parties

- Pluralism with representation of the different political and cultural positions in the country

- Diversity and the trust of the public

- Stability and long-term management

As shown in table 5.3, the makeup of TVN's board shares certain characteristics with that of the BBC. The BBC Board of Governors is named in a consensual manner not by the British Parliament, but by the Queen (King) in Council. The governors are not politicians or members of Parliament. They are drawn from the senior civil service and are named by the Crown in agreement with the leaders of the government and the opposition. The prime minister designates the president of the board. The governors do not serve at the pleasure of the government but have fixed terms and a staggered turnover. Through a somewhat different mechanism both the BBC and TVN attempt to guarantee pluralism, consensus, stability, and protection from political and administrative whims.

Table 5.3 / Characteristics of the TVN Board

Position	Characteristics
President of the board	Nonremovable
Director representing TVN employees	Nonremovable nonvoting member
Six directors	Closed list, absolute majority of the Senate nonremovable staggered turnover

The reform law extends some of these characteristics to some higher-level management positions in TVN. The vice president of the board should have the confidence of *all members* and must be elected by a majority of five of the seven members of the board (art. 13, no. 1).

The executive director of TVN is the highest administrative authority of TVN and serves at the pleasure of the board. The support of at least five of the seven members of the board is required to name or remove the executive director. This mechanism is designed to guarantee that the executive director has the confidence of the board as well as stability in his or her functions. The executive director is present but is not a voting member of the board (arts. 17–21). By making the executive director responsible to the board of directors, the law safeguards against any influence on TVN by external political powers (see table 5.4).

The higher-level managers of TVN can be present on the board when they are called to participate in the discussions, but the board makes the final decisions. Following modern management guidelines, the reform law foresees the need for a separation between directorial and executive functions in order to guarantee full transparency in the different functions. For this reason no TVN employee (including the executive director and the representative of the employees) is a voting member of the board.

TVN, like the BBC, draws the distinction between the governing board

Table 5.4 / Higher-Level Positions in TVN

Position	Means of Selection	Characteristics
Vice president of the board	Named by board of TVN	Named or removed by at least 5 of 7 votes
Executive director	Named by board of TVN	Named or removed by at least 5 of 7 votes Nonvoting member
Higher-level managers	Named by board of TVN	Named or removed by at least 4 of 7 votes Nonvoting member

of the organization and the administration of the company. The governing board represents the political and cultural diversity of Chilean society and for this reason should be stable and independent of the executive or legislative branches of government. The real autonomy of the governing board of TVN contrasts with the relative autonomy of other so-called public media in Chile.[4]

The administrative and management functions of a public television system require stable professional personnel who are accountable in terms of financial and social-cultural indicators to both the board of directors and the audience. The business of television requires an efficient management system with the necessary continuity to develop and carry out mid- and long-term planning. None of this is possible under a changing, partisan political administration.

Financial Autonomy

The reform of TVN emphasized self-financing. TVN has always accepted commercial advertising. Traditionally the Chilean state gave higher priority to public funds for other expenditures such as health, education, social security, and infrastructure than it did to television in general and TVN in particular.

TVN is a state-owned company that is publicly incorporated as a non-profit organization (arts. 1, 4, 26), similar to a public utility company. TVN, however, is required to be entirely self-financing within the new context of competitive private television stations.

In the public hearings on the law reforming TVN the private stations argued for true competition—in other words, that TVN not receive government subsidies, subsidized loans, or advertising. The drafters of the reform accepted these limitations (arts. 2, 25). At the same time, TVN cannot provide services to private individuals, companies, or to the state without just compensation at market value (arts. 27, 28). The only exception is when TVN broadcasts public service announcements without charge. ANATEL, the National Association of Broadcasters, usually coordinates this decision.

The financial autonomy of TVN is important for free and open competition with the other television stations. It also is a guarantee of political autonomy. Any government funding of TVN would imply yearly budget negotiations with the Executive Budget Office and with the parliament. It is highly likely that these drawn-out yearly negotiations would have led to a slow loss of autonomy, a regular tendency in public funding.[5]

The need to be self-financing has moved TVN toward more modern commercials, productions, programming, news, and technical management. TVN has rationalized costs, sought new business and coproductions, and created a new international channel sold to cable systems throughout the region.

Administrative Autonomy and Management Stability

TVN's financial self-sufficiency made the company more competitive in both programming and management, while the reform law gave it a series of measures that strengthened it administratively. Some of these measures already have been described—a stable board of directors and top management that enjoyed the confidence of the government.[6] Others gave TVN the flexibility to operate in a competitive television market. TVN is not required to follow the rigid administrative norms of a state-owned company but follows those of a private corporation (art. 24 and 35). It can set up associated companies (art. 22) such as the company that delivers the international satellite channel, TV Chile.

As private-sector employees, TVN employees have the right to form unions and strike (art. 29). Employees, however, must be selected in open competition, thus increasing the professional level of the staff (art. 31).

Authorized external auditors guarantee the corporation's economic responsibility and transparency (art. 24). TVN also has internal auditors under the board of directors, separate from the executive direction of the company. In 1999 the internal auditors put out a handbook of standardized administrative procedures of special relevance to the company's external suppliers.

TVN is audited by the Chilean Securities and Exchange Commission with trimester financial reports and is treated as a private sector corporation (art. 33). It is not under the Government Accounting Office any more than any other private sector company (art. 34) that does business with the government.

Article 26 of the television reform law allows for yearly earnings to be returned to the national treasury except when the board votes to keep earnings as a capital reserve according to prior authorization from the finance minister. (A weakness of this article is that it potentially allows pressure to be put on the company through manipulation of the strategic aspect of its capitalization.)

Political and Cultural Pluralism

Article 3 of the television reform law describes TVN's public service mission. All Chilean TV companies are required to operate according to the law that created the National Television Council. In addition, TVN has the special obligation of pluralism and objectivity in its entire programming and specifically in news, analysis, and programs of public debate. TVN's requirement for pluralism is based on the importance of television as a news source in comparison with other media. A 1996 audience survey conducted by the National Television Council with a sample of 2,400 individuals confirmed the importance television had acquired since the 1970s in relation to other information sources.

Table 5.5 / Most Frequent Source of Local, National, and Global Information (in percentages)

Your City			Chile			The World		
TV	RADIO	PRESS	TV	RADIO	PRESS	TV	RADIO	PRESS
66.5	10.5	18.5	75.5	8.0	14.7	77.3	5.8	16.1
70.4	16.5	12.1	77.4	13.9	8.1	81.4	10.8	7.1
70.9	17.2	8.9	79.7	13.2	5.4	83.1	10.1	4.7

Source: CNTV 1997 (Santiago, Chile)

Table 5.5 shows that television is the main source of information about the nation, the world, and the locality for seven out of every ten Chileans. The same study shows that television news programs play a key role as a source of information. Television news also receives higher ratings than radio and the press for veracity, amount of information, and political objectivity. This positive perception of television, however, does not rule out criticism of television's sensationalistic tendencies and its frequent irrelevance to the interests of the audience, among other things (cf. SGG 1999).

On the basis of their own past experience of Chilean television and of others' experiences in other countries in the world, the framers of the television law concluded that a pluralist board of directors for TVN was the only guarantee of effective pluralism within television. This hard-won pluralism, however, cannot exist without financial autonomy. And financial autonomy is not possible without flexible, competitive, externally reviewed management structures. In order to ensure these objectives, the board of directors approved two complementary documents: the Editorial Policy of October 1993 and the Programming Directives of April 1997.

TVN hopes to achieve active political pluralism through the expansion of sources of information and the limitation on editorializing on the part of the station. TVN should present a diversity of opinions for public debate, but it should not take sides or omit, distort, or challenge conflicting opinions. Pluralism, however, is not only a function of political debate. It also covers different values, cultures, tastes, and religions. Cultural pluralism, therefore, should be evidenced in a variety of television genres, reflecting the different interests and tastes of all segments of society.

TVN's pluralist mission must be achieved within the station's vocation to serve a mass audience with general content. Otherwise, programming aimed at the interests of a small elite audience would create an elitist station, in direct contradiction to TVN's mission to contribute to pluralism and to the legitimate diversity of the country.[7]

The TVN reform law did not establish any other additional public service missions for the company. Today public service programming for television is a subject of much debate as a result of the crisis of the systems and of audiences' lack of satisfaction (Fuenzalida 2000). The reform law preferred leaving decisions on the types of public service programming to be aired to the broadcasters, the specialists, and the creative forces behind this dynamic and changing industry.

Some Results

From the perspective of providing diversity of information, TVN has expanded the amount of time it devotes to news and increased the variety of formats for the transmission of information. According to its statutes, TVN's mission of providing a medium for pluralism and balance cannot be achieved without a significant quantity and variety of high-quality news programming that its public accepts as credible.

TVN airs five news broadcasts, totaling three and a half hours a day, on weekdays, and two news broadcasts, totaling an hour and a half, on weekends. In addition, TVN broadcasts *Medianoche,* an interview program for debate and discussion of the news, daily and *La Entrevista del Domingo* weekly in prime time on Sundays. TVN also runs two programs of investigative journalism: *Informe Especial,* an in-depth look at issues; and *Historia de la Noticia,* on breaking news.

Table 5.6 shows the evolution of news programming on the three most important television channels in Chile. It gives a clear indication of the expansion of TVN. The data cover the period 1993–99. It is based on the People Meter system of TIME-IBOPE, the only rating system in operation in the country under a joint contract with the TV channels and ACHAP (The Chilean Association of Advertising Agencies).

Table 5.6 / Total Annual News Broadcasts
(in hours)

Year	TVN	TV 13	Megavisión
1993	697	566	437
1994	785	585	451
1995	776	564	511
1996	904	560	567
1997	949	589	612
1998	1,031	638	605
1999	1,285	992	631

Source: People Meter/TIME-IBOPE

As reflected in table 5.7, the Chilean public's increased viewing of news programming on TVN is the most important indicator of public confidence in the information services of the channel. As mentioned above, in 1989 the central news program on TVN had a rating of 13.7 percent, compared with 30 percent for Channel 13.

Table 5.7 / Hours of News Programming Viewed by Households Annually

Year	TVN	TV 13	Megavisión
1993	68	91	41
1994	84	88	37
1995	85	80	51
1996	107	91	51
1997	126	100	52
1998	152	104	61
1999	171	127	69

Source: People Meter/TIME-IBOPE

According to table 5.8, during the 1990s, ratings for TVN's news programming increased, reaching a level competitive with Channel 13 by the end of the decade.

Table 5.8 / Average Annual Household Ratings for Prime Time News

Year	24 Horas/TVN	Teletrece/TV 13	Meganoticias/Megavisión
1993	13.2	20.6	9.0
1994	15.9	19.2	8.0
1995	15.4	17.7	9.1
1996	18.3	20.7	8.6
1997	19.4	22.2	7.6
1998	21.6	22.1	12.3
1999	22.0	19.5	11.3

Source: People Meter/TIME-IBOPE

The growth of the audience for TVN's news programming is an important indicator of its increasing credibility and public confidence. Among the public TV stations in Latin America, this audience growth is unique to TVN (Fuenzalida 2000).[8] Table 5.9 shows the growth of the average annual ratings for TVN compared with Megavisión and Channel 13, for many years the most popular television station in the country. By 1999, TVN had taken first place in audience ratings, ahead of Channel 13.

Table 5.9 / Average Annual Household Ratings for Main Channels

Year	TVN	TV 13	Megavisión
1994	8.4	10.0	7.5
1995	8.6	9.3	7.4
1996	9.2	10.0	7.0
1997	9.7	10.5	6.1
1998	10.7	10.5	8.7
1999	11.1	10.5	8.3

Source: People Meter/TIME-IBOPE

The Securities and Exchange Commission requires standardized financial information from the television stations three times a year. TVN has been the only channel that did not show a yearly loss and had variable earnings, depending on the economic cycles and the corresponding adjustment in advertising. If TVN were to show a loss, it must be absorbed by the company and cannot be passed on to the state.

The Chilean case is unique in the region. The Catholic University of Chile and the state own the two leading channels in the country, TV 13 and TVN. With the increased competition in the 1990s, the newer channels, not the traditional leaders, suffered serious economic difficulties and low ratings. As a result, the newer channels were partially or totally sold to the large international networks: Televisa, TV Azteca, Venevisión, and others.

Need for Three-Pronged Social Legitimacy, Management, and Industrial Legitimacy

The Aylwin-Navarette reform law inserted TVN in a competitive market by requiring that it be self-financing. This decision provided the material base for TVN's autonomy in the face of outside political pressure. The obligation to pay its own way, however, has led to creative tensions throughout the organization.

First, the tension to modernize the management and workings of TVN has led to stability in management, governability, a long-term vision both nationally and internationally, planning and evaluation, cost effectiveness, social responsibility, and independent auditing. The fear that pressures from advertisers could exert a negative influence on programming has been balanced by the competitive size of the company and the fact that the company as a whole and not each individual program is self-financing. The pressure from advertisers also is balanced by TVN's non-profit status, its vision of public service, the diversity of its advertising sources, and finally, the search for new business in the face of declining advertising revenues.

Another tension centers on serving an audience that has no obligation to tune in to a TVN program. TVN pays attention to the audience in order to achieve higher ratings as well as to provide for viewers' preferences and expectations rather than supposing that these are already known. The self-financing requirement has directed TVN's attention to the social and cultural needs of the viewer. This requirement was aimed at creating a public service channel better adapted to the needs of the Chilean audience.

These creative tensions contribute to the social legitimacy and sustainability of TVN. Today in Chile and increasingly in Latin America any public television network that is inefficiently run and loses money is illegitimate and unsustainable. The commercial success of TVN and the improvements in its management are thus key components of its social legitimacy.

On various occasions the current executive director of TVN, René Cortázar, has observed that TVN's insertion in the market has both virtues and limitations.[9] Chile's small market cannot permanently finance the national production of a wide variety of programming, including children's programs and programs of history, science, and culture. Nor can it support the regionalization of TVN. State subsidy is needed as a complement and correction in an imperfect market. This subsidy provides substantial financing through the Fund for the National Television Council; the TV channels and independent producers compete for these funds, which are awarded based on evaluations of audience ratings and satisfaction. TVN aspires to become a modern company that can take advantage of the market's possibilities and virtues, correcting its imperfection with state subsidies and the contributions of private individuals, foundations, and corporations. TVN's sound management and competitive strength are necessary but not sufficient conditions of its social legitimacy.

Public Legitimacy

A public network also requires the legitimacy and backing of the political system. The law assigns TVN responsibility for the balance of public information to sustain democratic governability as a basic public good (art. 3). The reform of TVN was aimed at forming an independent company that would "support a model of television whose key value is to provide service to all Chileans with a criteria of pluralism" (TVN 1993). The lawmakers' emphasis on TVN's mission to ensure political and cultural pluralism reflects an immediate past history of a country marked by deep political strife.

Today a more modest mission of avoiding misinformation and contributing to the governability of a democracy has replaced the government-controlled TV's previous mission of supporting specific political causes, ideologies, and government propaganda and smearing the opposition. The concept of pluralism has expanded beyond politics to include a diversity of cultures, tastes, regions, and religions.

In striving to achieve this mission TVN has recovered credibility and become an important news presence. The massive and active presence of TVN has obliged the other media to become more pluralistic. This is the "TVN effect" that the reform law sought. Within this new information context any attempt at misinformation is now practically impossible.

Conflicts were inevitable around this new approach of pluralistic information. It is not easy to give up the old ways of propaganda, the quick silencing of the opposition, or the facile cover-up of corruption and social problems—tasks formerly assigned to TVN. Dispensing of misinformation is a great temptation amid situations of political conflict, unmet demands in health and education, and a host of other social problems that plague developing (and developed) countries alike. This tension is historical and occurs throughout the world between politicians and the press in any democratic society with a free press. The new respect for different cultural values also generates inevitable tensions and discrepancies in newly pluralist societies. As cultural diversity increases, so too do the demands that different social actors place on public television. The question of quality of information becomes more complex because the different social and cultural strata have different interests and different definitions of quality with regard to news. Satisfaction with public television paradoxically can decrease under a pluralist society given television's inability to satisfy all these demands. The framers of the new television reform law, however, recognized that balanced information and cultural pluralism were necessary for the mid- and long-term success of democracy in Chile.

Legitimacy with the Audience

An actively engaged audience is the third pillar supporting television's social legitimacy. Chilean public television requires a large audience and the affection and respect of this audience. The affection of the audience goes beyond good management and political pluralism. It requires good satisfying programming that the audience considers useful. Rather than attempt to regulate this type of programming, the reform law left these decisions in the hands of the TVN staff, which allowed for flexibility within the dynamics of the television industry.

Audience surveys in Chile (Fuenzalida 1997; 2000) found that expectations for public service programming were closely tied to education in order to compensate for deficiencies in everyday life in the family and surroundings.[10] The home is the location of many of the problems that most affect the audience: the lack of basic goods and services, physical and mental illness, abusive relationships, domestic violence, drug and alcohol abuse.

According to the UNDP, about a third of the population of Latin America lives in conditions of physical and emotional poverty. Evidence exists that, rather than turning to television as a source of formal education, many look to the medium to assume a role in the home of providing emotional support and fostering self-confidence. This support is indispensable to the overcoming of attitudes of self-pity and lack of confidence that lead to passive behaviors. The educational potential of television is consistent with an assets-based approach to poverty reduction that looks at the capacities and resources of the population in order that they become active subjects of their own progress (Parker 1999). The majority of the problems related to the quality of life now are considered the responsibility of society as a whole and not only the responsibility of the state. Today strengthening an active role for civil society is a desirable objective of public television in Latin America.

Data show that people learn differently from television than they do from formal schooling. Formal education is systematic and conceptual. TV teaches with anecdotes and stories that facilitate identification with personal experiences. Television teaches by identification and affection rather than by logical argument. This form of learning explains the popularity of soap operas and reality programming. Here the audience is able to identify with the people and situations that are shown. Television audiences do not like to be lectured at. They like to be kept company and talked to—in other words, they like to be entertained.

Many television programs weave the educational content into the entertainment format, making audiences more receptive. This form of entertainment-education opens new doors for public television that may better fit the needs and possibilities of the Latin American audience.

Epilogue

The reform of TVN initiated by President Aylwin was a case of policy-making to form a public television channel within a new context of pluralism, diversity, and economic self-sufficiency. The process is not finished. Much still needs to be accomplished in the areas of balancing the limitations of the market and improving the service to meet the needs of the audience.

The reform described above has three characteristics.

1. TVN falls under a regulatory regime similar to the Central Bank, the Supreme Court, or the Government Accounting Office, all of which have a permanence and goals that go beyond the elected administration.

2. TVN is a self-supporting, publicly owned nonprofit company that operates within a competitive environment.

3. TVN addresses the demands of three competing actors: the administration, the audience, and the different social sectors, each of which has different relations with a public broadcasting station. These can be described as follows.

- the administration needs sustainability

- the audience needs satisfaction

- different social sectors have different requirements

The Need for Sustainability

The management of TVN needs to guarantee the sustainability of the company. This requires that various functions be put in place, or capacities developed, if they do not already exist. These include:

- to produce quality programming in different genres and administer the company

- to project the company nationally and internationally

- to become a competitor in the television market

- to position the station with an identity within the market

- to communicate with the audience to produce and broadcast attractive programming that is economically sustainable, thereby becoming a significant actor in the national cultural arena

- to facilitate a socially legitimate response to the demands of the different social actors and fulfill the obligations to these actors.

Audience Satisfaction

TVN's explicit social mission is to foster political pluralism. TVN has been relatively successful in achieving this mission. Audience demands, however, suggest other missions for the public station, including specifically for regional audiences an educational mission. This wider "educating" mission is related to improvements in daily life, empowerment, and increased self-confidence, especially for adults, youth, and children living in poverty, in order to help them face the challenge of social and economic development with high self-esteem and self-confidence. This is an area where public television needs to radically reconceptualize new forms of entertainment-education programming that will be useful and attractive to the audience.

Requirements of Different Social Actors

Audiences must be satisfied, and different social actors must be recognized. Finally, political forces, the "owners" of the station, must be heard.

The Chilean political class is complex. Some sectors of political power accept pluralism in theory but find the practice in the short term to be more challenging. The executive branch tends to perceive communication instrumentally for its own purposes. The natural reaction is to give less importance to pluralism or audience satisfaction. For the legislative branch, in daily competition in defense of constituencies, the tendency also is to perceive public television instrumentally; legislators, used to defending their plans and attacking their opponents, seldom favor pluralism and balance. Although the different branches of political power support the broader mission of public television in theory, the daily grind of politics puts a higher value on the missions of public relations, advertising, or propaganda.

Supporters of the free market feel that public television is unnecessary. In the long run, they believe, the forces of the market will automatically correct any concentration of ownership in the television field and naturally lead to pluralism. Others defend the need for the "TVN effect" within the Chilean television market in order to stimulate diversity of information. This diversity is an absolute requirement for complex societies where the old solutions no longer provide answers to the multiple new challenges.

The reform of TVN took place smoothly throughout the decade of the 1990s under the administrations of Presidents Patricio Aylwin, Eduardo Frei, and Ricardo Lagos. It even received support from the opposition. Joaquín Lavín, for example, a former leader of the center/right-wing party, has had nothing but praise for the achievements of TVN. No drastic changes in the system are foreseen for the future. TVN's strengths are its managerial and industrial energy, largely unperceived by its mass audience, and its pluralism, not always considered a strength by all politicians.

It is difficult to predict the future of TVN. Public stations can be privatized if they fail and become a drain on the public sector, and if they succeed they may get a high price on the auction block. Finally, in addition to what TVN already has achieved, it needs the continued and massive support of an audience satisfied that TVN's programming enriches daily life in Chile.

Notes

1. In Latin America these channels are under the legislative branch and are government funded. In 2000 the Chilean annual budget for the two TV channels in the houses of parlia-

ment was $1.2 million. In the United States, Cable Satellite Public Affairs Network—C-SPAN for the House of Representative and C-SPAN 2 for the Senate—are cooperatives of private companies (Murphy 2000).

2. In March 1990 the TVN accounts presented by Jorge Navarrete showed a disastrous financial situation carried over from the previous administration of TVN under the military government. The company had lost 83 percent of its capital. Faced with this situation, the stations did not appear to be economically viable without some government funds, which were authorized by parliament for a single time under the new law. Even with this one-time subsidy, without autonomy or credibility, TVN would not have been viable in the competitive television market. A few lone political voices supported the use of TVN as a government information channel for the new administration of President Aylwin. This suggestion was seen as out of step with the new democracy, as well as inefficient as a communication strategy. Director Navarrete promised to transform TVN into "a truly national" channel at the service of the needs and problems of the Chilean population, reestablishing and improving its autonomy and guaranteeing its credibility as a source of "truthful, timely and balanced information" (Navarrete 1990).

3. The first drafts of the law proposed the agreement between the executive and the Chamber of Deputies. The Aylwin administration changed that to an agreement between the executive and the Senate, the legislative body specializing in the achievement of consensus.

4. TVN autonomy starkly contrasts with the statutes governing the government daily, *La Nación*, which besides TVN is the only public medium in Chile, with the exception of the *Diario Oficial*, which has specific characteristics. *La Nación* is a newspaper with a low circulation in comparison with the other national newspapers. Its board and director are named by the president—in other words, it is more a government organ than a public medium.

5. In the book *The Vanishing Vision: The Inside Story of Public Television* (1995), James Day, former president of the Public Broadcasting Service (PBS) in the United States, describes how political pressure was applied through the budget process.

6. The seven-member board of TVN has been criticized for its size and for not representing all the cultural and political groups within Chilean society. On the contrary, this small size demonstrates that in setting up the board, the designers wanted to create a body with the ability to govern. A broader representative body would be more an advisory than an executive body. This is the difference between the board of directors of TVN and the National Television Council (CNTV)—a supervisory body with eleven members. Because of this difference, the direct executive responsibility of CNTV is held by its president and not by the Council. The president of CNTV is the chief executive of the service, and as such plans, directs, organizes, coordinates, and supervises the operations of the service, and hires and fires at his or her discretion, the employees of the service (Law 18.838 art. 14, bis of CNTV).

7. According to James Day (1995), the PBS network in the United States, in contrast with the BBC, has not achieved a massive audience in the country. It has become a marginalized system with little social and cultural relevance. Michael Tracey (1998) also has criticized the cultural marginality of PBS. With the exception of BBC, European public television systems are considered increasingly at risk of becoming minority and marginalized television systems (cf. UNESCO 1996).

8. A widely held hypothesis among Chilean academics and politicians is that the influential and pluralistic presence of the TVN news service has a double-edged effect: it provides massive amounts of diverse information to the audience and also tends to diversify the totality of the Chilean information system. There are, however, other unexpected types of effects. Guillermo Sunkel (1999) associates the increased credibility of television news after the return of democracy with the terminal crisis of the newspapers and magazines (e.g., *Fortín Mapocho* and *La Época*, and the magazines *APSI, Análisis*, and *Hoy*) that were created under the military government to fight for the return of democracy. That crisis would show that the more politically combative media do not draw large audiences except in time of crisis. Otherwise, readers prefer a more complex and balanced publication. The crisis of these outlets also is tied to their poor management.

9. "Una contribución a los desafíos futuros de la Televisión Chilena" (paper presented to the Special Commission to Study the Present Conditions of Chilean Television of the Chamber of Deputies, Santiago, Chile, July 1999).

10. Family is understood in the widest sense, as the unit of affection of a group of individuals. Public TV could not impose one, single cultural or religious definition of the family.

CHAPTER SIX

The Colombian Media

Modes and Perspective in Television

Fernando Calero Aparicio

COLOMBIAN broadcasting is changing rapidly in response to national and international developments. The most obvious change is an increase in the availability of more varied television content, supported by innovations in distribution and production technologies and the formation of new audiences.

At the national level, the changes in broadcasting are the result of the redesign or breakdown of the so-called hybrid Colombian model. In this hybrid, the state controlled the distribution channels and, at times, the content of programming. At the same time, the state also guaranteed relatively harmonious competition within the advertising market, supported national productions, and guaranteed coverage of a large portion of the population. This arrangement also provided a legal framework for private sector operations and guaranteed a fairly competitive market. A positive outcome of this mixed system was the high quality and quantity of national television productions and a secure time slot for their broadcast.

The Colombian model of broadcasting supported national programming and ensured the coverage of a wide sector of the population. It also created a Colombian cultural industry of considerable economic strength, both as a vehicle for advertising and as an employer of talent. Colombian television has its own star system, but it also worked closely with national theater groups and intellectuals and was responsible for training many professionals in the field. It was possible to make a living working on Colombian television, and it became a refuge for audiovisual expression and experimentation. The recent regional decentralization of Colombian television enabled broader groups to gain production and reporting skills. The regional channels fostered regional cultural industries and audiences independent from the central hub of the capital city, Bogotá. Colombia's experience is unique in Latin America. No other country in the region had a similar experience in terms of coverage by regional stations, regional production facilities, and local reporting independent of the national networks as part of public service broadcasting provided by the state.

At a national level, the redesign or breakdown of the Colombian model set off a struggle that is yet to end. The new players in this struggle are two commercial channels owned by the two largest economic concerns in the country; two mixed public-private channels, holdovers from the previous model; a public interest channel that attempts to revive the broadcasting commitments of the state in terms of content and production; eight regional channels; nine local public service channels; one privately owned local channel; and over 300 community-access and cable channels, reaching about 4.5 million households. Commercial advertising finances the majority of these stations. The same advertising investment that once supported Colombian national productions today is not only divided among many new players but as a whole is lower as a result of the financial crisis.

In order to understand Colombian television in the 1990s and beyond, it is necessary to understand the dynamics of television in Latin America. Heriberto Muraro (1985) has described Latin American television in the following terms: "The historical evolution of Latin American television demonstrates the weakness of the states and the influence of the multinational groups through direct ownership and production. The major battles for control of television have ignored the role of television in economic and cultural development."

Colombian television appears to have been the exception to this pattern in its avoidance of monopolization of ownership and production. With the exception of technological dependence, Colombia's television model was different. Television, of course, is an urban phenomenon that needs sufficient population numbers to be effectively exploited, as well as certain economies of scale for production. Technologically, television requires an infrastructure as well as a sufficient advertising base if it is to operate commercially. Television, however, is not independent of politics. Colombian television should be understood in a context of highly concentrated populations with regional poles of development, a centralized political structure and fairly nonparticipatory political system, and a virtual dictatorship by the two hegemonic political parties. The distribution of news and information in the country is politically motivated.

Colombia has a movement for constitutional reform, a market economy opening to the world, and a deepening political, economic, and social crisis.

The previous model of Colombian television, created as a compromise between the state and the broadcasting industry, was based on an idea of a public service with the following characteristics:

- A finite radio spectrum

- State-guaranteed national coverage and financing of programming through private, commercial programmers in a hybrid public-private system

- Television understood as a political tool

- Administrative, political, and technological centrism

- Special conditions identified by Elizabeth Fox (1988b) that included: a fragmented private sector, a political balance between the ruling parties, weak reform movements, and a relative absence of foreign investment and educational services.

- A high percentage of national production—legally at least 50 percent, in reality over 70 percent

- Regional stations and regional participation

- Until 1995, delegated authority in Inravisión, a decentralized institution that was part of the executive branch of government

- Community participation in television policymaking

- State control and regulation of television

- State-owned infrastructure and transmission facilities

- A philosophy that public interest prevailed over private interest

- Special treatment in the Constitution of 1991 and the creation of an autonomous entity, the National Television Commission

- Guarantees of freedom of expression and right of reply

- Viewed, in effect, as a public service that, according to Tremblay (1988), should guarantee continuity of service

• Continuous improvement of services as a function of the needs of the population served and changes in technology

• Equal access for all citizens

Under the pre-1995 structure Colombian television fulfilled the conditions of a public service, albeit imperfectly. Continuity of service was guaranteed despite uncertainties with each new administration. Quality of service and production was generally high, with exceptions, although the system was not as responsive to changes in technology as perhaps it could have been under wholly private or public ownership. Colombian television fell short in terms of guaranteeing equal access to all citizens, but it provided far more access to different points of view, artistic expressions, regional diversity, and freedom of expression than occurred in most other countries in the region. The protected national market and the centralized political system engendered a broadcasting system that covered 92 percent of the population, supported a consolidated national industry, and allowed for regional participation and diversity of viewpoints in news programming.

A clearer understanding of the development of the new Colombian broadcasting system can be gained by looking at the beginnings of the system in the 1950s, the transformations that occurred under the Constitution of 1991, and the new legal and regulatory conditions put in place in 1995.

The Beginnings of Television in Colombia

Colombian television began in 1954 in the capital city Bogotá, when a dictator put in place the new medium as a way to consolidate his government, reach the population with his message, and give his regime a symbol of modernity. At first, television services were limited to the urban center. This fit well with the centrist regime and its need for political control. As occurred in most Latin American countries, the technological limitations of early television accorded well with the needs of the political leaders. Colombian television expanded slowly from Bogotá, following the accelerated urbanization of the regional poles of development in Cali, Medellín, Barranquilla, and elsewhere.

The government programmed, produced, and transmitted what went out over Colombia's airwaves. Content was based on a somewhat elitist view of culture and included classical music and great works of literature. The Office of the President directed all news reporting. The professional level was not high, most if not all the technology was imported, and reception was often spotty.

In the 1960s the relationship between broadcasting and the state was framed by the hegemony of the two traditional political parties—the Liberals and the Conservatives—that, in response to the earlier dictatorship, had agreed to alternate in office. During this period the state set up an educational television service as a way to educate the new arrivals to the cities from the countryside, improve literacy, and consolidate a "national identity." The expansion of broadcasting under the government-controlled system was shaped by all the limitations of a developing country and the difficulties of covering a wide geographic area with large sectors of poverty and a traditional agricultural economy. Television's growth also was limited by the absence of direct national and foreign private investment and the incapacity of the system to train sufficient personnel for production and to maintain adequately the transmission facilities.

The search for private sector participation in Colombian television occurred at the end of the 1960s and was limited to the local channels that covered only Bogotá. The rest of the system remained under state ownership. What emerged from this period, however, was a mixed public-private model in which the state owned the broadcasting frequencies and the infrastructure for production and transmission and controlled programming by bidding out time to private companies who in turn sold advertising time. The introduction of color television in Colombia provides an example of how state control of the medium functioned. In Colombia, the decision whether to adopt color television was made by Congress and the president rather than by the private sector, and this innovation was introduced only after a long debate in Congress. It was a political rather than an economic or technological matter.

By the mid-1960s Colombian television had been moved out from under the direct control of the presidency and placed under a decentralized institution of the Ministry of Communication as a slightly more autonomous organization. The move, however, did not signify a reduction of Presidential control over television, especially news. The field of TV news most clearly demonstrates how the Colombian state's relationship with the private sector effectively guaranteed the dependence of television and denied a voice to those sectors of the population outside the traditional system of political power. The Colombian hybrid system, although many layered, was basically closed and static in regard to a news function as well as programming decisions. In the late 1960s and early 1970s the Colombian government, as part of its education policy, set up a third television channel dedicated exclusively to adult education and cultural programming. This channel also was placed under Inravisión. Finally, as a way of ensuring state control of news, the government set up its own news program on the national network.

For most of Latin America, the 1980s were a "lost decade" in terms of economic growth. For Colombia, however, the decade was a time of relatively stable economic growth and political transition. The hybrid model of public-private television matured, with an additional nuance of increased state control but decreased control of television by the successive administrations. At the same time, private sector programmers consolidated their commercial management of the medium. The government gave the programmers new guarantees in terms of longer contracts, which in turn allowed for more stable investments. It established a minimum and maximum number of time slots that each company could control and placed national productions in the most favorable positions, while requiring a minimum of 50 percent national content. Finally, in order to increase quality through greater competition, the government programmed the most popular genres—news programs and soap operas—against each other on the different channels. During the 1980s Colombian television came into its own in terms of production quality and began to open the door slightly to greater independence from government control over news. In contrast to other countries in the region, Colombia had a higher percentage of national content, close to 70 percent, a proportion exceeded only by the larger countries, Brazil and Mexico.

Colombia also experimented with some different ways to increase community input to the direction of television policy, an interesting but failed example of which was Law 42 in 1985, which attempted to place representatives of different groups in society on the National Television Commission. Although this was interpreted as excessive government meddling, it was followed by the initiation of a process of decentralization in the television industry—a taboo subject for previous Colombian administrations. The first regional channels—Teleantioquia, Telecaribe, and Telepacífico—began in 1985 with a mixed formula including the central and state governments. The decentralization of television production and transmission, especially news, coincided with the decentralization of the Colombian state and increased popular participation in elections, including for the first time the direct election of local mayors. The region-

Television System before 1995

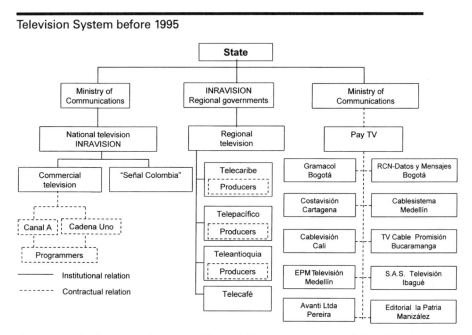

alization of television also coincided with an opening up of the Colombian economy engendered by the arrival of new technologies including cable and subscription television in the late 1980s. The new distribution systems brought new content and formats to Colombians' TV screens. The model of Colombian television before 1995 is indicated in figure 6.1.

Colombian Television in the 1990s

The opening of markets and the increasing political crisis brought new challenges to Colombian television in the 1990s. Colombia began the decade with a new constitution that would have profound repercussions on broadcasting. Article 20 of the Constitution of 1991 states: "Everyone is guaranteed freedom of expression and to inform and be informed truthfully and impartially, and to establish media of mass communications. These media are free and have a social responsibility. The right of reply is guaranteed under equal conditions. There will be no censorship." This article would have enormous impact on the public broadcasting services provided by the state and by the private sector. The new constitution dedicated three articles specifically to television.

Article 75. The radio spectrum is a public good under the inalienable control of the State. The State will guarantee equality of opportunities to its access and under the terms of this law. In order to guarantee pluralism and competition, under this law the State will intervene to discourage monopolies in the use of the radio spectrum.

Article 76. State intervention in the management of the radio spectrum used for television services will be under the control of a body with independent legal, administrative, technical and financial standing. This body will carry out the programs and plans of the State in the services referred to above.

Article 77. This body will be in charge of television policies under this law, without ignoring the freedoms guaranteed by this Constitution. Television will be regulated by an autonomous entity with a national mandate with its own regulations. The actions of this entity will be under a governing board made up of five members who will name the director. The members of the board will serve for a fixed period. The federal government will name two board members; one member will be selected from the legal representatives of the regional channels. Law will establish the remaining members and the regulations and functions of the board.

From these articles and their corresponding legislation (Law 182 of 1995 and Law 335 of 1996) emerged the present situation of Colombian television. The two principal results of the new legislation were (1) the formation of the National Television Commission (CNTV), an autonomous body independent from the government but part of the Colombian state, that regulates, develops, and executes television policies; guarantees equality of access; manages the distribution of the radio spectrum; and discourages the monopolization of its use; and (2) the subsequent creation of a diverse television service with at least six different types of models (as is seen in figure 6.2) that are the product of the legal and administrative directives of CNTV.

A significant difference under the Constitution of 1991 is the status of CNTV, which is a state organization but is not part of the executive branch of the government, as had been the case of Inravisión in the past. Another difference under the new constitution is that there is no higher authority than CNTV itself in regard to television. This autonomy given it by the constitution breaks with a long tradition of government management of the media. The participation of the private sector is yet another difference in the new situation of Colombian television. For the first time the private sector was responsible for the entire operation of a channel—not merely the tenant of rented time slots—under a system that established a certain balance of content and information, distribution of advertising, and equality of coverage of the population.

Structure of Contemporary Television

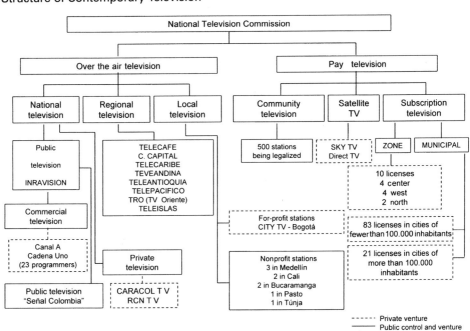

For some, especially those supporting the economic liberalization that began in the 1980s, this augurs a new era of progress and modernization of Colombian television with competition leading to improved quality. According to this theory, up until 1995, Colombian television was a case of backward state interventionism that did not fit with the rest of the emerging Colombian free market economic model.

Under Law 182, Colombian television continues to be conceived as a public service with the objective of educating, entertaining, and protecting children, family values, women, minorities, and others. With the previous arrangement, the government was both operator and regulator of this public service. Under the new constitution, for the first time there are private television services in the country, including channels covering "zones" or municipalities and satellite, subscription, and other forms of pay-TV. Obviously, the changes in Colombian television were seen not only in its regulation under an autonomous body but also in the possibility of new providers and the breakup of the state monopoly on television services.

The privatization of Colombian television was built on the idea of competition in an open market. Yet, the state continues to have the obligation to guarantee access and equality in television services through

CNTV. This has been interpreted to mean that the state is obligated to guarantee equality of access to the programmers of the former state-controlled channels by giving them conditions equal to those under which the new private channels operate. These new conditions include the promise of decreased interference in their commercial operations—for example, relaxing requirements of coverage and increasing flexibility of programming, including requirements on domestic content quotas. At least formally, the private channels are required to work within a basic framework of respect for viewing times for different audience types (e.g., children, general) and to provide airtime for institutional announcements. In return, the operators of the private channels must pay the Colombian state $95 million a year to operate the frequency.

The new system of competition in the Colombian television market still has not resolved the perennial questions of how to address issues such as quality of production, national production, and protection of audiences. Other unresolved issues are how to finance the system and the role of the state as regulator, a role that includes defining the different types of television services. In the case of over-the-air broadcasting, the question of access might be determined by the licensing procedure that involves a process of selection and meeting certain requirements. After licensing, the channel must conform to the legal and contractual requirements that come from the concept of public service with the concomitant guarantees to the audiences.

By law, CNTV also has a role to play in guaranteeing competition. Even in a free market economy, the state must intervene to avoid distortion of the market. In Colombia, this task is made more difficult by the need to maintain the balance in the market between the center and the different regions and between the state and the private sector and is further complicated by the recent introduction of new forms of over-the-air and subscription television services, many of which are tied to some of the strongest economic groups in the country.

Different Modes of Colombian Television Today

Colombia has two types of national television networks: public and private. Even on the public networks, the time slots are put up for bid to private programming companies and operated commercially. In 2000, twenty-two programming companies were operating in the country. The national cultural channel, Señal Colombia, is a public service financed by the state, for the most part through CNTV and its fund for the development of public television. This fund is fed by the contractual payments from the programming companies, the license fees for the private channels, and a monthly percentage of subscription payments to cable operators and other pay systems.

The two new private channels awarded in 1995 under the new regulation are owned by Radio Cadena Nacional (RCN), a powerful economic group that is in turn owned by Ardila Lule with wide-ranging investments including a national radio network and a television programming company. The other channel was awarded to Cadena Radial Colombiana (Caracol), which is owned by the Santo Domingo group, also with wide-ranging investments including a national radio network. The ten-year renewable licenses were awarded in open, competitive bids. The cost of the licenses was an initial $95 million each plus an annual payment of 1.5 percent of advertising revenue paid in three payments a year.

The regional television channels that began in 1995 have grown from four to eight. Regional channels are administered independently and in a decentralized fashion, with no relation to national public television, although Inravisión is a partner in most of the regional channels. The stations are both programmers, administrators, and responsible for the transmission of the public service channel.

Local television was authorized in 1995 and regulated in 1997 and has only been set up in the largest cities—Bogotá, Cali, and Medellín—although local channels have been authorized in smaller cities such as Bucaramanga, Pasto, and Tunja. Local channels must operate in a contiguous geographic area and are not allowed to broadcast either beyond a municipal or metropolitan area or beyond an association of municipalities. Local channels can be nonprofit and as such can be awarded to individuals in those municipalities with populations larger than 100,000. Only one channel can be awarded per person, and national license holders and programming companies on the public channels cannot hold local licenses. By the end of the 1990s only one local commercial channel was in operation, City TV, owned by the *El Tiempo* newspaper group, the largest national daily in importance and circulation. City TV covers only the capital city, Santa Fe de Bogotá, with a population of approximately 7 million residents. The other local channels are nonprofit and have been awarded principally to cultural and educational organizations. With limited financing, these channels have not been able to develop effective local productions, and their impact as alternative media has been limited in a competitive market.

Pay or subscription television began as early as 1980, but its growth in the last five years has been spectacular. Only 5 percent of the approximately 4.5 million subscribers, or about 225,000 households, however, are legally connected and pay the established subscription rates. The remaining 95 percent pertains to "informal" or illegal systems. Pay television is predominantly urban, and by November 1999, ten companies had been established—two each in Bogotá and Medellín and one in Cartagena, Cali, Bucaramanga, Ibagué, Peireira, and Manizales. After November, another eighty-three pay-TV concessions were awarded to municipalities under 100,000 inhabitants and twenty-one concessions to municipalities over 100,000 inhabitants, and ten to zones (four to the center, two to the north, and four to the western zone).

Direct broadcast television (direct to home, or DTH, and direct broadcast satellite, or DBS) was authorized in 1996 and began to be regulated two years later. A DTH system needs authorization from CNTV and must be awarded to a Colombian citizen or organization. A tenth of earnings must be paid to CNTV. Two companies are operating in Colombia—Sky Latin America and DirecTV—both set up by Colombian groups with international capital and support from companies in Mexico, Venezuela, Brazil, and Argentina that provide continent-wide distribution of programs by satellite.

Community television, which appeared in the country in the 1980s, is currently in a state of confusion regarding coverage, forms of distribution, commercialization, and financing of programming and production. Ideally it should be a television service provided by organized communities as a nonprofit operation taking advantage of national and international television and its own productions. Community television can cover a contiguous geographic area that ranges from urban residential communities, to neighborhood associations, developments, and rural areas and must be distributed by a physical network such as cable. Community channels can run commercial advertising, though the advertisers must be from the geographic zone served by the system. The difficulty has resided in the definition of an organized community, which should consist of individuals linked by proximity or collaboration; in reality this has been difficult to prove and the systems have become commercial for-profit operations.

In addition, most of the content on the community channels is taken from over-the-air and satellite channels, which has led to cable systems competing for distribution on community channels without a legal basis.

What began as a good idea for local or community television has degenerated into a chaotic situation where channels mostly carry international programming despite the founding principles of community service. Nevertheless, the new Constitution guarantees the basic right of freedom of expression, as well as the right to set up mass communication media—rights that are the basis of community demands to establish channels.

A Perspective on the Colombian Situation

Colombia in the 1990s experienced two situations that had a serious impact on the development of television. The first was the presidential period between 1994 and 1998, which was marked by strong national and international pressure for the resignation of President Ernesto Samper as a result of charges that he had accepted funds from the drug mafia during his political campaign. The second was the deep economic crisis and recession that began in the country after 1997.

During almost his entire administration, Samper was under indictment for allegedly receiving campaign contributions from the drug cartels. This resulted in a series of political efforts to guarantee his survival in office consisting of favors and counterfavors within the executive and legislative branches. This maneuvering most affected television in terms of the selection of the members of the National Television Commission as patronage, ignoring the spirit of wider representation in which it was set up. In addition, the president's political troubles affected many of the decisions regarding the distribution of television licenses and the relationship between the government and the media. The analysis of this period in Colombian politics has just begun (Rey 1998), and future scholarship will be able to identify more clearly the different impacts on television.

The model of private, competitive television that was set up after 1995 with the introduction of the private sector into national television networks and the different models of television service described above were based on a projected economic growth rate for the country of 4.5 percent. When the country entered into a recession in 1997 and advertising revenue plummeted, it became apparent that these models were not viable in either a short or medium time frame. Advertising revenues for the national networks in 1999 were slightly below $160 million. Costs of the national networks in that year easily passed $280 million. (This leaves a sizable deficit that is projected to remain constant over the next six years.) More than the result of a reduction in the license fee or in the rents paid for time slots, this deficit points to the need to modify the costs of programming and the model for debt financing that drained almost $55 million from the private channels in 1999, representing 74 percent of earnings. Such a level of loss is impossible for any company to sustain, even in an economic boom.

The Colombian model of television, however, is more complex than what is suggested by Figure 6-2. Colombian television needs to be considered not only from the perspective of the state, that is, from CNTV. There is a tension between the market and the state. On the one hand, the state created a new element, the private stations, in the model. On the other hand, the state has a constitutional obligation to control, regulate, and finance television service. Also, it seems as if the state, not the market, is the only entity that guarantees competition. This is paradoxical and important to recognize as a sui generis practice in television policy in the Colombian context. Meanwhile, the market has experienced important changes in terms of commercialism, the consolidation of audiences and private stations, and the concentration of advertising and production in the hands of private stations. The restructuring of Colombian television, however, needs to be seen from the perspective of the audiences—that is, how television is received in a context of specific aesthetic, symbolic, and communication conditions, conditions that cannot quite be grasped through quantitative analysis. Audiences have not typically been taken into consideration in the development of television, and in terms of the responsibilities and answers that the state needs to give them regarding diversity, plurality, formation, and participation. It is also important to think about the model of television from creation to production given that it is impossible to conceive television without addressing its evolution and history as a cultural industry. Perhaps it might be possible to articulate the roles of the market and the state better along the lines of regulation regarding audiences and production. In the construction of a more equitable television model, it is necessary to take into account the issue of representation in decision making, access, distribution and production, decentralization, and financing.

Under these circumstances, it looks as if the only organization operating at a profit is CNTV, which in 1999 brought in about $85 million in earnings. About $23 million of this came from the operations of the public channels, about $38 million from licensing rights and tariffs from the private channels, and about $12 million from surcharges on subscription

Context of Contemporary Television

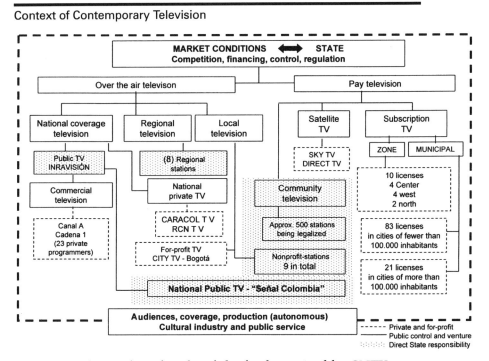

television. Almost three-fourths of the funds received by CNTV came from the private television sector. Half of these funds will be used for improvements in the television transmission network and equipment and in the control and regulation of the public television services.

From the above we can infer that the Colombian model of television set up in 1995 is not viable from either an economic or a political standpoint. Although the economic recession has touched all sectors of the economy and broadcasting, the private networks have tried hard to defend themselves, allegedly using practices such as only advertising their products on their own channels and excluding other programming companies from benefiting from their investments. Another defense is the purchase by the private channels of the rights to the most popular programs, even if another company produced them. Under different circumstances, this could benefit national production, but in the crisis economy it has hurt the smaller channels and programming companies by concentrating the best talent in the private channels. The private channels, furthermore, are the only channels that can attract international investment to improve their programming and services. About 15 percent of Caracol, for example, is owned by Grupo Cisneros from Venezuela, and

Caracol is negotiating to sell a one-fourth share to the Prisa Group from Spain. Another source of revenue for the private channels is the international export of their programs; in the case of Caracol, such exports represent 5 percent of earnings. Colombian productions, however, do not have a high profile in the export market, despite the good performance of some of their products. Finally, the private channels cover the richer urban markets, about 68 percent of the Colombian population.

The programming companies on the public channels have requested more time to pay their rents and the elimination of some of the signal transmission costs. They also have suggested other cost-saving measures such as cutting down on transmission time. What has become apparent is that the public channels—Canal A and Cadena Uno—are betting their future on the commercial television market. This has direct implications for the survival of a public television service that is based on a wide variety of programming, plurality of information sources, and the needs of the audience.

The hope is that subscription television services will change with the evolution of technology that will use the existing infrastructure to offer new services such as telephone, PC, and Internet. Colombia, however, keeps these telecommunications services legally separate, and there has been little advancement in combining services and optimizing resources. In the short and medium term, the 114 new licenses for subscription television in the different municipalities under 100,000, over 100,000 and other zones might establish a sufficiently firm base for subscription television, but in the long run the benefits for these areas are more likely to come from the new Internet-based technologies.

Regional television channels, once in the vanguard in terms of decentralization of television and news reporting as well as local and regional production, today are struggling to find their market position in terms of programming specialization and are suffering from economic difficulties. Their economic survival depends on their ability to find an equilibrium and maintain income from (1) renting time slots for specific programming, (2) the transfer of funds from the regional governments, and (3) contributions from the Public Television Fund of CNTV. At the same time, the regional channels are losing audience share although they are still the favorites for regional news. The shrinking audience has become a factor that pushes the regional channels to become more efficient in their services, to reduce the costs of their operations and the risks involved in the different productions, and to produce programming that is more commercial and that fits better in their competitive niche. Some feel the regional channels eventually will disappear or merge to form larger entities.

Local television, at first glance, appears to be a likely counterbalance to the commercial tendencies of national and transnational television. Upon closer inspection, however, there is little evidence with which to measure the impact of the local channels. There is only one commercially operated local channel, City TV in Bogotá. Meanwhile, nonprofit local television such as Telemedellín, although a good proposal for urban programming, is subject to the political and budgetary pressures of the city of Medellín. Perhaps nonprofit local television with specialized programming aimed at specific audiences will be part of the future of television in Colombia, a country that has shown interest in education and culture. The bets for educational and cultural television, however, are on Señal Colombia as a national network directly financed by the state but as of yet unable to define its style although it has become the focus of highly prized national productions. Señal Colombia, however, is centrally administered, with a passing glance at the cultural activities of the regions. The channel's operations and administration are defined within the structure of the national government, putting its priorities in terms of education, culture, and financing at the mercy of the state. Señal Colombia's coverage is around 60 percent, compared with 92 percent for the commercially programmed public channels. Part of its limitations are the result of transmitting in UHF, a frequency that continues to have difficulties for reception in Colombia.

Regarding technology, it is doubtful that Colombia will enter the digital era in the next ten years. All investments in distribution networks are analog technologies, yielding a situation that will limit the integration of different services in the immediate and medium term. Satellite uplinks are digital; however, the microwave network and distribution system are analog.

Most of the audience measurement in Colombia is done by Instituto Brasileiro Opinião Pública and Estadisticas (IBOPE), a Brazilian firm that replaced the services of Nielsen. Although the service is scientifically based on samples of the population, the data are less accurate in the regions. Moreover, the criterion of audience size alone does not conform well to the concept of public service, although increasingly it is these measurements that inform the decisions of the state and CNTV.

Despite all the above, it is important to point out that in a recent survey of Colombian television programming from 3 July to 30 July 1999,

by the author, about 70 percent of the programming on the public channel and on Caracol and 69.4 on RCN was domestic. This level of domestic production has held about the same for the last thirty years. In other
words, despite the crisis, national production continues to predominate
on Colombian broadcasting and, despite multiple offers, continues to be
preferred by audiences. This constitutes a cultural fact in this complex
and contradictory country, full of uncertainty in the present and for the
future, but with certain clear demands on and expectations of what it
means to be a Colombian.

CHAPTER SEVEN

Mexico

The Fox Factor

Rick Rockwell

A NEW era dawned for members of the media on 3 July 2000 when they realized Vicente Fox Quesada was truly the country's president-elect, the first opposition presidential candidate to gain power through an election since the Mexican Revolution. But most could not begin to guess what the outlines of that new reality might look like until many months later.

Fittingly, one of the first casualties of the changes to come in the Fox era was one of Mexico's oldest newspapers, *Excelsior.* A month before Fox's inaugural, the newspaper's cooperative board, made up of employees, ousted longtime owner Regino Díaz Redondo, who was attempting to sell the paper (Lloyd 2000). The employees took over all operations, with no guarantees it would survive in what was shaping up as a classic newspaper war to control access to the millions of readers in the megalopolis of Mexico City.

Employees pulled off their internal coup because they were the main shareholders in the newspaper's operation. But with the takeover came the truth about *Excelsior.* Total access to the publication's financial records revealed to employees that their newspaper was in dire financial straits, and had been for years. *Excelsior* owed the Mexican government $70 million in back taxes. The paper had only enough ink and newsprint to continue operations for another week (Lloyd 2000). More importantly, as the staff considered whether to fold *Excelsior* for good or to sell it, employees also discovered the paper's circulation was actually 65,000 daily, not the 180,000 the newspaper had publicly claimed.

Excelsior's circulation figures have been debated for years, because circulation is one way to measure the influence and worth of a particular publication. In 1994, *Excelsior* claimed an official circulation rate of

200,000 copies daily. Media watchdogs, like Raymundo Riva Palacio, a former reporter with *Excelsior* and now the editor of *Milenio*, along with columnist Raul Trejo Delarbre, noted those figures were suspect. In the mid-1990s, the figure many critics of the paper thought was a closer estimation of its real impact was 86,000 for daily circulation (Fromson 1996). Few realized it was even smaller.

Excelsior's circulation and impact inside Mexico's media system are important because it was viewed as the leading morning newspaper in the country, at least by the older generations. For decades, Mexico's ruling party had seen it in a similar light. Mexico's Institutional Revolutionary Party (PRI, by its Spanish acronym) had never lost a presidential election until Fox's victory, a reign of more than 70 years. For many of those years, the PRI had used *Excelsior* as a sort of propaganda organ for the party. The government conveniently overlooked the paper's tax debt, while surreptitiously backing the paper financially. The government pumped millions of pesos in advertising into the paper and kept reporters happily writing the PRI party line by giving them illicit payoffs (Mandel-Campbell 2000). When other papers modernized during the 1990s, especially *Excelsior*'s main competitor, *El Universal*, another paper founded during the Revolutionary era, *Excelsior* stuck to its old ways (Fromson 1996). On the brink of *Excelsior*'s closure, London's *Financial Times* criticized the Mexican paper for its "cramped and shoddy presentation" and for how the paper "toed the party line" for the PRI (Mandel-Campbell 2000, 3). "It was the most important newspaper in the last century," Riva Palacio said of *Excelsior*. "But now the demolition of the old regime is taking its toll and the newspapers that rely on government financing are having second thoughts" (Weiner 2000). "It's change for change's sake," Díaz Redondo said after his ouster. "These days, people think that if you don't change the established order of things, you're not democratic" (Sheridan 2000).

Importantly, *Excelsior*'s troubles could presage a major change for newspapers in Mexico. Members of the PRI, who claimed to finance completely some of Mexico City's newspapers, predicted that the Fox era would mean closure for most of the newspapers in the capital, because the government would no longer prop them up (Weiner 2000). Joel Estudillo, a media analyst at the Institute of Political Studies in Mexico City, confirmed that viewpoint. "All those papers that have been characterized by their tight relationship with the government will start to fall," he said (Lloyd 2000). Indeed, Fox's campaign and victory on democratic principles, and his insistence on ending the corrupt and fraudulent ways of the PRI, mean the system of corporate and party control of Mexico's media is about to enter a time of unprecedented upheaval.

The Fox Factor

In the following pages, the Mexican election of 2000 and what it means for the media will take center stage. Media practices, before and during the election period, will be examined to sketch a picture of the current semicontrolled environment for the media in Mexico. Finally, Vicente Fox's victory will be analyzed for what it means for the next stage of evolution for Mexico's media structure.

Fox's win is significant beyond the context of the media structure because his triumph holds out hope for the end of a type of soft authoritarianism as practiced by the central government in Mexico City. Mexico is one of the cornerstone states in Latin America. With a peaceful transfer of power there, reformers have new hope, throughout the hemisphere, as they try to promote a wave of democracy.

Arrogantly, members of the media like to say that the weight of free expression as practiced in the modern media often pushes nation-states toward a freer democratic system. Certainly, changes in the media in Mexico in the 1990s affected the structure of the 2000 election campaign. However, Fox's victory may well spell the reverse of the notion that the media are the catalyst behind democracy. In the end, Fox's victory means a new formula for the media: a cataclysmic break with the past that inexorably pushes the modernization of Mexico's media forward. A truly democratic administration in Mexico City will send a message to the media, both politically and economically, that the old days are over.

Fox let the media know that in no uncertain terms when he told reporters after the election they would have "to follow the rules of ethics and responsibility, in an open and transparent way" (Weiner 2000).

In a way, Fox showed Mexico's media what a modern candidate could do inside the country's tradition-bound system by breaking the rules yet adhering to a personal code of ethics. Fox took great pains to begin his campaign on the weekends, time he saw as his own while he was governor of Guanajuato. Unlike other candidates in Mexico, he drew a sharp division between his time to serve the public as governor and time that was personal for his campaign. While imposing these personal restrictions on his conduct, Fox broke the rules for candidates in Mexico's very traditional system by starting his campaign three years before the election (Allyn 2000). He became a candidate of the paid media: buying a fortune in billboards and time on television and radio, well before he even secured the nomination of his party (Guggenheim 2000). Fox and his advisers felt this strategy would build momentum for the candidate. That momentum not only secured Fox the nomination of his party, the National Action Party (PAN, by its Spanish acronym) but also led to his eventual triumph. Rob Allyn, one of Fox's media consultants, writing about the race a few months later, remarked that one of the main challenges was to find ways to show off Fox's personality and leadership style "without the filter of the PRI-controlled press" (Allyn 2000). It was no coincidence that Fox, a former executive for Coca-Cola, ended up marketing himself like a soft drink, to break through the protective walls the media had erected around Mexico's presidency.

Fox's strategy appealed directly to Mexico's younger voters, who did not remember the 1988 crusade of the leftist opposition candidate Cuauhtémoc Cárdenas. Cárdenas was making his third run for the presidency in 2000. As in the U.S. election of 1992, all of the candidates, but especially Fox, reached out to the nontraditional media (talk shows, entertainment shows, even children's programming) to make their case. Because Fox's major opponents were stiff and "painfully charmless," said Delal Baer of the Center for Strategic International Studies (CSIS) in Washington, Fox's personal charm and ease showed through on these television appearances outside the extremely structured and controlled news environment. Stunts like doing rodeo rope tricks on a popular entertainment program allowed Fox to capture the imagination of the younger voter, she noted (Baer 2000).

Candidate Fox also decided (correctly as it turned out) to project his personal image through what clothes he wore on the campaign trail. He did not want to be viewed as another technocrat headed to Mexico City in a suit. "His natural bent for boots and jeans underscores his outsider populism," wrote his media adviser, Allyn (2000). Fox gambled on the notion that his country was ready for a cowboy in Los Pinos, the Mexican White House.

The President and the Media

With Fox's victory it is now politically feasible for Mexico's allies to admit that for decades the electoral system was a sham meant to prop up the PRI. The PRI's great success was in projecting an image to the rest of the world—using the forms of democracy to hide its authoritarian core. In that system, elections were held to constantly reinforce the PRI's mandate. Never mind that the elections were often fraudulent. Likewise, an uncensored media was necessary to give the illusion of a lively Fourth Estate. Never mind that the media was compromised ethically and beholden politically to the PRI. In the funhouse mirror that was democracy under the PRI, the media's real role was to act as public relations agent for the central government. As Sallie Hughes of the Center for U.S.-Mexican Studies at the University of California at San Diego said, "The press was seen as a subsidiary of the government" (Kammer 2000).

For this reason, the PRI often employed a corporatist strategy against those in the media who did not succumb to this viewpoint. Owners who operated media outlets deemed to be overly critical of the central government were offered political or financial deals to become partners, of sorts, with the PRI. Those who would not bend to political accommodation could be bought. This was certainly how the PRI operated in other parts of Mexican society, and it also proved successful in gaining control of the media.

So, for example, in 1976, the PRI moved aggressively to mute the voice of one of its critics, the daily *Excelsior.* At the time, President Luis Echeverría supported a hostile takeover of the newspaper by financiers friendly to the PRI. Publisher Díaz Redondo was installed to head the paper, and twenty-four years of collusion with the central government began (Mandel-Campbell 2000).

Mexico's ruling party seemed incapable of brooking much opposition, but there were exceptions. A few publications, such as *La Jornada*, have existed for years as bastions of left-wing thought in Mexico. However, this seemed to be a sop to Mexico's intellectual class rather than a publication that anyone in government actually cared to heed—a safety valve for releasing heated rhetoric that could always serve as an example of Mexico's supposedly uncensored and free press. Few realized *La Jornada* existed largely on government subsidies, as did many of the other daily newspapers in Mexico City. Like other newspapers in Mexico, *La Jornada* routinely inflated its circulation figures from the 40,000 daily copies that it actually circulated, although in times of crisis the paper's circulation had in fact jumped beyond 230,000 (Fromson 1996). Because of these credibility problems and deals with the government, *La Jornada* was suspect—a critic operating, it seemed, within very prescribed boundaries.

Any media outlet that mattered to the central government came under pressure to sell out or was offered some sort of political accommodation or both. Like the Mexican bureaucracy, legislature, and judiciary—indeed the entire political system—the media were to provide a means of supporting Mexico's president. As President José López Portillo said in the 1980s, "I don't pay them so they can beat me up" (Weiner 2000).

Corruption and Collusion

The PRI's great success at controlling a system with little prepublication restraint from the central government was largely due to its multifaceted system of bribery. For media owners, the stakes were high: government subsidies, low-interest loans, reduced import duties, and tax breaks, if not a blanket amnesty for not paying back taxes. In a system where the central government is still the largest advertiser, having the government steer millions of pesos in legal and official advertising to a publication could be beneficial. This was one way the government also disguised its subsidies to publications.

Government and party propaganda also shows up regularly in the news in what are called *gacetillas*. These are planted stories that are paid for just like an ad, except they are not set off in any special way from the rest of the editorial product, so the reader cannot discern what stories are advertisements. The *New York Times* says at least 65 percent of Mexico City's newspapers still use this way of generating ad revenue disguised as legitimate news stories (Weiner 2000). However, the amount of funds pouring into newspapers in the form of *gacetillas* has steadily declined over the past decade, ever since President Carlos Salinas de Gotari decided to cut back all forms of government advertising, including this veiled public relations mechanism (Lloyd 2000).

Another hidden subsidy the PRI-controlled government gave to publishers was to allow them a free pass when it came to paying taxes. As in the case of *Excelsior*, the paper had been allowed to pile up a $70 million tax debt since 1994. During the administration of President Ernesto Zedillo Ponce de León, when *Excelsior*'s main competitor, *El Universal*, reformatted and became a more independent-minded daily, the PRI went after the paper's owner, Juan Francisco Ealy Ortiz. In 1996 and 1997, the government aggressively pursued charges of tax evasion and tax fraud against Ealy Ortiz. Their pursuit included a spectacular raid: fifty federal agents charged into the offices of *El Universal* (Rockwell 1999). This episode showed the PRI was willing to collect from media owners who stepped out of line.

For reporters, most of whom make less than $10,000 a year in salary, financial controls are also important (Weiner 2000). The system for bribery is so complex in Mexico for reporters that there are a variety of names for each type of payoff. A simple, one-time payment—to plant a story, twist a story's point of view, or spike an embarrassing piece—is sometimes called by the generic slang term for bribery in Mexico, *la mordida*, "the bite" (Fromson 1996). Riva Palacio of *Milenio* claims these "bites" can sometimes be more than a mouthful. He claims Gen. Absalón González, the former governor of Chiapas, once paid $40,000 to have a story killed (Weiner 2000).

For reporters on the regular illicit payroll of the government or the PRI, there are other methods. The *embute*, or "envelope," arrived for reporters like a regular paycheck, a weekly bonus to make sure reporters on specific beats were beholden to the agencies or bureaucrats who kept them on the special payroll (Fromson 1996). Another system, which quadruples the pay of specific reporters, is referred to as the *chayote*. According to the *New York Times* it is named "after a small and tasty squash that fits in the palm of the hand" (Weiner 2000).

Not all bribery in the system is in the form of cash. Bureaucrats, politicians, businessmen, and even drug lords often cut elaborate deals with reporters and editors as a way to guarantee that coverage is spun in a particular fashion. The methods of payment are almost too numerous to list but include free, all-expenses-paid vacations; free long-distance calls (a significant item since Mexico's phone system is notorious for charging high rates); free meals; breaks on importation fees or luxury taxes for expensive items, especially cars; free or discounted gasoline; free cars; gifts of luxury items, like expensive watches or cases of liquor; airline tickets; and prostitutes (Fromson 1996; Weiner 2000). At one time, reporters covering the president in Mexico could expect the government to pay for all their expenses incurred during the president's travels, no matter where the president traveled in the world. This system was slowly dismantled during the past decade, until Pres. Zedillo put a firm stop to all payments of travel expenses to reporters (Lloyd 2000).

"The reason we cannot expose this system of corruption," said reporter Armando Guzmán of Univisión, the Spanish-language network based in Miami, "is that nine out of ten reporters from Mexico have accepted some bribe or compromise at some time in their career" (Guzmán 2000). A survey conducted before the 2000 election by the Center for U.S.-Mexican Studies at the University of California at San Diego showed 52 percent of Mexican reporters admitted knowing someone who had skewed coverage for a bribe (Kammer 2000).

Outsiders to this corrupt system often cannot comprehend its complexity or byzantine nature. During the 2000 campaign, Josh Tuynman, the national editor of Mexico's only English language daily, the *News*, made waves when he tried to expose the corruption at his paper. The *News* is owned by the O'Farrill family, supporters of the PRI. Tuynman claimed the O'Farrill family had ordered him not to run positive stories about Fox or display pictures of the candidate. Tuynman also claimed the paper was accepting *gacetillas* from candidates (Anderson 2000). Three weeks before the election, the *News* published a special eight-page pull-out section on the elections, called *Political Profiles*. Inside the section, there were no pictures of Fox and one of the major articles focused on allegations of illicit dealings between the PAN and former president Salinas, generally reviled now as one of the most corrupt presidents in recent Mexican history. The *News* prominently displayed the allegations, repeated by PRI presidential candidate Francisco Labastida Ochoa, that President Salinas had rammed through an amendment to the Mexican Constitution that allows the offspring of foreigners to run for president (O'Farrill Avila 2000). Some in Mexico snidely referred to the amendment as "the Fox law," because Fox's mother was born in Spain (Guggenheim 2000). Tuynman's resignation from the *News* came less than a week after the special section, filled with pro-PRI propaganda, was printed.

The "Mavericks"

Not all of Mexico's newspapers were complicit partners with the government. For decades, a small but influential group of publications has bucked the trend and tried to usher in a different ethical standard for journalism. Many point to Alejandro Junco de la Vega and his newspaper group as leading the "Mavericks," as they have been called. Junco may be the most prominent publisher separating his publications from the government, but he is not the first.

Proceso, a weekly newsmagazine, founded by Julio Scherer in the 1970s, evoked rage from the central government because of its irreverence and its investigative reporting (Kammer 2000). *Proceso*, like all of Mexico's publications, obtained its newsprint through a government agency called PIPSA, which sold the paper at a greatly reduced price, another subsidy for publishers. When President Echeverría ordered PIPSA to cut off *Proceso*, Scherer was forced to cultivate more expensive, private suppliers of newsprint outside the country. But the magazine persevered.

President Echeverría's feud with Scherer over paper supplies was not the first time the two had tangled. Scherer was the publisher of *Excelsior* whom the president moved to depose with the help of Díaz Redondo (Blume 2000). Scherer had founded his magazine with some of the best reporters who left *Excelsior;* hundreds of employees quit the newspaper in solidarity with Scherer when the pro-PRI team took over (Lloyd 2000).

In the sprawling border city of Tijuana, J. Jesús Blancornelas founded a critical publication called *ABC,* but President López Portillo moved to have the publication closed and banned from distribution. When Blancornelas surfaced again with a new publication, a weekly tabloid called *Zeta,* featuring his brand of thorough investigative reporting and acidic political commentary, he printed the weekly in the United States and smuggled it across the border (Rockwell 1999). *Zeta* is still considered to be in the forefront of critical publications in Mexico, a place where the journalists say they do not succumb to the temptations of the Mexican system.

Not far away, in the state of Sonora, the daily newspaper *El Imparcial* has battled the PRI-dominated system since the 1960s. Publisher José Santiago Healy is the third generation of his family to run the paper, which does not accept the largesse of the government. Healy also recalled how his family fought against the chokehold of the PIPSA newsprint monopoly: "Our newsprint shipments would be delayed, or we would get less than what we needed" (Kammer 2000).

From these traditions of newspaper activism, Junco in Monterrey also began to battle the PRI. Junco took over his family's newspaper *El Norte,* at the age of twenty-four, and two years later he was already locked in a battle with President Echeverría. The president used PIPSA to keep *El Norte* from getting paper. The government also poured funds into Junco's competitors, allowing them to print in color (Fromson 1996). The PRI often used this tactic to marginalize strong critical voices. By supporting friendly newspapers, or creating newspapers friendly to its views, the PRI was able to fragment readership in various regions and cities as a means of guaranteeing that the influence of one newspaper would not grow too strong (Weiner 2000). To compete, Junco was forced to pay for paper from the United States and to forgo the subsidies usually doled out by the government, but he battled onward with a publication that distributed 30,000 copies in one of Mexico's important industrial cities of the north.

Today Junco's newspaper empire stretches across four metropolitan areas. Besides *El Norte,* he owns *Mural* in Guadalajara, *Palabra* in Saltillo, and *Reforma* in Mexico City. The group of newspapers has a combined circulation of 460,000, making it one of the most important and influential in the country, and the newspapers employ 1,070 reporters (Anderson 2000). Junco's papers also offer some of the highest pay for reporters in Mexico because they also have one of the strictest ethics codes, banning reporters and editors from accepting any sort of favor or gift from sources.

But like his early battles, when Junco expanded, especially into Mexico City, he had to fight the system. When *Reforma* began operations in Mexico City, the news vendors union, which is closely aligned with the PRI, refused to carry the paper. Junco was thus forced, in what was essentially a controlling measure of the PRI-dominated central government, to establish his own private system of newspaper distribution, again at an additional cost (Fromson 1996).

During the 2000 elections, Junco's papers were notable for how they tracked the campaign. The newspaper group devoted 100 reporters to election day coverage, especially to track charges of voter fraud. The *Washington Post* called the group's polling operation one of the most reliable and respected in Mexico (Anderson 2000). The papers also established a special unit of eighteen reporters to monitor radio and television coverage.

The Electronic Media

The need to monitor Mexico's electronic media was twofold. First, PRI candidates in the past had been known to exceed agreed-upon limits concerning campaign advertising, and during these millennial elections, Mexico's new independent election-oversight institution was imposing stricter limitations on campaign spending for advertising. Second, Mexico's electronic media have long acted as unapologetic shills for the PRI and the central government.

For decades, Televisa, a programming behemoth with four networks on Mexican television, had been run by Emilio ("El Tigre") Azcárraga Milmo, an open supporter of the PRI. "I am a soldier of the PRI," Azcárraga Milmo said, and he ran his television operations like a general (Fromson 1996).

With that underlying philosophy, it was not surprising that Televisa was considered by some analysts as a potential buyer of the financially strapped paper *Excelsior.* As the television operation looked to diversify into radio and the Internet, the newspaper with its history of supporting the PRI also looked like a likely acquisition target.

But the media climate that resulted from the 2000 elections was very different from that during El Tigre's prime as the leader of Televisa. His death in 1997 and the competition from Mexico's upstart network, TV Azteca, had resulted in a less powerful Televisa, one not so beholden to or openly interested in supporting the PRI. However, both networks had shown they still tilted news coverage toward the PRI. In the 1997 elections for the Mexican Congress, gubernatorial seats, and mayor of Mexico City, both networks gave most of their positive coverage to PRI candidates (Valverde 1997).

One of the great questions of the 2000 elections was whether Fox could overcome the bias on television and still win. Some experts openly wondered if the system was biased any longer.

London's *Financial Times* said El Tigre's successor Emilio Azcárraga Jean had converted the Televisa networks into a more objective force that "embraced democracy and greater transparency" while "winning plaudits even from human rights groups for its even-handed coverage of the elections" (Tricks 2000).

Less than a month before the elections, the *New York Times* reported that Mexico's Federal Elections Institute (IFE, by its Spanish acronym) had determined "Televisa was fair in covering the race" (Preston 2000). This clearly contradicted what the paper had written about a month earlier, in the wake of Fox's initial win in the nation's televised debates. In that report, the IFE was quoted as saying the mainstream news shows on Televisa and TV Azteca retained an overwhelming bias against Fox. Furthermore, in that report, the *New York Times* said Fox was receiving four times as much negative publicity as the PRI's candidate, Labastida (Dillon 2000).

In the intervening weeks, perhaps Mexican broadcasters did respond to early criticism of their coverage of the campaign. *New York Times* correspondent Julie Preston wrote that mainstream national broadcasters had tried to react to criticisms of impartiality, but the traditional pro-PRI slant of broadcasts remained strongest from local affiliate stations spread throughout the country. She said that this tainted local coverage of the campaign tilted the IFE's statistics to show television broadcasters still favored the PRI (Preston 2000).

Reforma's tracking of the electronic media for the entire election period proved to be enlightening. On Televisa, all three major candidates received comparable airtime: Fox of the PAN with 8.64 hours; Cárdenas of the Revolutionary Democratic Party (PRD, by its Spanish acronym) with 8.46 hours; and the PRI's Labastida with 8.28 hours. However, Fox received three times the negative coverage of Cárdenas, and twice as much as Labastida. On TV Azteca, only the top two candidates received comparable time: Fox had 10.62 hours; Labastida had 10.52 hours; and Cárdenas trailed with 7.7 hours. But Fox's negative coverage was twice the total of either of his major competitors on TV Azteca (*Reforma* 2000). *Reforma*'s tracking of the election clearly showed a bias against Fox among the country's main broadcasters.

"The TV news is getting worse and worse," complained writer Homero Aridjis, the president of PEN International. "It's like watching a channel run by the Ministry of Propaganda" (Anderson 2000).

Mexico's main broadcasters also showed their partisan bias when it came to the IFE. This independent government institute wanted to launch a television campaign to combat voter fraud and inform voters about new conditions meant to promote a free, fair, and secret ballot. The IFE was depending on the government's ability to place free advertising on the national networks as the backbone of this voter awareness campaign. The Mexican networks, backed by the PRI-dominated Chamber of the Radio and TV Industry, demanded the IFE pay expensive commercial rates, since they regarded the IFE as autonomous, and not part of the government. After much stalling by the networks, the Interior Ministry finally brokered an agreement between the networks and the IFE, but the end result was a shortened period of advertising for the campaign (Dillon and Preston 2000).

On radio, Fox may have commanded the most time nationally, more than 34 percent of all coverage, but much of it was negative (*Reforma* 2000). And in some regions, like the state of Chiapas, which gave most of its votes to Labastida, coverage of the race on radio was slanted. The *Washington Post* reported that in Chiapas 57 percent of all radio news time was devoted to PRI candidates, compared to just 11 percent for Fox's conservative party, the PAN, and 18 percent for the left-wing PRD (Anderson 2000).

Intimidation

No Mexican election cycle would be complete without clear cases of intimidation of the media. One of the more controversial cases during the 2000 elections was the case of Lilly Téllez, a popular anchorwoman for TV Azteca. Ten days before the balloting, Téllez was attacked in her chauffeur-driven car. Three men opened fire with handguns on her car and the car carrying her bodyguards. Her chauffeur and bodyguards all were wounded but Téllez escaped unharmed (Rodríguez and Sánchez 2000).

Although the attack on Téllez was linked to threats against her by narcotics traffickers, some saw the attack as a political message. Sowing the seeds of fear before an election and causing voters to think about instability that could increase with a different government is a tactic often linked with the PRI in the past.

Even if the assassination attempt on Téllez was not linked to national politics—and was not meant as a nationwide warning of instability—many believed the hit had more to do with politics than with investigative reporting. As revealed by the tracking statistics, TV Azteca was clearly slanting its coverage—reporting negatively on Fox and cutting coverage of Cárdenas. The undercoverage of Cárdenas related to his time as mayor of Mexico City. Prosecutors under Cárdenas's direction had opened an investigation into links between Mexico's powerful drug cartels and TV Azteca, after the murder of the network's popular comic Paco Stanley. This feud between Mexico City's prosecutors and the network spilled over into TV Azteca's editorial decisions during the campaign (Preston 2000). Whether the Téllez shooting was connected to the cocaine deals and murder of Stanley or was a result of her reporting has yet to be determined. However, the sensational headlines and massive coverage it generated settled like a pall on the final days of the election campaign.

As in past election years, the death toll for journalists in Mexico ticked upward during this presidential race. On 28 April radio reporter José Ramírez Puente of Ciudad Juárez was stabbed more than thirty times. Ramírez was the host of *Juárez Hoy*, a program about politics and local news on radio station FM Globo. Although police said they found marijuana in Ramírez's car at the scene of the crime, journalists alleged the drugs had been planted to make it look like Ramírez was involved in the drug trade. Mayor Gustavo Elizondo of Ciudad Juárez also stood up for Ramírez's integrity (CPJ 2000a).

Also in April, U.S. Border Patrol agents retrieved the body of Pablo Pineda, a reporter for *La Opinión* of Matamoros. The agents watched two men cross the Rio Grande and dump Pineda's body. Pineda's head had been wrapped in a plastic bag, and he had been shot in the back of the head. He had written about the police and drugs along the border (CPJ 2000b).

Although all these cases had more obvious connections to the dangerous climate for journalists reporting on drugs in Mexico, they also had a chilling effect on election coverage. The Committee to Protect Journalists (CPJ) felt so strongly about these and other incidents in Mexico that a letter was sent to President Zedillo expressing concern about the climate of free expression before the nation's important elections (Cooper 2000).

Into the Fox Era

Although Fox's administration represents the beginning of a media era in which journalists will not be shackled directly to the government, some members of the media are looking upon the beginning of the new millennium with trepidation.

Undoubtedly, *Excelsior* is only the first media outlet with strong financial ties to the PRI to feel the tremors of the new era. Of the more than thirty daily newspapers in the capital, most will not survive without the financial backing of the PRI, predicted the *New York Times* (Weiner 2000). Chappell Lawson, of the Massachusetts Institute of Technology, issued predictions about the demise of specific papers: *Excelsior* would fold and along with it such longtime publications as *El Día* and *Unomasuno* (Gaddis Smith 2000). For PRI-backed media outlets—dubbed *globos inflados* (inflated balloons) by media critics—the era of easy payoffs for simply owning a way to distribute information and news was quickly coming to an end (Mandel-Campbell 2000).

Marta Sahagún, Fox's media spokesperson, said that in a Fox administration the entire relationship between the media and government would be reexamined. Government payouts to the media—legal and otherwise—along with government control of newsprint and newspaper distribution would likely be curtailed if not abandoned. Likewise, the government news agency, Notimex, would probably become autonomous of the central government, or at the very least not have to deal with political interference from a Fox administration (Jordan 2000).

Other *panistas* besides Fox may also make waves in a government run by the PAN. Senator Javier Corral of the PAN heads the Mexican Senate's Communication Committee. He plans to look at how television licensing is regulated. He wants to see if Televisa and TV Azteca need to have specific regulations for how they program, especially in standards for news and information programs (Tricks 2000). Such sentiments have analyst Baer of CSIS predicting "pernicious" regulation of Mexico's media "is right around the corner" (Baer 2000).

Blancornelas, publisher of *Zeta*, also warned that not all members of the PAN are to be trusted. Although Blancornelas supported the PAN in his state of Baja California Norte, and was instrumental in bringing the first *panista* governor to power, he noted that some *panista* politicians have learned too well from the PRI. He said some members of the PAN in state and local governments have used bribes to control the content of stories. And like the PRI, the PAN has also used advertising as a way to buy influence with media outlets (Gaddis-Smith 2000).

Other journalists warned that all rules of politeness or respect for the president will be ignored in the Fox era. "Expect a more confrontational press," predicted José Carreño (2000), a correspondent for *El Universal*. Without financial support from the government, some journalists may turn their anger about the changes in the system on the new administration, he added. That anger could be significant, with publications and jobs disappearing.

Fox's own personality could be fueling this heated relationship between his administration and journalists. During the election campaign, Fox was known for confidently shooting from the hip with the media, and although he was quotable, much of his coverage was negative. Even some of his off-color remarks made it into the coverage and became part of the discussion about whether Fox was really "presidential material." This debate contributed to the perception that Fox beat not just the PRI but the party's media lapdog when he triumphed unexpectedly in the election. Some see Fox's macho attitude adding friction to the tense atmosphere surrounding the president and the media. "The Fox government will be arrogant," said Carreño (2000). "They have not reached out to the media since the election."

But some in the media feel it is long overdue for journalists to clean up their own mess. In a postelection speech, publisher Blancornelas noted: "I dream of a journalism without bribes . . . that pays for its newsprint, that pays its taxes. More ethical, more responsible, more professional. We need fewer presses and more journalism" (Gaddis-Smith 2000).

If Fox keeps his promises and does not succumb to the political pressures around him to fall back into the cultural ways already imprinted on Mexico's media by the PRI, after a rough shakeout period, he could begin the changes that eventually deliver the journalistic utopia of Blancornelas's dreams. How the various institutions inextricably linked to Mexico's presidency react in the Fox era can only be the subject of conjecture now. But the early signals indicate Mexico's major media institutions will not disappear. There will be the noisy crashes of the dinosaurs who fail to adapt and thus collapse. The stress of change will inevitably hasten the disappearance of other media outlets. But it will also bring opportunities for innovation, advancement, and exploration of new niches in Mexico's rich culture. And more than likely the intelligent leaders of many of Mexico's media institutions will find ways to slowly adapt, proving they can find the keys to evolution amidst the maelstrom of Fox's political revolution.

Mexico and Brazil

The Aging Dynasties

John Sinclair

I N B O T H Mexico and Brazil, television is the medium with the great-est reach, and the one most attractive to advertisers. There are sev-eral close parallels between the companies that dominate those respec-tive national markets, including a strong dynastic character in their ownership and control, and an unusual level of both vertical and hori-zontal integration in their structure. Taken together, these features have constituted something of a "Latin model" of television, but the growth of unaccustomed competition in domestic markets as well as the height-ened activities of global companies in the region during the 1990s raise the question of how well they can adapt to a new game in which they are no longer making the rules.

Mexico

As the 1980s came to a close, the beginning of the end of Televisa's golden age of domestic market domination presided over by the patriarchs of the oligarchical Azcárraga, Alemán, and O'Farrill families, was becoming ap-parent. The costs of international expansion had been taking a toll on Televisa, with a large debt to carry and substantial losses in both 1988 and 1989. This brought to a head a struggle for power between the family-based factions within the management group that had been going on at least since 1986, when Televisa had been obliged to divest itself of its national network of stations in the United States, a major setback in cor-porate fortunes. In an internal restructuring of holdings in 1991, Emilio Azcárraga and his family greatly increased their share in Televisa, while Rómulo O'Farrill completely sold out his 24 percent interest, and left. Miguel Alemán also left the business, after ceding his share to a son still within the administrative council. Azcárraga took over the video, radio, and dubbing divisions, while the cable division went to his sister Carmela

(Acosta 1991, 14; "Big Shuffle in Mexican TV Ownership" 1991; Sánchez Ruiz 1991, 35).

It transpired that this consolidation of Televisa's control under the Azcárragas was in preparation for a public float on both the Mexican and New York stock exchanges in 1992. Presumably O'Farrill and Alemán had chosen not to endure with Televisa into this new era, while Azcárraga had determined that it was the only way he could raise the capital needed to meet debt obligations and fund his further ambitions for international expansion. For as well as dealing with the immediate liquidity crisis, Azcárraga displayed his eagerness for sufficient finance to make a return to the U.S. market, as well as to establish some presence in South American markets. These concerns can be understood in terms of the NAFTA (North American Free Trade Agreement) then imminent, in anticipation of which Azcárraga had been lobbying to have the foreign ownership provisions over U.S. broadcasting modified in his favor. In any event, he was obliged to enter a partnership with a U.S. majority owner and another Latin American network in order to restore some direct control over the major Spanish-language television network in the United States that the Azcárragas had previously owned, by then known as Univisión. The float had meant that Televisa was in a strong cash position to be buying back into the U.S. market, as well as making several new investments throughout 1992 and 1993.

Thus, in July 1992, on top of the announcement of Televisa's intended return to its former network in the United States, came the news that Televisa had acquired 76 percent of Compañía Peruana de Radiodifusión, Peru's second-ranked network ("Televisa anunció" 1992). Already at the end of 1991, Televisa had bought 49 percent of Chile's first private channel, Megavisión ("Televisa compró" 1991). Such selective direct investments in other Latin American countries were something quite new for Televisa, and perhaps also related strategically to extensions of NAFTA provisions then mooted. Also in 1992, Televisa announced a noncompetitive program-distribution and licensing agreement with Venevisión, owned by Grupo Cisneros, its Latin American partner in the U.S. network (Morgan Stanley 1992).

Direct investments continued in 1993, notably with Televisa paying $200 million for a noncontrolling 50 percent share in PanAmSat, the international satellite venture it had initiated in the 1980s, but from which it later had been obliged to withdraw. There were also some strategic alliances with international media corporations announced. An agreement to produce and distribute a Latin American version of the Discovery cable channel was put into effect, and a program production and distribution arrangement with News Corporation was commenced (Mejía Barquera 1995, 71–73). However, as the following section will show, such internationalization of television services coincided with yet another economic reversal in Televisa's domestic market, leaving both in a greatly weakened position.

Thus, the quincentennial year of 1992 marked a high point in Televisa's development, particularly in its ability to fund international expansion. Just five years later, by 1997, Televisa was in crisis. It was almost $1 billion (U.S.) in debt and was desperately engaged in selling down prime assets; its management had become unstable; it was facing real competition in its domestic market for the first time, and it was being subordinated to foreign-based partners in its international ventures. On all of these counts, Televisa was subjected to fundamental changes that, taken together, amounted to a major downturn in its fortunes precisely at a time when the stakes were being raised by global players in Spanish-language markets.

The "Tequila Effect"

The drastic devaluation of the peso in late 1994 and the accompanying inflation had drastic effects for Televisa, as for other Mexican companies. The business magazine *Fortune* estimated that Televisa's value dropped $3.8 million from 1994 to 1995 (Puig 1997b, 16). More than this, the devaluation also plunged Televisa deep into debt, and curtailed its ability to generate income. Largely because of its international activities, Televisa's considerable operating costs and expenses in U.S. dollars meant it had to earn so much more in pesos to meet its U.S. dollar commitments.

Furthermore, because the Mexican government's austerity program in response to the fiscal crisis was having a simultaneous adverse effect on the domestic consumer market, part of the so-called recessionary "tequila effect," Televisa's income from new advertising revenues decreased drastically. Most of Televisa's advertising revenues are obtained under the "French Plan," in which advertisers pay a year in advance at an agreed-upon rate. This system is most advantageous to Televisa's financial planning and liquidity. However, since the crisis, Televisa has been sorely testing the loyalty of its advertisers with steep increases each year, up to 80 percent, in nominal advertising rates (Grupo Televisa 1997, 30–37).

In order to meet its debts (almost $1 billion U.S. in 1997), and the cost of servicing them, Televisa began in 1995 to sell down its interests in some of its strategic assets. First was the sale of all of its interest in the Peruvian station it had acquired in 1992. Next came the sale of 49 percent of Cablevisión, its cable division, to a subsidiary of the privatized Teléfonos de México, or Telmex (Grupo Televisa 1997, 71). Then, toward the end of 1995, PanAmSat was converted from a limited partnership to a public company, diluting Televisa's former half-share to 40.5 percent. Another significant sell-down occurred in the following year, when also as a result of a public float, and the opportunity to realize $190 million, Televisa's former 25 percent interest in the U.S. Univisión network and 12 percent interest in the corresponding station group were reduced in total to a less than 20 percent interest in the restructured Univisión (Grupo Televisa 1997, 73).

Thus, within two years of the 1994 devaluation, Televisa had given up most of what it had gained in the 1992–93 wave of expansion. Even if the Peruvian channel was not a significant loss, the reduction in its command over Cablevisión meant a weakened position in the domestic cable market with regard to its competitor Multivisión. As to the dilution of its participation in Univisión, the crucial toehold in the U.S. Spanish-language television market that it had regained only in 1992, this meant that Televisa's position was once again weakened in this key strategic market, although its program supply agreement continued to hold.

The PanAmSat restructuring of 1995 had not been so great an obstacle in Televisa's international maneuvers, but that was not the end of it. The subsequent merger of PanAmSat with the U.S.-based satellite division of General Motors, Hughes Electronics, in September 1996, effectively meant that Hughes acquired most of Televisa's interest in the restructured, publicly traded company that resulted, the "New PanAmSat" (Grupo Televisa 1997, 73). The outcome of Televisa's agreement with Hughes was that it received $650 million for its former share in PanAmSat, which it applied mostly toward its debt of $988 million. Televisa retained a 7.5 percent interest in the restructured PanAmSat, with the rights to acquire more equity in its DTH (direct to home) satellite television operation, Sky Latin America (Cardoso 1997; González Amador 1997).

In May 1997 this arrangement was announced formally as part of Televisa's "Televisa 2000" plan, in which the company committed itself to increasing its audience share, developing its DTH service, and improving its financial results over the three years to follow (González Amador

1997). Televisa's sell-down of its participation in PanAmSat, like its previous dilutions of interest in the other ventures, was rationalized in terms of getting back to its "core business," to invoke the business cliché of the time, or in the words of the announcement: "The fundamental business of the company has always been the production of programming, and it doesn't necessarily need to be the owner of program distribution companies" (quoted in Cardoso 1997).

Certainly, as the history of Televisa's development has shown, program production for the domestic market has always been its stock-in-trade, but this has been augmented significantly by its vertical integration with distribution systems, principally its own networks in Mexico, but also, if less consistently, with Univisión and its predecessors in the United States, and PanAmSat at the international level. It is difficult not to see "Televisa 2000" as an attempt to make virtue out of necessity.

After "The Tiger"

Another significant internal problem for Televisa in 1997 was its difficulty in establishing a stable and effective management structure following the retirement of Emilio ("The Tiger") Azcárraga Milmo as president of Televisa on 3 March, and his subsequent death from cancer on 16 April. Given the degree to which Azcárraga had consolidated all power and decision making over Televisa within his own person, and the patronal style of management that he cultivated, his succession was clearly going to be a problem. It is believed that Azcárraga had known of his illness for some years, but he seems to have vacillated in his choice of a successor. At one stage, during the 1991 reshuffle, Azcárraga Milmo had anointed his nephew Alejandro Burillo Azcárraga (Martínez Staines 1991), but he soon fell from favor (Puig 1997b), so that on his retirement it was his son, Emilio Azcárraga Jean, whom The Tiger named to be president of Televisa.

At the same time, Guillermo Cañedo White became the chairman of the board. Together with his brother José Antonio, also a member of the board, the Cañedo Whites had 10 percent of Televisa shares. Their father, Guillermo Cañedo de la Bárcena, had been a Televisa vice president, and it was his membership in the International Soccer Federation that had twice brought the World Cup to Mexico (and thus to Televisa). He also was president of the Organización de la Televisión Iberoamericana. The father also had died in 1997, in January, so there was a major generational change taking place with the accession of both Emilio Azcárraga Jean and Guillermo Cañedo White.

However, this generational transition to the sons of the dead fathers was tempered by oligarchic tradition, in that Miguel Alemán, one of the triumvirate of Televisa's golden age, and son of the Mexican president who had granted the first television licenses, returned to the board. Explaining this move as the fulfillment of a promise to the late Azcárraga, Alemán took care to ensure it was on condition that the shares held by him and his son, also on the board, would exceed the holdings of the Burillo and the Cañedo White family members (Puig 1997a).

While the return of Alemán typifies the dynastic character not just of Televisa but of media ownership in Latin America and beyond, it can also be read as an attempt to balance the youthful vigor of Emilio Azcárraga Jean (who was twenty-nine at this time) and Guillermo Cañedo White (then thirty-seven) with maturity and continuity, which Miguel Alemán represented, so as to rebuild confidence on the stock exchanges in Mexico and New York. Whatever apparent stability was achieved with this arrangement was broken by June, however, when Alejandro Burillo Azcárraga, having gained an additional packet of shares from a former wife of his late uncle, succeeded in having the Cañedo White brothers put off the board (Celis Estrada 1997).

Little wonder that the London *Financial Times* commented that the internal struggles of the company were coming to resemble the plot from one of its *telenovelas* ("FT: La batalla por el control en Televisa parece 'una telenovela'" 1997). For Televisa, this is not a joke: such perceptions of "the market" are a significant obstacle for an internationally listed company desperate to maintain the capital it needs to deal with recession and competition at both the domestic and international level.

New Players, at Home and Away

For nearly all of its existence, Mexican television has been run as a virtual monopoly. The original licensees first merged to form Telesistema Mexicano in 1955, and then, as a bulwark against government intervention in the industry, merged with a competitor to form Televisa in 1972. Thus, Televisa has been formed in an uncompetitive environment, effectively protected by the Mexican government and its weak participation in the industry through Imevisión, its former network (Sinclair 1986).

This was the "Mexican formula" until 1993, when the Government sold the licenses to its Channel 7 and Channel 13 networks, together with production studios and some cinemas, to Ricardo Salinas Pliego and his partners in the Saba family, as TV Azteca. Salinas Pliego, the majority owner, is from the Salinas y Rocha family of retail store owners. He owns Elektra, a chain of hundreds of electrical parts stores, and other retail chains throughout Mexico and Central America, and TV Azteca is an integral part of their development ("Azteca into El Salvador," 1997).

Before the government sold it off, the former Imevisión had been obtaining around 2 percent of the domestic TV market (Moffett and Roberts 1992, 1). By 1995, the new TV Azteca had about 14 percent of the audience, rising to 22 percent in 1996 ("Avanza TV Azteca," 1997), and by the end of that year, it was claiming 37 percent of the prime time audience, and 23 percent of television advertising revenue. There were also substantial increases in the amount of its own production, and in profits—up by 51 percent, compared to Televisa's losses ("TV Azteca gana mayor audiencia" 1997). In 1997 it was claiming 33 percent of television advertising revenue (Sutter 1999). Even if its audience share later leveled out to around 20 percent (Sutter 1999), this still represented a tenfold increase over its performance as Imevisión.

With the advent of TV Azteca, programming has become the basis on which competition is conducted, and quality, in the broadest sense, has become an issue. For all the wealth that Televisa's productions have generated both at home and abroad in the past, this success has been on the basis of quantity rather than quality. Many of the obituaries that appeared upon Azcárraga Milmo's death recalled this frank comment from a 1992 press conference: "Mexico is the country of a modest, very wretched class, which isn't ever going to stop getting screwed over. There is an obligation for television to bring diversion to these people and take them out of their sad reality and difficult future. . . . [T]he rich, like me, are not clients because we rich don't buy a whole lot. In short, our market in this country is clear: the popular middle class" (quoted in Puig 1997b, 15).

As well as being a rationalization for the characteristically low intellectual and production values of Televisa's output—that is, the *telenovelas* that dominate their production and program schedules—this comment alludes to the absence of credibility that has always dogged Televisa as a news and information source. This has been the price of the close relations it has cultivated with the ruling party and the state, and also of its readiness to commercialize the content of its information programs (Zepeda Patterson 1997). Yet so long as Televisa was a virtual monopoly, audiences had no means of expressing their dissatisfaction with Televisa programs, and Televisa could claim to be giving the people what they wanted.

At the beginning, TV Azteca's competitive strategy had been to offer a range of imported programming (Mejía Barquera 1995, 88), and although it is significant to observe that TV Azteca has since moved toward showing much more of its own productions, it is also notable in Mexico for the introduction of some of the same programs that aided the rise of the Fox network in the United States, namely Los Simpsons (The Simpsons) (Godard 1997). Although the relationship later turned sour, from 1994 until early 1997 TV Azteca also enjoyed the benefit of the program content, technology, and prestige of a formal relationship with a major U.S. network, NBC (Enríquez 1995; Ramón Huerta 1997; Rebollo Pinal 1997).

Another notable association formed by TV Azteca has been with the U.S. Spanish-language network Telemundo, which is the competitor of Univisión, the network in which Televisa has an interest in the United States. TV Azteca has been utilizing the studios it acquired, now known as Azteca Digital, and producing programs in collaboration with Telemundo that each of them can show on their networks (Strover et al. 1997, 20). Thus, rather than compete on the basis of imported programming alone, as it first intended, TV Azteca now seems to be looking for the most part to an attractive balance of imported and local programming, offering a wider and more innovative range than Televisa did throughout its unchallenged years.

It is important to appreciate that Televisa is facing competition not only on its traditional ground of broadcast television, but also in its cable distribution service, Cablevisión, a company it established in 1966, and in which it still maintains a majority share (Crovi Druetta 1995). Yet competition is not so new in the cable field. In 1989 Multivisión was launched, and as of the second half of 1996, although Cablevisión had a total of around 450,000 subscribers, Multivisión was well ahead with 720,000 (Olivas and Lince 1996, 8). Although continuing to compete with cable services, both Cablevisión and Multivisión are now looking more toward the new satellite distribution/delivery technology of DTH, and it is in this field that the Mexican companies are becoming involved in strategic alliances with major U.S.-based and continental Latin American companies.

The Global League

While DTH satellite television transmission can be seen as just a new phase of development of existing satellite services and similar in concept to other kinds of pay-TV systems, there are certain qualitative differences that are being emphasized by the largely U.S.-based satellite and programming interests that are promoting the medium in Latin America and the rest of the world. Digital decompression technology on the current generation of satellites now being launched permits a much greater number of channels to be carried than has been the case in the past. In turn, this not only allows for a greater variety of channels dedicated to certain kinds of programming, but allows the same channel to be transmitted in more than one language. Thus, there is a much lower technical barrier against programs *produced* in languages other than those used for transmission. This is a challenge for those companies that have exploited linguistic differences in the past, notably Televisa and Grupo Globo. The subscriber requires a small receiving dish (about 60 centimeters in diameter) and a set-top decoding box. This means that the DTH market is attractive not just to the satellite industry and program suppliers, but also to the manufacturers and retailers of this domestic consumer hardware, such as the Salinas chain, Elektra.

Even at the end of 1995, DTH in Mexico had been assuming the character of a duopoly. In November of that year, Rupert Murdoch's News Corporation announced that it would lead a panregional DTH consortium including not only Grupo Televisa, but also its counterpart in Brazil, Organizações Globo, and the U.S. cable company TCI (through its international division, TINTA). News, Televisa, and Globo were to have 30 percent each, and TCI the remaining 10 percent. Apart from the scale and the cross-cultural links it brought about, the new consortium represented a decision in favor of international corporate collaboration rather than competition between Televisa and Grupo Globo. This move was remarkable considering that Televisa had been planning such a Latin American service in conjunction with PanAmSat, while News Corporation had previously announced, in July 1994, a similar venture in partnership with Grupo Globo (Brewster 1995; Francis and Fernandez 1997, 36).

Whatever opportunities Televisa saw in the deal for its further internationalization, it also would have been motivated at the level of the domestic market by the fact that earlier, in May 1995, Multivisión had announced it would join a similar panregional project led by the U.S. satellite manufacturer Hughes Electronics, which incorporated also TV Abril in Brazil (Grupo Globo's main cable competitor), and Grupo Cisneros of Venezuela (which in other areas is a major collaborator with Televisa) ("Country Profile: Mexico," 1996, 7).

Thus, by the end of 1996, Multivisión had signed on with the Hughes project, known as Galaxy, and received its license to launch its service in Mexico, which was to be known as DirecTV, the same name as Hughes's DTH service in the United States. It was set to be carried by one of Hughes's own satellites. Like TV Abril, its cable counterpart in Brazil, Multivisión has 10 percent in Galaxy, Grupo Cisneros has 20 percent, and Hughes, the dominant partner, has 60 percent (Strover et al. 1997, 8).

Around that same time, the corresponding Televisa service based on Cablevisión began transmission. This was called DTH Sky, in line with News Corporation's satellite ventures in other global regions. It began with more channels than DirecTV, including the Latin versions of U.S.-based channels such as Discovery (as modified by Televisa) and MTV, as well as News's own FLAC (Fox Latin Channel) and Televisa's terrestrial network channels (Toussaint 1996a; Francis and Fernández 1997, 38). The plan was for 20 percent of programming to be supplied by Televisa and its international partners in the venture (García Hernández 1996). For its part, the Mexican government had cleared the way for all this DTH development by signing an agreement with the United States just a month before, under which Mexican and U.S. satellites could transmit into each other's national space (Olivas and Lince 1996; Francis and Fernández 1997, 30, 36).

The company that manages DTH Sky is called Innova. As a joint venture with News Corporation, Televisa has a 60 percent share in Innova (Grupo Televisa 1997, 74). While this formalizes the Cablevisión/Multivisión duopoly at the national level, there is a global level to be taken into account. In this regard, it is important to recall that PanAmSat, the satellite venture associated with Televisa, and Hughes Electronics, the leader of the competing Galaxy group, in fact had merged in September 1996, under the name PanAmSat, months before the launch of their respective services in Mexico. In the sense that both Galaxy and PanAmSat are owned by Hughes, DTH in Mexico at one elevated level has become a monopoly, but one that represents itself to consumers on the ground as competing services. At least for the present, it appears that the company's intention is to maintain both of them (Francis and Fernández 1997, 34). Put another way, there is a monopoly at the level of hardware, but apparent competition in terms of software, all under the same corporate umbrella.

The pay-TV industry association in Mexico, CANITEC, estimates that the maximum number of subscribers that the DTH industry can hope for in the next few years is 2 million, at least at the initial level of cost

(Toussaint 1996b). No doubt prices will continue to fall, with DirecTV aiming to bring the installation charge down to compare with the cost of a VCR (Olivas and Lince 1996). However, the growth of DTH depends on the recovery of the Mexican economy as a whole, and if the market proves too small to be profitable for both competing services, the company that controls the distribution of both of them at a global level, the new PanAmSat, can either close one or the other down, or oblige them to merge. Either way, Televisa has become most vulnerable to the strategies of both its global and regional partners.

Brazil

Although the new networks created in the 1980s have not been able to overtake Grupo Globo's dominance of television in Brazil, it nevertheless faces more competition now than in its heyday under the military rulers, and more than Televisa does now or has in the past. Yet as of the early 1990s, Globo was well ahead of its competition on all indicators. Only SBT, and far behind it, Bandeirantes, have continued to offer meaningful competition in broadcast television (Hoineff 1993, 50; Fox 1997, 64–65). By 1997, Globo was claiming an audience share of 74 percent in prime time (probably more like 60 percent overall), and a commensurate 75 percent of all advertising revenue (Rede Globo 1997).

Beyond Broadcasting

Although Grupo Globo's dominance of domestic broadcast television seems unassailable, it has met stronger competition in the realm of subscription, or pay-TV, services as new modes of transmission have been introduced on this basis. The first of these was the opening up of the UHF (ultra high frequency) band for broadcast-delivered subscriber services. The first full such service to be offered was TVA (Televisão Abril), a joint venture of a financial and industrial group, Machline, and the television division of Grupo Abril, Brazil's other major media conglomerate. Launched in 1991, TVA offers CNN and ESPN from the United States, and RAI (Radio Audizioni Italiane) and Canal Plus channels from Europe. Grupo Abril had already launched a narrowcast channel prior to this, its own Brazilian version of the U.S. music channel MTV (Bahiana 1994, 21; Straubhaar 1996, 233).

Grupo Abril has grown from a strong base in print media: in fact, it is the largest publishing operation in Latin America. It did not enter television services until 1990, with the advent of the new distribution technologies, although it had been heavily involved in video distribution since the beginning of the 1980s. The publishing division, Editora Abril, was founded in 1950 by an Italian refugee, Victor Civita, who came from the United States with the rights to publish Disney comics in Brazil. The business was built up on comics and magazines, including some foreign titles, but most important has been *Veja*, a well-regarded newsmagazine with the highest circulation of any publication in Brazil. The group is now managed by Roberto Civita, son of the founder, who died in 1990, and has wholly owned subsidiaries in Portugal and Spain and majority inter-ests in publishing houses in Argentina and elsewhere in Latin America (Pickard 1991).

With Grupo Abril opening up subscription television as a new area, Grupo Globo soon responded, meeting Abril's MMDS (multipoint multi-channel distribution service) venture with its own four-channel service, Globosat; transmitted via BrasilSat, Brazil's domestic satellite, this chan-nel could be received directly by a small satellite dish (Bahiana 1994, 22; Straubhaar 1996, 233–34). Both competitors secured foreign programming alliances and sources of capital (Glasberg 1995, 35–36B).

Meanwhile, a number of "hardwire" cable subscription franchises had been established in the main cities, notably by Multicanal. This was begun by a mining entrepreneur, Antonio Dias Leita Neto, and offered programming from several other Latin nations: Televisa's ECO from (Mexico); TV Nacional (Chile); Telefe (Argentina); Radio Televisión Espa-ñola's TVE (Spain); and RAI (Italy) (Hoineff 1993, 62). With attention shift-ing to cable and the Brazilian Congress preparing to regulate it, in 1993 Globosat established a subsidiary, Net Brasil, to be its cable distribution arm, with the programming function being left with Globosat (Bahiana 1994, 22).

By mid-1997, subscription television had grown rapidly, so that there were 2.5 million pay-TV homes in Brazil, a nation of 34.5 million tele-vision households total. Of the pay-TV households, 67 percent had cable, 22 percent had MMDS, and the remainder were DTH. Grupo Globo had caught up Abril's early lead and achieved preeminence in the subscrip-tion television market through Net Brasil, by then the largest MSO (mul-tiple system operator) in Brazil, having 700,000 subscribers compared to TVA's 350,000. While this is not as decisive a lead over its competition as it enjoys in broadcast television, Globo also had acquired a 33 percent stake in Multicanal, and this brought in a further 650,000 subscribers. At that time, North American investors such as the Bank of America and Bell Canada were showing interest in new cable and MMDS licenses that the government had promised to auction, in anticipation of imminent approval for foreign investment in the cable sector, but attention was shifting yet again to another new delivery technology, DTH (Cajueiro 1997, 28).

Brazil is a major market for both of the panregional schemes under which DTH is being established in Latin America, and each of them incorporates one of the key competitors in subscription television: Grupo Globo is aligned with News Corporation, Televisa, and TCI in the Sky project; while Abril is allied with Grupo Cisneros and Multivisión in the Galaxy Latin America/DirecTV venture led by Hughes Electronics. As with the subscription television market in general, it was Abril rather than Grupo Globo that made the first move into this new area, although Grupo Cisneros of Venezuela has been the front-runner in the Galaxy consortium in Latin America, and Venezuela was the first nation to commence the service. Brazil followed soon after, however, ahead of Mexico, and by mid-1997, Brazil was believed to have more than half of the 200,000 subscribers in the twelve countries where Galaxy was operating. The relative importance of Brazil as a market for DTH was also reflected in the fact that half of the transponders on the Hughes satellite carrying the service were dedicated to programming in Brazilian Portuguese (Bulloch 1997: 20; Paxman 1997).

"My Three Sons"

Just as Televisa has had to face a crisis of succession with the death of Emilio Azcárraga Milmo, the question must be asked as to how Grupo Globo will fare after the death of founder Roberto Marinho, now in his nineties. However, because Globo's management has been less dominated by Marinho alone than Televisa reportedly was by Azcárraga, there should be less of a crisis of transition. Long-serving Globo executives responsible for successful strategies in the past are still there, such as José ("Boni") Bonifacio de Oliveira Sobrinho, the programming specialist, or have returned, as is the case with Joe Wallach at Globosat. Roberto Marinho has three sons, each of whom is a vice president of a separate major division of the organization—television, radio, and newspaper—although one of them, Roberto Irineu, has been designated the "heir apparent." This would indicate that a more solid basis for succession has been laid than at Televisa, but some well-placed observers predict the outbreak of tense rivalries between the brothers, particularly as Grupo Globo faces ever stronger competition from SBT. On the other hand, an American communications journalist who visited Globo in 1997 reported:

> My requests to interview Marinho were ignored, and one Globo official told me that "at age 92 the man was no longer transmitting on all channels . . . day-to-day control of the private company has passed to his three sons. . . . Now the next generations of Marinhos . . . have accepted that Globo will lose its near monopoly on Brazilian media as multinationals move in, and are counterattacking by going global: Globo has courted deals with AT&T for cellular phones, Ted Turner for cable, and Rupert Murdoch's News Corporation for satellite television. (Symmes 1997, S14)

Thus, as in Mexico, generational transition has coincided with the opening up of new modes of delivery beyond broadcasting, admitting new players of substantial weight at both the national and international levels. This has obliged the traditional broadcast market leaders to defend their turf through joint ventures in the new convergent technologies with global partners, occasioning an interpenetration of global, regional, and national capital. The degree to which Televisa and Grupo Globo will be able to assert themselves within these alliances will be much more circumscribed than in their glory days of relatively unchallenged dominion.

CHAPTER NINE

The Transitional Labyrinth in an Emerging Democracy

Broadcasting Policies in Paraguay

Aníbal Orué Pozzo

ANALYSIS OF media policy and media politics in Paraguay, a common practice in the country's cultural and intellectual circles, is not an easy task. During the last eleven years of democratic life, as Paraguay experienced important political advances, the mass media, particularly broadcasting media, have had an important presence. The mass media are important mainly because of their potential to provide spaces for public discussion.

Scholarly analysis on the contemporary mass media is both complicated and challenging. It is complicated because despite important developments in media industries in the recent years, little or almost no academic research has been done on the subject in ways that can inform present analyses. Although the social sciences paid a great deal of attention to political developments before and after the coup d'état that overthrew the Stroessner dictatorship in 1989, media research has made little progress. Unfortunately, communication scholars have made only a few contributions to debates about media processes. Research on mass communication (systems, mediations, and reception) is practically nonexistent (Orué Pozzo 1997). Media analysis is also challenging given the need to have a multidisciplinary approach to the study of the media. Media studies require the incorporation of concepts and theories from other social sciences. Only then would it be possible to advance our understanding of the complexities of mass communication and mediation in Paraguay.

This article analyzes media politics during the democratic transition period in Paraguay (1989–98). In the context of this book, this chapter also intends to contribute to a more systematic analysis of media developments and trends in contemporary Latin America—legal, technological, and commercial. It focuses on changes in the broadcasting media where the *"guerre des images"* (war of images) currently takes place (Gruzinski 1994). The analysis examines the historical evolution of communications legislation and media policies in Paraguay. A historical overview provides the necessary framework for understanding the changes and characteristics of the present media, particularly during the transitional period after Stroessner was ousted in 1989. Many of the new media developments have been crystallized in election campaigns. The political parties' intense use of the media while campaigning reflects the transformations that the media (particularly broadcasting) have experienced and the introduction of novel political practices.

The legislation that existed before the current democratic period set the basis for these changes, which in turn were accelerated by laws that were passed during the 1990s. Media legislation remained practically unchanged since the 1940s and throughout the Stroessner dictatorship. After the regime collapsed, there was a period of adjustment to changing political circumstances until new legislation was approved in December 1995. With the 1995 Telecommunication Law, a new era began. To some observers, this law indicated the conclusion of the transition regarding media issues; to others, the new political democracy does not necessarily imply the democratization of the media. The decade of transition is crucial, then, to understanding the present and identifying future trends.

The Labyrinth of History: Media Systems and Legislation

A historical reconstruction of the way radio broadcasting developed in Paraguay could be done in two ways. One is to analyze the processes of media development and consumption throughout the country (Martín-Barbero 1987). Another possibility is to take an institutional perspective, examining the different moments in which the state used its administrative power to regulate the mass media, and the negotiations and different positions of the actors involved in broadcasting (McChesney 1993). This distinction is important because it allows us to understand different stages in the building of a broadcasting system in Paraguay. This chapter integrates both approaches, looking at media consumption (the reappropriation of contents and messages) and at different state actions to consolidate a specific media model.

An important aspect to consider is the authoritarian tradition of Paraguayan politics that shaped the evolution of media systems. According to Miranda,

Paraguayans accepted strong types of authoritarian rulers since national independence. José Gaspar Rodríguez de Francia (1814–1840) initiated a period of almost total isolation from the outside world. Presidents Carlos Antonio López (1840–1862) and Francisco Solano López (1862–1870) reinforced authoritarian structures within their vision to give Paraguay a larger role on the world stage. The three dictators made Paraguay a self-sufficient nation during the nineteenth century, perhaps creating the notion that such governance promoted stability and progress. (1990, 3)

From the beginning of 1936, and again in 1940, the army took control of the political administration of the Paraguayan state. Authoritarianism was evident in three contexts: the political structure, psychological dispositions, and political ideologies (Bobbio, Matteucci, and Pasquino 1988). The long authoritarian tradition reinforced these three elements in Paraguay. Authoritarianism has been expressed through the presence of the military in politics. In the name of the national interest, the military regularly took over the state and controlled its institutions.

There have been many landmark moments in broadcasting history. The 1927 and 1936 legislation harnessed the development of radio broadcasting and gave power to the state to control and regulate other aspects of the media. It was only in 1944 that legislation that specifically regulated broadcasting and telecommunication was approved.

The first experimental radio transmission was initiated in the 1920s. Radio was introduced in an extremely delicate situation: the beginning of the conflict between Paraguay and Bolivia over the Chaco territories, Paraguay's western region that Bolivia disputed as its own.[1] The development accelerated after the war. The 1927 radio legislation laid the foundations of broadcasting for years to come. Radio was organized as a private business, without any provisions for public service as was the case in Europe (McQuail and Siune 1991).

The 1936 law reflected the belief that broadcasting was an instrument of political action in the service of the Paraguayan military. Despite the uncertainty over the Chaco situation, the internal political situation was relatively calm after years of continued military conflicts. The need to regulate the airwaves and bring the country into the modern era provided the impetus for the new legislation. This was a unique period in Paraguay's history. Fifty years after the "Triple Alliance War" (1865–70) was finished, in which the country was almost destroyed, it was necessary to reinvent Paraguay and prepare it for modern times.[2] It was necessary to construct anew feelings of national identity, which had been badly damaged by the defeat in the war.

In this context, the radio became an instrument for nation building. The intensive use of radio during the war with Bolivia put the new technology in a privileged place.[3] During the Chaco War, the army command introduced a national radio network that aired daily broadcasts about the actions of the Paraguayan military. To reinforce national sentiments, most of the information was in Guarani. As Jesús Martín-Barbero (1987, 165) has written about the process of national formation in Latin America, radio in Paraguay played a political and ideological role "in the nationalization of the popular masses."

Regarding the media, for example, military government made intensive use of the mass media particularly since the rise of National Radio in the 1940s until the implementation of the mandatory daily National Radio Network during the Stroessner era. During the 1930s and 1940s, radio broadcasting was expanded in support of the goal of national integration. State-owned Radio Nacional and the official newsreel showed in theaters reflected the intention to develop and consolidate an ideal nation. Guarani broadcasts were intended to expand linguistic identification nationwide.

Radio was also at the center of the construction of a modern, mass society. The 1940s became the golden years of radio broadcasting. An observer writes, "Whoever didn't listen to the radio in Asunción during the forties, was someone, as a friend of mine at the time used to say, out of this world or living in a stratosphere." Most stations covered urban areas. Notwithstanding the urban reach of radio, a military historian complained in the late 1950s that "our radio stations had a small reach, covering only parts of the national territory and some borders" (Bejarano 1963, 221). At the beginning of the 1970s, there were nine private and one official radio stations. Six out of the nine private stations were in Asunción, the country's capital.

The Morinigo Years

The fundamental basis of the media system and the cultural market were established during the Morinigo government. That basis was consolidated during the decades of Stroessner's dictatorship. In 1941, the Morinigo administration (1940–48) created the National Department of Press and Propaganda (DENAPRO). During a period that has been described as national-populist, the government ran several industries, including the media. The administration was committed to economic independence and development, and to orgainizing a state presence in several social areas.[4] The DENAPRO was the first state agency to organize and structure the broadcasting spectrum in the country, in one of the first official efforts to articulate a media policy. The state organized and administered the official propaganda and broadcasting frequencies. According to decree 9829, the DENAPRO was "dependent on the Presidency of the Republic in order to coordinate and centralize propaganda." At the same time, the state also created the Paraguayan National Radio to manage official propaganda. The DENAPRO was organized in four sections: Press, Propaganda, Broadcasting, and Tourism and Culture; this structure was later continued by subsequent governments.[5]

In December 1944 the Morinigo government passed law 6.422 that "establishes a legislation in matters of telecommunications in the Republic of Paraguay." The law defines the first legal regime for telecommunications in the country that included telephony, radio, and television. From this point on, all the legal apparatus for the operation of electronic communications were directed by the DENAPRO and through application of the 1944 Telecommunication Law, the legal regime that organized the system. By this law, the granting of broadcasting licenses was under the jurisdiction of the executive. It was the president who, using his own discretion, authorized, gave, or denied permits and concessions for radio station operations. The law defined broadcasting services as those that have "the duty of transmitting cultural, educational, artistic and informative programs, geared toward the general public." In 1948 the National Administration of Telecommunications (ANTEL) was created. An office of the Ministry of Public Works and Communications, ANTEL was in charge of administering the Telecommunication Law.

The Stroessner Years

After Morinigo, different governments strengthened this legal order. Little can be understood about the evolution of the media in Paraguay without paying attention to media policies during the Stroessner dictatorship. Gen. Alfredo Stroessner ruled Paraguay from 1954 to 1989, when a military coup led by Gen. Andrés Rodríguez, the second-highest-ranking officer in the army command, deposed him, bringing to an end the longest dictatorship in Paraguay's history.

During the Stroessner years, radio and television licenses were manipulated according to the motto that ruled the administration: "peace, work, and well-being." Media censorship was in the hands of the DENA-PRO and the Subsecretaría de Informaciones y Cultura. Among the duties of the DENAPRO were the "centralization, coordination and censorship of the national and international official propaganda, carried out by the press." Some sectors of the opposition regularly protested the way in which licenses were granted. They criticized the dictatorship for having absolute control of the media and preventing any kind of criticism of the government.

During the Stroessner regime, and into the mid-1980s, the DENAPRO was central to media policies. In the 1950s, it established the production of an official newsreel, a short news summary on the activities of the government but mainly of Stroessner himself. Movie theaters were compelled to show the national newsreel at the beginning of film presentations. The DENAPRO's broadcasting division was in charge of establishing the National Radio Network. The latter was an extension of the network started during the war with Bolivia, and was officially installed in 1940, under the presidency of Gen. José Félix Estigarribia, the former military commander during the Chaco War. The mission of the Network was to "establish a permanent information radio program" and "arrange broadcasting network transmission for those official activities that according to their importance require broad diffusion." Also, Stroessner's Colorado Party had its own radio network for more than twenty years. The head station was National Radio, to which other stations had to be linked "voluntarily."

In terms of infrastructure, Stroessner radicalized the fundamental principles established by Morinigo. The modernization processes undertaken by Stroessner included the formation of a consumer market of cultural goods. Television was introduced in 1965 following the radio model, but the regime never went as far as establishing a mandatory daily connection to a national television network as it did with radio.

During Stroessner's regime the stability of the broadcasting system was based on the fact that the various actors involved in the process *shared responsibility* and were satisfied with the situation. Provided that the media did not question the dictatorship's sociopolitical scaffolding, they were bound for eternal glory. This *consensus compromise* worked through the dictatorship.

While the consensus compromise was implemented among media owners, the population created its own consumption and reception structures. Early communication research took into account this phenomenon. In the early 1960s Dominguez (1966, 59) studied the behavior of the people who lived in the countryside, and concluded that the radio set was something highly valuable, like the leather jacket and the cowboy hat. His data documented the increasing presence of radio and other media in the daily life of the rural population.

The "economic boom" during the construction of the Itaipu hydro-electric dam in the 1970s redesigned once again the consensus compromise in Paraguayan society.[6] At that time a substantial number of popular sectors joined en masse the consumer market of cultural goods. In the early 1980s a second television company was founded, a company that currently is an important media group with interests in print, radio, and television. Television companies expanded geographic coverage, and radio stations also increased their transmitting power, achieving a national reach. With this expansion, the integration of the country was completed. Only then was it possible to speak of one country under a government that claimed to stand for national "peace and progress," although in order to accomplish these goals, there were no state-funded stations.

The economic crisis of the 1980s began after the construction of the Itaipu dam was complete. The crisis was responsible for why some factions of the hegemonic sectors moved away from the Stroessner government. During the mid-1980s, the dictatorship "hardened" its consensus compromise with certain media interests. Some broke the agreement and started a slow political movement away from the dictatorship, disclosing secret aspects of the government. Several dailies were temporarily closed. *ABC Color* was shut down in March 1984 and not reopened until after the coup d'état in 1989. Some time after the shutdown of *ABC Color*, ANTEL closed radio station Ñandutí on the grounds that it did not have all documents required to operate legally. It too was reopened after the 1989 coup.

However, the Stroessner government only hardened its political position as the foundation of the media system remained unchanged. There was no economic conflict that might have caused media entrepreneurs to look for allies in the popular movement to confront the government politically. The consensus policy manufactured throughout these years brought benefits to media and communications interests.

In summary, the system can be characterized as a *mixed broadcasting system* dominated by a spectrum of private companies. There are some public radio but not public television stations. National agencies control broadcasting operations. All the power to administer media frequencies is held by CONATEL, the collective of institutions that in 1995 replaced ANTEL. The state continued to provide the infrastructure of the broadcasting media system. It owned transmission lines and microwave towers for transmitting television signals.

The basis of this communications system still works in Paraguay, though almost nothing has changed in the last fifty years. Despite large political changes, the media field continues to be ruled by what the government negotiates with the largest economic groups. Nowadays, a new consensus policy is being designed for media communication in the country.

Mass Media and Democratic Transition: Paraguay during the 1990s

The political transition unleashed the possibility of building a society based on the principles of representative democracy. For the first time in the country's history, there is the possibility of creating democratic institutions to favor and strengthen citizens' participation. It is one of the scarce moments in Paraguay's history when an elected president finished his term and also a civilian president was elected by popular vote. Before Juan Carlos Wasmosy replaced Gen. Rodríguez in August 1993, only twice (in 1916 and in 1928) had democratically elected presidents replaced their predecessors in the country's history. After the crisis of March 1999, when President Carlos Cubas was impeached and the president of the National Congress, Luis A. González Macchi, took over, the democratic transition finally passed its final exam.

During its first years, the political transition was very dynamic. General elections were called in May 1989, only three months after Stroessner was overthrown. The first mayoral elections in the country's history took place in 1991. In December of that year, new elections were held to elect candidates to write the country's new constitution. In June 1992 the new constitution was approved, and the basis for the official recognition of a state of rights in the country was established. In two years, three democratic elections were held with extensive participation of diverse political and ideological groups. These elections gave a new face to the emerging Paraguayan democracy. In 1993 a new president and Congress were elected in general elections. The establishment, represented by the Colorado Party, won the election for president, but opposition parties won the majority of the seats in Congress. With a level of participation of almost 90 percent of eligible voters, the second elections for municipal government were held in November 1996. The third presidential election after the 1989 coup was held in May 1998.

In all, six elections on different levels helped consolidate the emerging system begun in 1989. Most politicians considered that finally the transition was over. From now on, the process of consolidating the democratic institutions that were born after 1989 was under way. The country now has a democratic constitution, one of the most advanced in the region, as well as new institutions. It would seem that everything is running marvelously.

The democratic transition went hand in hand with the new communication technologies. Fast-paced changes took place during the first two years after Stroessner was deposed. Soon after Stroessner went into exile in 1989, cable television and mobile telephony arrived. Cable television rapidly expanded throughout the country.[7] The postcoup government espoused neoliberal policies that opened communications markets, with the exception of telephony. The changes that have taken place since 1989 took old-guard nationalists by surprise. As the country moved toward democracy, it was also moving away from the nationalist positions of previous governments.

The expansion of new technologies required changes in the legal structure, namely the adaptation of the 1944 legislation. During the early days of the transition, however, Congress was powerless to make the radical changes that the system needed. Not until after the general elections of 1993 did Congress decide to change the legislation, and it approved a new Telecommunication Law in 1995.

Despite its relative modernity, the 1995 Telecommunication Law basically keeps the structure of the 1944 law. Whereas it establishes that "the emissions and generation of electromagnetic communication signals are of public domain of the State," the 1944 law stated that the telecommunications spectrum "belongs to the national jurisdiction." While the executive continues to control the granting of radio and television frequencies, the 1995 law introduced some modifications. According to the new legislation, the National Commission of Communication (CONATEL) took on the political administration of telecommunications, replacing ANTEL. The law also created the Broadcasting Council, strictly as an advisory board to the CONATEL, and integrated it through inclusion of representatives from different areas of civil society (including workers). The executive appoints the members of the CONATEL Council and the Broadcasting Council. The law requires that CONATEL "elaborate and apply the National Telecommunication Plan and the National Frequencies Plan in order to regulate the free access to the electromagnetic spectrum."

The context in which the 1995 law took effect was far different than previous periods that witnessed the passage of communications legislation. Beginning in 1993, the Congress debated the need to have a new law to regulate broadcasting and telecommunications in the new democracy. Official agencies, legislators, businesspeople, nongovernmental organizations, and other segments of civil society engaged in a debate about the need for a new broadcasting law that would provide the country with a democratic regulatory instrument for the media. Over a more than two-year period, they gathered periodically to debate policy proposals. The big commercial interests carried the most weight in this process, with the result being that the 1995 legislation was practically designed by the business community interests. AM and FM radio frequencies are basically owned by private companies. A small number of low-power stations, which comprise so-called community radio, are allow to function as long as they do not interfere with commercial signals.[8]

The 1995 law thus has made little progress toward effective democratic control of the media in Paraguay. The goal of a telecommunications law that was the product of an effective discussion with wide participation from different social actors collectively creating a comprehensive national policy did not happen. The democratization of media use and access is one of the most sensitive areas not just in Brazil but in the Mercosur countries as well (as the chapters on Argentina, Brazil, and Uruguay demonstrate).[9]

Since 1996, under the new Telecommunication Law, more than 120 new radio frequencies (AM and FM) were put up for bid. With those new licenses, coupled with three new television licenses and the coming of cable television, the broadcasting landscape experienced substantial changes. Currently, there are 42 AM and 107 FM radio stations, four television stations, 77 cable providers, and one MMDS. All licenses have been issued directly by the executive.

Despite the strong pressure of big economic groups, the main telephone company remains a state monopoly in the hands of ANTEL. The nationalist leanings of the governing Colorado Party are still much too strong to let the political patronage and clientelism embedded in state companies be broken. Mobile telephony, which was introduced in 1991, shows a different ownership structure as eight companies, all subsidiaries of transnational corporations, offer services. Pressures to privatize the state-owned company, as well as other state-run services, are very strong. The 1995 Telecommunication law established that basic telephony is a public service operated through concessions. The fact that state-owned companies work as a source of patronage fends off privatization anytime soon. The current administration has promised, however, that all utilities will be privatized within two years and has set up a commission to design proposals for future actions.

Overall, the changes experienced in the 1990s have largely favored corporate interests. The old system developed during the long years of dictatorship was replaced by a more dynamic one but kept the same economic and political interests. Media policymaking continues to be short on diversity and pluralism in terms of access and control.

The Media Break into the Electoral Process

The Stroessner government's 1960 electoral law, the Estatuto Electoral, had ruled the elections during the dictatorship. Modified in 1965 and 1981, the law made no references to media campaigns. Two possible reasons explain the absence of media regulations in the different versions of the Estatuto Electoral. First, neither Congress nor the executive considered the use of mass media; second, facing the prospect that diverse parties might use the media, Stroessner may have preferred to avoid any use of the media for electoral purposes. Consequently, electoral propaganda was absent from the media during the electoral processes under Stroessner. However, the regime daily bombarded the population with messages from the National Radio Network, the irrational use of the National Radio, the Noticiero Nacional in movie theaters, and the Colorado Party's broadcasting network.

The political situation radically changed after 1989. In March 1990, a new electoral code was approved. This code introduced important changes in the use of the mass media during the electoral process. Article 306 gives permission to "parties, political movements and alliances to carry out different kinds of propaganda activities on the mass media to make people know their doctrine and to transmit information to their members and public opinion." This law also defines how mass media spaces are to be used.[10] For the first time, the country's political and electoral advertising entered the mass media. A 1995 modification of the electoral code maintained basically the same principles stipulated in 1990, but clarified and regulated some ambiguous situations. It defines the meaning of election advertising and restricted media airtime. It establishes two areas for media advertising: free advertising equally granted by the Supreme Electoral Justice, and paid advertising. The code regulated thirty-second spots, which became the staple of election campaigning. It also establishes rules that political parties and the media must observe during the electoral process. The big business that political advertising represents—especially during the electoral campaign, and principally on radio and television—is, surely, an emerging product of the liberalization of the social and political system in Paraguay.

During the Stroessner era, several journalists were persecuted and others went to prison. After the coup d'état in 1989 these journalists won space in the mass media, especially television. As Mitchell Stephens observed, "Radio gave newsmongers back their voices, television restored their faces" (1988, 280). The political transition introduced well-known radio journalists to a television audience. Although radio and the print media were important political actors during the last years of the dictatorship, television emerged as the central medium during the transition.

Research conducted months after Stroessner was ousted showed that radio was the most credible medium, at 51.8 percent; followed by television, at 35.2 percent; and print, with 10.6 percent (Fox 1990). At that time, radio was also the main source of information for the population. For some political parties, especially those founded during the transition, it was important to make their leaders known to the population. For these purposes, media and television campaigning was the chosen strategy. New forms of campaigning introduced the "new enlightened men" as the organizers of image campaigning; in a country without experience of political campaigns on television, media and advertising consultants became more important. The transition ushered in media consultants, technical advisers, and a whole new array of professionals working on image creation—the "technicians who purchased the airtime, checked the lighting, supervised the make up, arranged the set, and timed the speech," as Kathleen Hall Jamieson (1988, 35) writes about the U.S. experience.

The 1993 presidential elections were a laboratory for the media and the "new enlightened men." According to the report of the delegation of the Latin American Studies Association that was sent to observe the election, "a low estimate of the total campaign expenditures of the three major contenders in the election was around $27,500,000" (Riquelme et al. 1994, 38). This approximate amount included radio, television, and print. The two leading candidates "spent approximately one third of their campaign funds in TV," the report added. No question, then, that in only four years the audiovisual media had become central to the electoral process.[11]

During the 1993 election, opposition party Encuentro Nacional invested heavily in television advertising with the intention of creating a modern image. This was in sharp contrast to the two traditional parties, the Colorado Party and the Partido Liberal Radical Auténtico. But this strategy was at first not tremendously effective, judging from electoral results. Encuentro Nacional came in third in the final count, far behind the second-place Partido Liberal Radical Auténtico. However, in 1998 the Colorado Party invested a great part of its budget on broadcasting media and won the elections.

The electoral process that began in 1989 is a hybrid in communicational terms. The traditional ways of politicking, which centered on the candidate's interpersonal communication such as face-to-face campaigning, converged with the use of audiovisual media—mainly television and lately the Internet. During the August 2000 election for vice president, both candidates had their own home pages on the World Wide Web. The *multitemporary heterogeneity* of the new citizenship spaces (García Canclini 1990) in which politics is battled out combines traditional practices and modern media.

Business, Politics, and Culture

During the 1990s, broadcasting and telecommunication systems have undergone important changes in Paraguay. Private business became more important, as reflected in legislation that favors commercial interests and the control that they have over broadcasting and print. The emergent media map also shows that political interests continue to wield power in the allocating of frequencies and by granting favors that benefit allied private interests. Commercial and political interests continue to be linked together in broadcasting. During recent years, several political groups close to the government have showed interest in owning radio licenses, particularly during election times. Patronage and clientelism underlie the allocation of broadcasting licenses, which have favored progovernment politicians and businessmen. To keep its friends happy, the government has reduced the transmitting power of radio stations to increase the number of stations in different regions and cities.

In this mixed system, it is clear that the private sector is stronger than the small public sector. The state owns the National Radio Network and two radio stations, but its presence, measured in audience and reach, is really insignificant. State-owned media is not a serious rival that can challenge the private sector media companies, which never complain of "unfair" competition from the state.

Media policy did not essentially change during the transition years. In fact, the foundations of the media system have remained substantially unchanged for two decades. Compared to previous periods, the changes introduced during the 1990s may seem rapid and radical; however, these changes have not been radical, but merely reflect a new agreement among different sectors of Paraguayan society.

The 1995 Telecommunication law mainly established a new framework for organizing communications, introducing procedures for granting new radio and television licenses and acknowledging new technological developments. It largely reflects a new consensus compromise among political and economic interests that allows them to remain dominant and continue going largely unchallenged.

The transition in the media, however, will not be complete without a consideration of the issue of control and access to the media by social movements and citizens' groups. The 1995 law only refers to services of small- or medium-size coverage, but no law has been passed yet. A proposal has been in Congress for more than two years at the time of this writing. Community radio stations have been authorized to function, but the allocation of the electromagnetic spectrum is far from egalitarian as those stations have very low potency. The law ignores community television channels and lacks provisions for citizens' access to cable and satellite television. The democratic transition has allowed new sectors of civil society to have a voice in politics, but they are denied access to television. The democratization of Paraguayan society will not be complete without the democratization of the media.

The process of media democratization needs to be analyzed within the context of the Mercosur Agreement. Media legislation in the member countries continues to ignore the integration process; for example, the Paraguayan Telecommunication Law, which passed four years after the Mercosur Treaty was signed, made no reference to it. As media flows and cultural exchanges intensify, it is all the more essential to address these issues.

Notes

1. The conflict between Paraguay and Bolivia began in 1928 but war was not officially declared until 1932.

2. This 1865–70 war was called the Triple Alliance War because of the alliance or secret treaty between Argentina, Brazil, and Uruguay to destroy Paraguay. As a consequence of the war, the country was almost destroyed economically, politically, and socially. Its population was reduced by approximately two-thirds by the end of the conflict (Whigham and Potthast 1999).

3. Print technologies had a similar role during the Triple Alliance War when a number of newspapers (*Cabuchu'i, Cacique Lambaré, El Centinela, La Estrella*) were founded. Those papers rescued Guarani, the indigenous language spoken by a large number of the population.

4. Other regimes similar to Morinigo's, other populist governments existed during those years in the region, such as those headed by Brazil's Getulio Vargas and Argentina's Juan Domingo Perón. Though embedded in fascist ideology, they were not precisely fascist. Although many members of those governments sympathized with the European fascist movement, in these Latin American countries, according to Hobsbawm (1995, 135), "we cannot speak of the same kind of movement."

5. The structure of the DENAPRO was subsequently transferred to the Stroessner government (1954–89) under the undersecretary of information and culture (Subsecretaría de Informaciones y Cultura), which was also dependent on the presidency of the republic. After the 1989 coup, the Rodríguez government redesigned the agency under the Office of Culture and Information.

6. Construction of the Itaipu hydroelectric dam, one of the largest in the world, started by 1974, and for more than eight years helped to consolidate the consensus among several sectors of Paraguayan society. The construction of the dam was responsible for "easy money years."

7. The issue of cable television and language is interesting to analyze in terms of the cultural changes in television reception. One cable company was authorized to operate in the city of Tobati. Located 75 kilometers from Asunción, it had a population of 9,014 according to the 1992 census. The majority of the population speaks Guarani (which became one of two official languages after the 1992 Constitution).

8. Articles 57–59 define the functioning of community radios as follows: "The main objectives of these radios are to broadcast cultural, artistic, educational and information programs with no interest in gaining any profit."

9. Signed on 26 March 1991, the Tratado de Asunción, also known as the Mercosur Treaty, began the integration process among Argentina, Brazil, Uruguay, and Paraguay. The treaty created a free trade zone and intended to push forward a stronger integration among its members. Currently, Bolivia and Chile are negotiating to enter Mercosur.

10. Article 319 states, "The law guarantees, to carry out the electoral propaganda, radio and television spaces, a minimum of one hour daily, on each of the social communication media public and private. In this last case, those who want to use private media, have to pay for it." Article 323 specifically defines how to use it:

1. In order to contribute to the country's democratic processes and therefore to the Paraguayan people's civic education, the mass media will allocate for free, three percent of their daily spaces to publicize the political programs of the parties, political

movements and alliances that participate in the election, during ten days before the end of the electoral campaign. For the same reason, and also during the same time, the print media will allocate one page in each edition. 2. The distribution of spaces will be controlled by the Supreme Electoral Justice equally of all the parties, political movements and alliances.

Article 290 establishes: "Electoral media advertising will last a maximum of sixty days, counting up to two days before the election." The 1990 Code says: "A minimum of one hour daily"—it should have said a *maximum* of one hour daily. Article 301 of the 1995 Electoral Code stipulates that "advertising will be limited, to each party, political movement or alliance to no more than half page per edition or its equivalent in centimeter/column in number, in each daily and magazine. As for television or radio propaganda, each party, political movement and alliance will be granted a maximum of five minutes on each television channel and radio daily."

11. At that time, there were 620,000 television sets, equal to about half the country's total population. According to the 1992 Population and Housing Census, 53.9 percent of the households in Paraguay had at least one television set, and 81.8 percent of households had at least one radio.

CHAPTER TEN

Peruvian Media in the 1990s

From Deregulation to Reorganization

Luis Peirano

Introduction

During the decade of the 1990s, Peru, under the presidency of Alberto Fujimori, entered an era of free market economic development and integration into the global economy. Over this turbulent decade the actions of the Fujimori administration were key to Peruvian history. This administration was closely tied to a specific concept and management style regarding the mass media.

For the two decades before Fujimori came to office, Peru had been ruled by populist and nationalist regimes that produced a series of original and independent-minded policies that drew the country closer to the nonaligned movement and away from either the U.S. or Soviet orbit. Alberto Fujimori appeared on the scene at the end of the 1980s when the country was experiencing a wave of hyperinflation and terrorism. Fujimori had little experience to distinguish himself in the political field, apart from being president of the Agrarian University and heading the National Assembly of University Presidents. In little time at all, however, Fujimori was leading the electoral polls and eventually won the 1990 election. He defeated Mario Vargas Llosa, who had the backing of all the opposition political groups and was the strongest candidate to replace outgoing president Alan García.

The political circumstances that made Fujimori's triumph possible can be better understood by attending to the different processes of communication and in particular the mass media in Peru. The same processes and media also help explain how he conducted his presidency once in office.

The development of the Peruvian communications media over the Fujimori decade can be divided into five phases. Specific political events and measures taken by the government in regard to political institutions and the economy mark each phase. The first and probably most important phase was Fujimori's open reinsertion of Peru into the world economy, following the failure of his predecessor, President Alan García, to maintain an independent economic position for the country. The next phase was Fujimori's coup d'état against his own government during the second year of his administration and his consequent dismissal of Peru's parliament. The third phase comprised the government's successful attempts to control hyperinflation and combat terrorism, which allowed Fujimori to be reelected for a second term with an absolute majority in parliament. Riding high on these successes, a newly energized Fujimori brought to his second administration, which constitutes the fourth phase, his own concept and style for managing the mass media. This style, while respecting the formal terms of the principle of freedom of expression, produced an authoritarian regime that tightly controlled the media. Fujimori's bizarre fifth and last phase—standing for election for a third presidential term—ended when he announced his resignation soon after.

The Fujimori Decade

The development of the communication media had a strong impact on the Fujimori decade, a period that was somewhat of an anomaly in a region of Latin America that after decades of military rule was rediscovering democracy and the regular renovation of elected officials. The specific characteristics of Peruvian politics, however, were what allowed Fujimori to remain in power for ten years. Little of the history of what made this possible has been written. The question of how Fujimori first came to power, defeating the well-known writer Mario Vargas Llosa, an intellectual closely tied to Peru's traditionally dominant political parties, is yet to be explained adequately in terms of either political or social theory.

The first Fujimori victory sheds light on the role the mass media played during a crucial electoral period. In the first round of voting, Vargas Llosa won 32.6 percent of the vote to Fujimori's 29.1 percent, making necessary a runoff election held a few weeks later. During the period between the first and second rounds of voting, the balance shifted toward Fujimori, a dark horse whose support came from an unusual group of voters, usually ignored by the traditional politicians—Protestant evangelicals, street vendors, slum dwellers, and a frustrated middle class. In the runoff Fujimori's supporters came together to give him 62.4 percent of the vote, thus soundly defeating Vargas Llosa.

The political pundits and consultants, including the U.S. public relations firms working for Vargas Llosa, had little understanding of the process of formation of public opinion and the voting habits and preferences among the groups constituting the wide Peruvian underclass. During the campaign, the mass media, in both their information and propaganda function, which included a deluge of political advertising, were under the control of the supporters of Vargas Llosa and the group called Fredemo. Yet, communication processes entirely outside the modern mass media—the rumors, jokes, and gossip of interpersonal communication—seem to have decided the election in favor of Fujimori. Students of communication would say that popular culture beat out the diffusion theory of the hypodermic needle. Was this a planned communication strategy? Did Fujimori recognize a force that his professional adversaries ignored? Probably not. Fujimori was among the first to express surprise about his victory. What is certain is that he followed his intuition concerning what resonated with his followers. Once elected, this intuition continued to serve him well.

After taking office with the support of the majority of the population and the backing of the armed forces, Fujimori had to face the problems left him by the previous administration of Alan García Pérez of the Aprista Party. These problems included an unimaginable administrative mess, skyrocketing inflation, and a national emergency brought on by the successful offensive of an armed guerrilla movement, Sendero Luminoso (the Shining Path), that threatened the capital and already controlled vast portions of the countryside.

Fujimori inherited a broken-down Cadillac of a government information or propaganda machine, the same that previous president Fernando Belaunde had received from the military when he was elected in 1980. In the 1970s, the military, firm believers in the efficiency of the mass media, had set up a powerful national information system to carry out their political objectives. National newspapers, television channels, and the leading radio stations, according to the military, should serve the "revolution." In consequence, the military expropriated newspapers, radio stations, and television channels from their private owners. In 1980, with the return of democracy, President Fernando Belaunde returned many of the main media outlets to their original owners. He kept several key outlets in the military's arsenal, however—including three newspapers, a few radio stations, and a news agency—which together made up the National Institute of Social Communication. The García administration continued to maintain the same structure of government and private media.

Fujimori also inherited a dense network of legal restrictions on freedom of expression that the military had imposed on at last half the country in order to combat the Shining Path movement and the Movimiento Revolucionario Tupac Amaru (MRTA), a smaller terrorist movement. In those regions declared Emergency Zones the military had the power to close and censure newspapers and prosecute journalists in the name of the counterinsurgency against the guerrilla movement.

Alternative Proposals

Once in office, President Fujimori had to balance a national emergency that demanded both a major counterinsurgency effort and the reorganization of the private sector. To further complicate this delicate balance, in 1991 the parliament soundly defeated the new president's proposal to create a Peruvian Council of Culture and Communication. Media owners, advertisers, and significant sectors of the press objected to the formation of the council on the grounds that it signaled a return to an authoritarian regime and government control of information. The proposal for the formation of the council was Fujimori's first and last attempt to regulate the mass media, arguing the public service function of journalism and the media. Other Latin American countries routinely had employed this argument in formulating media policies. All of Fujimori's subsequent efforts to impose limits on the media were done in the name of the struggle against terrorism, or simply against bad taste, and were perceived rightly as an even more serious threat against freedom of expression.

Insertion in the Free Market

The globalization of the economy and obviously of Peruvian culture, although not on the agenda of any administration, was inevitable. The government of Fujimori quickly joined the ranks of those supporting the changes occurring in the world economy. He enacted measures that brought Peru in line with different policies supporting global integration of the economy, in this way making his administration more acceptable to the international agencies and the governments they supported. In local terms, this meant the accelerated sale of the government-owned industries that had been created or strengthened by the military during the 1970s under a policy of self-sufficiency and central planning. The immediate impact of the sale of these industries was a boost to the national economy and a corresponding rise in the popularity of the president. In the telecommunications sector, beginning in 1991, the Fujimori administration kept in place the existing legislation, but initiated a process of gradual modification, especially concerning private investment and the privatization of services.

Up until that point the relationship between the new Fujimori administration and the mass media had been difficult, but no more so than the usual give-and-take that occurs in a democracy. Some observers, however, began to notice signs that this administration was going to be different from its predecessor in terms of tolerance of criticism. On the positive side, at the beginning, the new government did not respond to criticism with the classic military reaction—closing media outlets and deporting journalists. Likewise, the Fujimori administration did not react strongly to the accusations of corruption coming from associations of journalists, such as those of the Association of Foreign Correspondents, which in the past had mediated well between the government and the press.

Fujimori also appeared to pay little attention to the calls for change from different sectors of the population that were channeled through the media or, more surprisingly, to the attacks from different media, although these at times were hard-hitting. Probably no president of Peru had been more strongly attacked by the press without any apparent reaction on his part than Fujimori, perhaps a topic for future research concerning the presumed power of the press. Fujimori's strategy vis-à-vis the press, as soon would become apparent, was totally different from those of his predecessors.

In April 1992 Fujimori, finding his legislative initiatives blocked by parliament but with the full support of the armed forces, carried out an auto coup d'état. He dissolved the two chambers of parliament and sent soldiers to occupy the main opposition newspapers and radio and TV stations, as well as the media outlets that most interested him.

The New Regime

Following the coup, Fujimori announced that he would call elections for a constituent congress to write a new Constitution. More importantly, he decided to rule by decree, a move highly criticized in the past when carried out by the military, and now comfortably accepted by the supporters of the president. The rule by decree enabled Fujimori to modify the regulations on private investment in telecommunications and begin the process of privatization of the communications sector, bringing it more in line with the characteristics of the world economy. Fujimori established a regulatory body for private investment in telecommunications, Organismo Supervisor de Inversión Privada en Telecomunicaciones (OSIPTEL), of critical importance to the reorganization of the telephone sector.

The presence of soldiers in the streets severely damaged the image of the new government, a situation that registered in the unfavorable public opinion polls that followed the coup. A key incident, however, would change the political tenor of the country and improve Fujimori's image. On 12 September 1992 the government announced the capture of Abimael Guzmán, the supreme commander of the Shining Path movement, the group responsible for the wave of terror that had crashed over the central part of the country since the mid-1980s. Thousands were killed in the name of a Maoist-inspired revolution. The widespread violence reached into Lima itself; in the high-income suburb of Miraflores, incidents such as a car bomb explosion produced notable social consequences.

The capture of Abimael Guzmán kicked off an accelerated process of disarming and breaking up the Shining Path. The movement soon lost its protagonist role on the national scene and was reduced to a small, fragmented band of terrorists acting on their own. The other guerrilla movement, the MRTA, never had the same national prominence as the Shining Path. Nevertheless, MRTA also suffered the effects of the crackdown. All its main leaders except one, Néstor Serpa, were captured and sentenced to life in prison. The predominant image projected from Peru became one of peace finally reaching the Andes. Even if this were not entirely the case, government propaganda made sure that this was the message.

The next year, Fujimori's election slate, Cambio 90, won the majority of the seats in the Constitutional Congress. Later his supporters voted to accept the new National Constitution with a slightly more than 52 percent majority. In April 1993, a year after Fujimori's autocoup, the parliament discussed and rapidly approved a new Telecommunications Law, replacing the previous legislation and doing away with many of the responsibilities assigned to the state. An important paragraph on the new General Norms states: "[T]he services of telecommunications will be provided under a regime of free competition. All practices that restrict loyal competition are prohibited."

The new regulations led to substantive increases in the number of licenses to provide the public services of telecommunication, as can be observed in table 10.1.

Table 10.1 / Licenses Issued for Telecommunications Services

Service	1990	1993	1995	1997
Telephone	0	0	2	2
Cellular telephone	0	3	3	3
Paging	0	1	14	38
Cable TV	1	4	12	54

A similar process occurred in broadcasting. The Ministry of Transportation announced a significant increase in the number of stations between 1993 and 1994. In 1997, 202 new radio licenses were awarded, bringing the total number of radio stations in the country to 1,425, of which 839 were FM, 447 AM, and 139 shortwave. Fujimori's sale of the state-run telephone company to a Spanish company with monopoly rights for the next five years resulted in an enormous jump in telephone lines. From slightly under 600,000 lines in Peru in 1990, the number grew to 1.7 million lines in 1997, with most of the growth occurring since 1995.

Along with the reinsertion of Peru in the world economy, Peru's agreements with the IMF and the World Bank brought with them control over hyperinflation. In 1995, on the political front, the combination of peace and stability, iron control of inflation, and prosperity resulting from millions of dollars flowing into the state's coffers as a result of privatization resulted in Fujimori's overwhelming victory in the election. Fujimori and his supporters from Cambio 90–Nueva Mayoría received 64.4 percent of the vote, winning by a wide margin over his opponent, Javier Pérez de Cuéllar, former secretary-general of the United Nations. The Aprista Party of Alan García was severely punished with only about 5 percent of the vote. The left-wing coalition trailed further behind.

Fujimori's overwhelming triumph guaranteed him a large majority in the new Congress, reduced as a body by the new constitution to one chamber with 100 members. Abandoning the bicameral system radically changed the way business was conducted in the legislature. Specialized commissions assumed more importance, and fewer traditional debates occurred in open sessions. In practice, the Fujimori administration entered a phase of easy congressional management, enjoying broad support that quickly legitimized executive decisions.

The New Press Freedom

The reelection of President Fujimori proved that his political intuitions and communication tactics were correct, despite the growing opposition of a large sector of the population increasingly alienated from his regime.

Traditionally, the opposition had two basic forms through which to exercise its power—parliamentary debate and the mass media. The former was now out of their reach, with the unicameral parliament firmly in control of the president's supporters. Opposition to Fujimori on the mass media front was diverse and complex, but unified by the common objective of defending freedom of expression.

In the 1990s, for example, the center-left opposition newspaper *La República* provided space on its editorial page to opponents of Fujimori and provided leadership for the forces opposing his presidency. The paper started an investigative reporting unit that had notable success, for example, in 1992 with the identification of student murder victims from the Cantuta University of Education. *La República* also uncovered abuses carried out by the military linked to the intelligence services. The television programs that still preserved their independence within the increasingly limited television market picked up and ran these stories (Waisbord 2000). Paradoxically, the recession came to the aid of the government in terms of the management of the opposition media. Shrinking investments, a falling stock market, and increasing unemployment resulted in a decrease in the advertising revenues that had financed the independent media, especially in the case of television.

Starting with the second year of Fujimori's second presidential term, three separate government actions influenced the mass media. The first was the management of the distribution of advertising investment by the powerful Ministry of the Presidency, the most important political and administrative arm of the regime. Between January and May 1999, the Peruvian state spent $16 million in advertising, making it the single largest advertiser in the country, followed by the beer brewers in a distant second at $6 million.

The second action was the Peruvian government's support of various sensationalist tabloids, a subsidy that was not openly acknowledged, but came to light in later investigations. These papers, packed with vulgar accusations against the opposition, were available at a low price and sold well on the newsstand. Government support of the tabloids had begun in 1997 with an eight-page supplement dedicated to the well-known journalist Manuel D'Ornellas. Attacks on other distinguished professionals followed in an avalanche of yellow journalism. The most notable case was that of the weekly *Repudio*, a one-subject paper dedicated to insulting the director of the opposition paper *La República*.

The third government action against the opposition media was a series of measures proposed by the majority party in Congress to limit freedom of expression. Members supporting the president presented several projects that would limit the ability of the media to attack the government or carry out investigative reporting. These initiatives, however, did not prosper due to an apparent lack of support from the president.

Television continued to be the most important target of government censorship. Freedom of expression on television was limited in three ways:

1. Self-censorship by media owners, including the closing and cancellation of programs directed by opposition journalists and their teams on the leading TV stations. Soft news and human-interest stories with no political content often replaced these hard-hitting stories. In 1998 five programs covered politics on television; by November 1999 only two remained. The most-respected opposition journalists, including César Hildebrandt, were fired. In an extreme case of self-censorship, at the end of 1999, in a surprise move ATV Noticias announced it would not transmit any more political advertising from any party or candidate.

2. Indirect intervention, as in the case of Channel 13 (Astros), which ended up controlled by an individual close to the government by means of a convoluted legal process. Ownership of Channel 11 passed to one of Fujimori's ministers.

3. Direct intervention through ownership of broadcasting outlets, the most dramatic case of which was Channel 2, Frecuencia Latina. In September 1997 a court decision gave control of the station to minority stockholders. The first contracts the new owners canceled were those of the journalists in charge of the newscasts and political programs. The case went to the Inter-American Court of Human Rights, but Peru withdrew its membership from the court in protest against the decision of the judges in favor of the dismissed journalists.

Journalists and owners reacted vigorously against these measures described above, and various international organizations took up their cause. Newspaper owners grouped in the National Press Council and the InterAmerican Press Association denounced the actions of the Peruvian government under Fujimori. The Institute of Press and Society, a professional association, joined in the protests against the attacks on press freedom. A high point in the international protests came in June 1998 with a visit to Lima by a delegation of representatives from the Committee to Protect Journalists, the organization Reporters without Borders, the Freedom Forum, and the Association of Journalists of Argentina. Fujimori received the delegation, telling the group that Peru enjoyed wide press freedom. The immediate effect of the visit was a temporary lessening of attacks on the opposition by the tabloid press. Soon after, however, the attacks resumed. They now included television with short spots paid for by the tabloid sensationalist press attacking presidency opposition candidates Alberto Andrade and Luis Castañeda.

The accelerated growth of the Internet in Peru, higher than what has occurred in neighboring countries, offered an important outlet for the opposition news media. Peruvian newspapers, including the sensationalist tabloids that attack the opposition paper from a Miami-based Internet site, Aprodev, however, also offered their editions over the Internet.

In July 2000, as was expected, in an internationally disputed second round of voting Fujimori was reelected president for an unprecedented third term. His "victory" depended heavily on the government's control of the electoral processes and of the mass media—only one television channel even covered the campaigning of Fujimori's opponent, Alejandro Toledo.

The new Fujimori administration met with wide-scale national and international protests, including mediation by the Organization of American States first to resolve the electoral irregularities and then to negotiate conditions with the newly elected government. A third Fujimori administration would have meant the longest-ruling president in Peruvian history.

The opposition and what remained of an independent media were vocal in their attacks on the third Fujimori administration. They supported the candidacy of Alejandro Toledo, who had refused to participate in the second round, arguing voting irregularities and no guarantee of a clean election. The independent media were the only source of information on the enormous mass demonstrations against the new administration that occurred in most major urban centers, and especially in Lima.

The independent press and the new subscription television channel "N" demonstrated the best examples of investigative journalism to be seen in recent years in the country. "N" uncovered cases of systematic fraud and corruption, especially in the judicial branch of government.

Just when a third Fujimori administration seemed inevitable, "N" produced a journalistic scoop that shocked Peruvian and world public opinion alike. "N" interrupted its regular afternoon programming two months after the disputed elections with the transmission of a videotape showing presidential adviser and head of the National Intelligence Services, Vladimiro Montesinos, handing over a thick wad of dollars to an opposition member of parliament. The money was payment for the member of parliament to leave the opposition party, to which he was recently elected, and join the government's side. With this bribe, the government would ensure its parliamentary majority.

The media played a decisive role in the dramatic events that followed the airing of the tape. The revelation precipitated a series of political scandals that resulted in Fujimori's announcement that he would step down from the presidency and call new elections within the next year in which he would not run.

In the following days of political tension, Fujimori's adviser, Montesinos, escaped to Panama, returning weeks later and setting off a bizarre manhunt by his ex-boss, the president. The rapid political upheaval impacted the media. The government-supported tabloids quickly changed their tone, and some went out of business. The national broadcast television stations that had formerly closed their doors to the opposition, now opened their news and opinion programming to a wide range of views and political parties. The two television stations that had been taken over by the government were returned to their original owners. The Peruvian media were ready to run the story when Fujimori faxed in his resignation from Japan a few weeks later.

The media placed themselves at the center of the national debate that began to open up the country. Of the thirty topics placed on the table for the "Dialogue" convened by the OAS, seventeen concerned the mass media. This revealed the depth of the distortion of the media under Fujimori and the need to make important changes in the relationship between the media and the government. One change was the need to limit the use of government-paid advertising, and another was for new mechanisms to control the use of public funding for this purpose. Yet another change was the need to establish free time and space on radio and television and in the press for all parties during campaigns. Finally, there was a need to review the existing regulations and laws concerning the media.

The communication media in their role as sources of information and opinion were both witnesses to and supporters of Peru's process of transition.

Television and the New Uruguayan State

Roque Faraone

TELEVISION in Uruguay is not yet fifty years old. Channel 10 Saeta, the first commercial station, was founded on 7 December 1956, and Channel 4 Montecarlo, the second channel, was created a little over four years later, on 23 April 1961. Channel 12 began broadcasting on 2 May 1962, followed by Channel 5 public television on 19 June 1963 (CIIDU 1986).

At the beginning, television only reached Montevideo, the capital city, and within it, as in other countries, only well-off audiences. After a decade and a half, television expanded to the other main cities in Uruguay, which is 84 percent urban. At the beginning of the 1980s, color transmission began and the number of television households grew. The number of broadcast hours also increased without any state intervention. Although the 1973–84 military dictatorship passed decree 14,677 in July 1977 to regulate television content, including advertising time, it was not enforced. Only the market and technical developments set the limits for the growth of the industry. The small size of the national market determined some characteristics of the market such as dependency on foreign products (*telenovelas*, dubbed films, news, variety shows), high advertising costs, and scarce domestic production.

A key characteristic from the outset was the absence of legal regulation. Early on, the Uruguayan state was thus virtually uninvolved vis-à-vis private broadcasting. The executive branch, through its broadcasting arm (SODRE), approved a decree that established National Television Standards Committee norms. Aside from this decision, which linked the country to the importation of receivers and other equipment from the United States, there were no other policies until the beginning of the military government in 1974. Law 8.390, approved in 1928, was still enforced. This law was passed during the origins of private radio broadcasting and established in eleven articles and fewer than four hundred words all matters that pertained to the industry. Legislators at that time surely considered broadcasting a hobby and did not foresee the commercial development that, thanks to advertising, it later had.[1] No state agency showed any interest in legislation, in setting the basis for public television, or regulating private firms.

By the early 1980s Uruguay had four channels based in Montevideo plus seventeen local channels in the interior, some of which were owned by or linked to stations in the capital that were more consolidated both industrially and economically. The three channels in Montevideo developed a cartel policy in order to avoid competition about matters such as advertising rates, the purchase of foreign programming, and the broadcast of national news.[2]

Unlike Brazil, Uruguay lacked a coherent and systematic policy. The former had a developed electronics industry supported for two decades by the military government, and a private network closely linked to the state. The Uruguayan military dictatorship passed Law 14.235 that was validated in 1985, the main goal of which was to separate the administration of electricity from communications, which were unified in one company (Usinas y Teléfonos del Estado). This law created the National Administration of Telecommunications (ANTELCO), which, among other functions, was assigned to "administer, defend and control the National Radioelectric Spectrum [and] the technical and operative supervision of radiolectric transmissions" but was not given the power to authorize the installation and functioning of broadcasting stations. The executive retained this power with ANTELCO in a consulting role.

The centralization of power in communications was in contrast with the existence of at least one military official in each one of the public services (in addition to civilian officials appointed by the military government), even in public education. The difference was that the government was not interested, on the grounds that it was a strategic matter, in delegating the power it had to authorize the use of broadcasting. This was also expressed in the decision of the military government in November 1984, at a time when the transition to a civilian government had already been negotiated, to move the Dirección Nacional de Comunicaciones from ANTELCO to the Ministry of Defense. This office was key in the control of television broadcasts. When the military appointed ANTELCO administrators, it was not important where the Dirección was located. But given that the future civilian government would name ANTELCO officials, the military believed that this role had to remain in their hands.

Television in Democracy: Relations with Other Social Powers

A civilian government was elected in March 1985 after a peaceful nego-tiation with the military, which realized that its time in power was over amidst an unfavorable international climate. This "Uruguayan solu-tion" put many limitations on the actions of the new (and subsequent) civilian administrations. Although all remaining political prisoners were freed, most of the decisions taken during the twelve-year military gov-ernment were not changed. The extent of political freedom was some-what less than that which characterized Uruguayan society between the 1920s and 1960s. The fact that the military appropriated the Dirección Nacional de Comunicaciones had not only institutional but also sym-bolic value. Media owners who had temporary permits understood this decision perfectly well in terms of being careful about the content of future broadcasts.

In 1985, three months after the civilian government took power, the Senate unanimously passed a law that returned ANTELCO to Dirección Nacional de Comunicaciones.[3] Despite opposition from the executive during the debate in the House of Representatives, the majority in the latter approved the Senate's text on 3 November 1986. Two weeks later, the executive vetoed the law. Only 54 votes against 39, less than the three-fifths needed to override the veto, were cast at the General Assembly (the meeting of both chambers).[4] At that moment, the two traditional political parties (the Colorado and the Nacional) controlled 80 percent of the votes and representation in Congress. The process unequivocally re-vealed military pressures to change the location of ANTELCO as well as weak civilian opposition.

Under the civilian government, television improved technically, broadcasting more hours, over a wider reach, to bigger audiences. In terms of political information, television featured more interviews with politicians, members of government agencies, and military command-ers that reproduced official messages, but it did not search for controver-sial and critical information. Uruguayan television basically serves as a mouthpiece of power rooted in habits developed during the dictatorship and in fears of the military presence. The press, for its part, suffered a deep economic crisis, intensified by the impoverishment of the middle class. Whereas newspaper circulation during the 1950s and 1960s reached 500,000 copies daily, it was less than 100,000 during 1985–95, numbers that are more striking considering that population growth was at 10 percent during that period.[5]

The elitist function of the press, in turn, increased the weight of television as a mass medium, turning it into a power in its own right in contemporary Uruguay. In addition to the political power of the state and the politico-military power of the armed forces (at least in some issues), television holds almost omnipotent sway in ideological matters. The crisis of the press also made difficult the emergence of an opposition press. Therefore, the information environment, dominated by television, has been poor.

The military dictatorship's legacy includes the thousands of disappeared for which many officers were called to court. An amnesty law, which resulted from a political agreement in extremis, released them from any responsibility. Military pressure was so strong (or civil opposition so weak) that the decision was not even called "amnesty" (implying that crimes had been committed). It was called "caducidad de la pretensión punitiva del Estado" (expiration of the state's intention to punish). A popular referendum rejected this law in 1987. During the campaign for the referendum, in which the stability of the state was at stake, television restricted information about the opposition to the law even though there was no formal censorship.[6]

Since 1985 Uruguayan television increased the amount of "debate" programming, much like in other countries. The subjects of these shows were diverse, but the armed forces were never, directly or indirectly, discussed. National defense, pension privileges for officers and their families, the excessive number of personnel, the disappeared—none of these issues related to the military were ever debated.

Uruguay has a long electoral tradition. Since 1925, elections were held peacefully and without significant fraud due to Uruguay's legislation and systematic practice. Other reasons were also important in its tradition of being "the Switzerland of America," despite some interruptions—the most dramatic between 1973 and 1984. In a country with a secular, bipartisan tradition, the political parties are structured around mechanisms to capture votes. Partially due to ideological blurring, the parties became fragmented but, at the same time, kept an apparent unity that was favored by protective legislation.

In the face of partisan fragmentation, television responded pragmatically and followed clear lines. It offered spontaneous support for existing powers (government, obviously, and the leaders of the other traditional party) and opportunities to many middle-rank leaders, most from a leftist, third force that got a third of the vote. The leaders of the third force have access to television if they are moderate (the logic of social control) or colorful or scandalous (the logic of market audience), which serves television's intention to present the appearance of pluralism.

The Senate considered a proposal to assign free broadcasting access to all political parties in Congress and to limit the time for election advertising (forty days before primaries and fifty days before national elections). At the time when interparty negotiations on the proposal were progressing toward agreement, members of the ANDEBU (Asociación Nacional de Broadcastings Uruguayos), which represents radio and television owners, opposed it arguing that it was unconstitutional. They labeled the proposal "an intrusion in the power [of the ANDEBU] to organize and decide programming and space."[7] The association proposed "to substitute legal mechanisms for a legal compromise of those who represent the allocation of time for political parties in the broadcasting media." Furthermore, ANDEBU proposed the creation of a commission with party representatives who accept airtime according to this compromise and ANDEBU to fine-tune details for implementation.

A senator from the National Party in government and, later, a senator from the opposition Frente Amplio indicated, in a careful manner, that the mission of the Senate is to legislate rather than to encourage agreements or contracts between licensees and parties. Another senator added (also in a careful tone, to counter the argument that ANDEBU offered more time than the law stipulated) that an agreement or contract was necessarily temporary whereas legislation was permanent.[8] The National Party officially accepted ANDEBU's offer and the Colorado senators also agreed to withdraw their objections to the proposal. In summary, the Senate did not legislate on the free use of private broadcasting but only passed laws for the official station and limited election television advertising to fifty days. Records of the meetings between representatives of private stations and the Senate patently show the dependence of political power on the power of television.

State-owned Channel 5 captured 3–5 percent of the audience.[9] It is a very modest station, with minimal investments from limited state budgets plus some advertising.[10] For a long time it was not authorized to air commercials, and when it attempted to, it confronted strong opposition from the private stations represented by ANDEBU, the powerful association that defends corporate interests and also plays a political role.[11] The three private stations also developed commercial and industrial cartel-like ties in regard to national news, the purchase of telenovelas and other programs, and even for broadcasting (García Rubio 1994).

Every time the state intended to develop the official station, the private stations waged a public offensive to oppose it. This happened in 1967, 1985, and 1991. Private companies won all three battles between private and public television. The first of these battles resulted in the resignation of the board of directors of SODRE chaired by Irene Ramírez de Aguirre Roselló. The new members ousted Channel 5 director Justino Zavala Carvalho.[12] In 1985, the newly established civil administration of Julio María Sanguinetti appointed Carlos Maggi as director of Channel 5. Maggi invited several journalists to work in the official station, which prompted ANDEBU to accuse him of offering state propaganda, not information. ANDEBU's opposition, which had the support of the minister of culture, Dr. Adela Reta, brought about Maggi's resignation (*Búsqueda* 1990, 38–39; Faraone 1989). The government of the other traditional party tried to develop public television in 1991, but private television resisted. Juan Martín Posadas, who headed the SODRE, resigned because the government caved in to the power of the owners of private television.[13]

Relations between Political Power and Television

The relations between political power and television have been generally harmonious, although there have been moments of conflict that were easily solved, probably owing to contacts that never became public. The government does not intervene at all in the main business of broadcasting, that is, advertising. Limitations established by the 1977 law, passed by the military government, on advertising and on other aspects of programming such as language and percentage of national production go largely unenforced. Nor is the content of programming regulated. Typically, in the aftermath of a spectacular crime, for example, some representatives will address the subject and other media (press and radio) will chime in regarding media violence, but neither Congress nor the executive act.

An instance of this was a 1988 executive decree that established specific airtime for "children protection." This decree stated that "television stations have occasionally aired programs unsuitable for minors" and stipulated that any taped shows that were not news, political, sport, or advertising that were to be broadcast earlier than 9:30 P.M. had to be submitted to INAME (an official institution that deals with children's issues) to be approved.[14] This decree was doubly unconstitutional. First, the Constitution bans prior restraint, or censorship, and only authorizes the law to determine "abuses that were committed" in the exercise of freedom of communication. Second, the executive power cannot transfer a role to a subordinate agency. Also, the INAME, in charge of applying the decree, went beyond its mandate. Among other decisions, it created two "child protection" slots, defined pornography and violence, and so on. TV stations did not react, however, and the decree has not been applied. In a session of the Commission of Education and Culture in Congress, an INAME official declared that his agency lacks the means to monitor broadcasts.[15]

This example shows that when politicians need, for demagogical reasons, to appear to be doing something against violence or pornography on television, the stations understand and tolerate because, probably, their business is not at risk. The caption that reads "children's protection time" is shown daily (although it has no effect), and thus it benefits both the government and the private stations: the mass public believes that someone is doing something.

By contrast, when the executive proposed a law to regulate tobacco advertising that was signed by nine ministers and the president, television companies, together with all affiliate stations and the main newspapers, vigorously campaigned against it. The latter succeeded as the ruling government coalition, strongly supported by the opposition, removed most of the restrictions; and the proposal, even in such a diluted form, received approval only from the Senate.[16]

The political and television powers maintain relations as associates. Private television seems to say, "As long as you don't harm my business, you will receive coverage." The political power seems to say, "As long as you support power, you will be treated well." Both seem to say to the military: "You will not be touched."

This "marriage of convenience," which in some aspects is almost a ménage à trois, severely limits freedom of information. Four episodes, among others, illustrate the pressures that the political power puts on television news. First, television stations remained silent when former president Luis Alberto Lacalle was called to testify in a corruption trial of one of his collaborators.[17] Second, television host Jorge Arellano was ousted after a newscast showed police brutality against demonstrators (*Brecha* 1993). Third, police repression was excessive when three Basque citizens were extradited. Television filmed and broadcast the events that same night, but suddenly the subject was hushed up because it did not fit the government's thesis of an insurrection.[18] Fourth, Channel 4 journalist Guillermo Lussich was penalized for having inserted a businessman's criticism of official policies following clips of a high official praising economic policies.[19]

This last episode prompted CNN host Jorge Gestoso to send two public letters. In the first one, he denounced Channel 4 in Montevideo, not CNN, for censoring an interview with President Julio María Sanguinetti. Channel 4 was forced to rebroadcast the segment in its entirety the following day. Gestoso also said that a question put to Sanguinetti by the interviewer as to whether pressure on the press would be repeated during Sanguinetti's second term was censored.[20] In the second letter, Gestoso, who is Uruguayan but works in Atlanta, Georgia, says: "Let's take a minute of our time to think what happened that, as a nation, we allowed the monopoly of information in Uruguayan television not in the hands of public opinion, of the people. It is in the service of interest groups, pressure groups, opinion groups."[21] These letters were made public by the weekly *Brecha* but were not reproduced by any other media, and television stations ignored them.

Cable Television, an Appendix to Over-the-Air Television

At the beginning of the 1990s, the expansion of over-the-air television was almost complete. About 98 percent of the households had a television set in a highly urbanized country that has a network with national coverage. Only a few rural areas lacked television broadcasts. Meanwhile, the sale and use of videos expanded. The fact that movies broadcast on television featured many commercials contributed to that expansion. The consequence was that the three commercial stations in Montevideo promoted pay television and the government auctioned licenses.

Eleven companies made bids for the licenses. Five of them were linked to over-the-air television stations through a consortium formed by private channels. Three of them, owned directly by Channels 4, 10, and 12, gained authorization for laying cable and broadcasting. A fourth company that belongs to the consortium that offered MMDS also received a license. Finally, only one company that does not belong to that monopoly got authorization for UHF broadcasts. The first three firms can air 22 programs, the fourth 15, and the last 16.

Because there were other interests that vied to enter the cable business, there were criticisms in Congress and a campaign by the only opposition newspaper. The licenses were assigned by an executive decree on 11 November 1994, which stated that although all bidders met the requirements, "it was inadequate to authorize all eleven bidders because it would undermine the economic viability of all of them. It is reasonable to limit the number of licenses to five to allow healthy competition."

The outcome confirms what was said earlier about the tacit association between the political and television powers. Uruguayan television in the mid-1990s has been described as being in "an oligopoly situation as a reduced number of companies dominate the market. It would be possible even to talk about a monopoly given the actions that the three big groups carry out together. It is clear that there is no free competition in the national television market" (García Rubio 1994).

The existing parliamentary debate with its repercussions in the press needs to be understood within the limits given by the structure of the news media in Uruguay. The three private channels have a tremendous influence on public opinion, reinforced by the most influential daily newspaper, which belongs to one of the stations. This explains why the public debate was absent, except for opposition publications that have limited circulation.

Responses by the political parties to these problems were diverse. The parties in the government coalition (Nacional and Colorado) kept silence, as did El Nuevo Espacio, a growing small party that could take votes away from the opposition. The latter received strong support from television in the 1994 elections, support that was beyond its financial means. The opposition Frente Amplio, which does not own any newspaper, denounced cable concessions in Congress. A few months later during the election campaign, it was confronted with the application for cable services submitted by the companies that controlled television in the city of Montevideo. The authorization for cable services required a study. But an agreement was apparently reached: the Montevideo City Hall leaders (opposed to the national government) quickly authorized the private companies to lay cables, without consulting with any monitoring institution, and in return, they received lower rates for television advertising. After the election, won by the Frente Amplio, the city canceled the decision and struck a new agreement in which cable licenses were exchanged for a free cable channel granted to the local government. This channel was free of advertising and aired for eight hours a day.

Television News

There are no legal norms regarding television news in Uruguay.[22] Agreements among the three private channels determine that the most important newscasts (at the end of the day) start at 7:00 P.M. Monday through Friday. Newscasts last for an hour and fifteen minutes and are continuously interrupted by commercials. They feature international and national (mostly metropolitan or government) news, interviews with political leaders and clips of party meetings, crime, catastrophes, economic and financial, and sports (mostly soccer). Out of 75 minutes, 25 are advertising, 25 are sports (national and foreign), and only 25 are devoted to *substantial* information (economic production, trade, government regulation, and power, plus accidents and crime, which range from five to seven minutes).

Reporters cover crime news on the spot and interview neighbors or victims. Quick, subjective testimonies are presented as evidence that the audience is being informed (and being protected from crime). In this way, television stations achieve high credibility at a low cost: audiences feel informed and protected, while, at the same time, relevant information is virtually absent. As Bourdieu says, when such expensive space and time is devoted to trivial subjects, it is because those making programming decisions do not want the time and space to be used for more important issues.

Interestingly, the official government channel, which lacks sufficient means, cannot send reporters and offer coverage like the private channels. Consequently, its newscast, which features little advertising, is better overall than the news on private stations. In regard to international news, all stations had fewer resources than their counterparts in other countries; thus, they frequently rebroadcast clips from Spanish television and CNN. There is little work done locally, and the dependence on foreign news sources is absolute.

Conclusion

Privately owned television dominates the airwaves in Uruguay: it captures over 95 percent of the audience and attracts the lion's share of advertising. This allows the stations to make more technical investments, to purchase popular shows, and to have the kind of diverse programming that, in turn, contributes to larger audiences.

The absence (or deterioration) of the idea of public service explains why public television has been ignored in Uruguay. The state considered that television needed to be in the hands of profit-oriented entrepreneurs and that the market should regulate content, time, and advertising. Consequently, Uruguayan public television needs the help of foreign governments and other cultural, film, and television institutions (mostly from European countries) to get donations and loans of materials.

From a social control perspective, it is likely that private television has more ideological effects (in the sense of shaping or influencing ideas, values, beliefs, and stereotypes) than in other societies due to the reduced influence of the press, the small size of the society, and the cartelization of the stations. This is why television decisively contributes to the political power of the ruling social forces.

Most political leaders need frequent, individual appearances on television. This further atomizes the political forces as personal features and charisma become more prominent. Simultaneously, the power of television is overtaking that of political leaders. The role of the political parties continues to change: they need physically attractive leaders and images and slogans instead of ideas and programs. There is also a growth of spectacular programming, particularly sports and low-cost, foreign serials. Oligopoly and concentration characterize both broadcast and cable television and the media at large. The facade of pluralism and controversy is usually present, but the manipulation and the support of the status quo are ubiquitous, permanent, and spontaneous.

Notes

1. Some violations, for example, only received mild punishment (fines of about $50).

2. RUTSA, created in 1981, and Coloso S.A. are evidence of this policy (see García Rubio 1994).

3. *Brecha*, 7 November 1986.

4. *Brecha*, 28 November 1986, 4. *Búsqueda* mistakenly stated that "the General Assembly approve the veto" but offered the correct number of votes. 27 November 1986, 10.

5. Daily newspapers cost $1.50 (double the price in Madrid, New York, or Paris), and wages are three to five times lower than in those cities.

6. Senator Carlos Julio Pereyra, a moderate leader of one traditional party, denounced television ads aired in the interior for manipulating public opinion by linking his group to communists and tupamaros (the guerrilla movement of the 1960s and 1970s) with the intention of blackmailing those who voted to scrap the law. SERPAJ (Service for Peace and Justice) could not place *paid advertising* about the disappeared because the three private channels rejected it.

7. Senate, number 2299/98, 21 October 1998, 5.

8. Senate, number 2231, 2244, 2288, 2309; and Acts 57th session, 4 November 1998.

9. SODRE vice president Claudio Rama's declarations to the Commission of Education and Culture, Chamber of Representatives, 18 November 1996.

10. The 1964 budget law states that state commercial and industrial agencies must allocate 20 percent of their advertising to the official station, but this is not observed (Chamber of Representatives).

11. In 1998 ANDEBU, which links all affiliate radio stations in a private network, offered the president a five-minute weekly slot that is not offered to the leader of the opposition.

12. See Report of Vice-Secretary of Public Instruction, Dr. Fernando Oliú, and speech by Senator Luis Hierro Gambardella in the Senate, 16 August 1967.

13. *Búsqueda,* 12 November, 17 November 1991; and *La República,* 25 October, 28 November 1991.

14. Decree 445/88, 5 July 1988.

15. Julio Saettone, Chamber of Representatives, number 395, 24.

16. Senate, number 1292, April 1997.

17. *Búsqueda,* 16 November 1995.

18. *Búsqueda,* 11 November 1997.

19. See "Declaration of the Association of the Uruguayan Press against Political Pressures on Information." *Búsqueda,* 18 December 1997.

20. *Brecha,* 12 December 1997.

21. *Brecha,* 12 December 1997.

22. The European Union established that no half-hour newscast could be interrupted with commercials in any country members.

CHAPTER TWELVE

Venezuela and the Media

The New Paradigm

José Antonio Mayobre

OVER THE past two decades Venezuela has witnessed radical changes in its political, media, and broadcasting landscape. During this period a country with one of the most solid and stable formal democratic structures in Latin America lived on a political roller coaster. The ride included two attempted military coups d'état, the constitutional impeachment of an elected president who had been reelected to a second term after having been declared politically almost untouchable, and his trial, sentencing, and removal by the Supreme Court after being found guilty of corruption.

An interim government, appointed by Congress as mandated by the Constitution, followed the impeachment and removal from office of the president. Another former president, the oldest ever to be elected, followed the interim government. As the twentieth century came to an end, the caudillo who had led the first of the coup attempts in the 1990s came to power in a democratic election, signaling the almost total disappearance of Venezuela's two traditional national political parties.[1]

More specifically, with the election of Rafael Caldera in 1993 Venezuela seemed to have moved beyond surprises and was seen as ready to regain a slower, more stable pace (Mayobre 1996). The calm before the second Pérez administration, however, could not be recaptured so easily. Over the five years of the Caldera presidency the economic and political climates rapidly deteriorated. Oil prices sank to new lows, unemployment crept up, accusations of corruption piled up, not just against the government but also against the political parties and "the system" in general.

The media, in particular broadcast media, frequently and virulently denounced the faults and sins of politicians and the last forty years of democratic administrations, although not with the same degree of intensity as they had during the last years of the Carlos Andrés Pérez administration (Mayobre 1996).

The politicians and parties themselves seemed bent on self-destruction. In a lemminglike march, the level of public in-fighting and flurry of attacks by and within rival politicians and parties reached a degree never before seen in the country. Politicians and the media seemed unaware of the damage they were inflicting on the democratic system and its institutions.

Early in his administration, President Caldera, in what at the time appeared to some to be a brilliant political move, pardoned Lt. Col. Hugo Chávez, head of the 4 February 1992 attempted coup against Carlos Andrés Pérez, and had him set free. By then Chávez had become a public figure, receiving a steady stream of prominent opposition visitors and journalists in his cell in the grim prison of Yare. Some political analysts and media pundits believed that taking away Chávez's aura of martyrdom and setting him free to go into the streets to preach his homespun mix of populism and "bolivarianism" would finish him off in what seemed by now to have become a politically sophisticated nation.

To the surprise of most, after a few false starts, the Chávez movement and candidacy caught fire and started to develop and grow. Meanwhile, polls and pollsters kept reassuring the traditional political class that a movement of this sort could never really catch on in Venezuela.

Two phenomena need further study in the Venezuelan political context: (1) the outrageous mistakes in the pollsters' projections measuring Chávez's popularity, and (2) the changes that occurred in Chávez's image and communication strategies over the early years of his rise.

In 1998 the country elected Chávez president by a large plurality. In doing this, the electorate brought in what appeared to be a completely new and politically unknown leadership. Soon after, a majority voted to discard the 1961 Constitution, considered by some to be an almost flawless juridical model, and to elect a National Constituent Assembly charged with radically changing the country's institutional framework.

In July 1998 the election for members of the National Constituent Assembly gave Chávez an even more notable triumph. Of the 131 posts in the Assembly, 127 were known Chávez backers and only 4 could be called opposition.

Several possible analyses can be made as to how this could occur. One is that the opposition, reeling like a punch-drunk boxer, was never able to recover and react to the flurry of Chávez's actions and activities after the beginning of the match.

The new president's use of the media (he created his own newspaper and weekly "town hall" radio and television programs) was pervasive. The president also developed a series of highly symbolic visual elements such as the "People's Balcony" in the Miraflores Presidential Palace, held a large number of military parades, and made widespread use of military uniforms (including parachutist camouflage versions). These public displays were reminiscent of previous Latin American populist regimes such as that of Juan Domingo Perón's in Argentina.

By mid-1999, the new caudillo appeared to have concentrated all political power in his hands. During this time intellectuals and the Venezuelan upper and middle classes, a reduced and increasingly hard-hit minority economically, hemmed and hawed and gossiped and criticized Chávez for his discourse, looks, or even some of his ideas. Chávez soon let everyone know—for example, in his speech installing the new Assembly—that he could be magnanimous if people behaved. Chávez assured the crowd that he was a democrat, but an undercurrent of menace made it sound more like an offer that few Venezuelans could really afford to refuse.

Chávez's presidency easily and clearly divided the country into those who were for him—patriots and Bolivarians—and those who were not—corrupt and guilty of not being patriots. It was clear that if necessary, but only if he were forced, he would not abide the latter.

The Media

At this stage it is still difficult to understand the position of the media in the early 1990s. Venezuela had gone from a limited but increasingly powerful small group of media owners, especially in television (Mayobre 1993), to a wide range of outlets. These newer media seemed to turn into paper tigers under the onslaught of the emerging populist movement.

According to media researcher Prof. Gustavo Hernández Díaz,[2] during the last year of the Jaime Lusinchi presidency (Social Democrat, 1983–88), the dam gates opened and a flood of new media concessions were granted, basically to politicians or entrepreneurs friendly to the regime. Until close to the end of the Lusinchi administration, there had been little change in the radio and television broadcast situation in Venezuela. At this time Venezuela had four licensed VHF national television networks, of which two were private (Radio Caracas Televisión and Venevisión) and two government owned (Televisora Nacional and Venezolana de Televisión), and 158 AM radio stations—157 private and 1 government owned.

Starting around 1987, however, the Ministry of Communications began to allow FM broadcasting and the expansion of television into the UHF band. The government also gave permits to various forms of satellite and cable reception and transmission. By law, the reception and distribution of satellite signals had been a government monopoly controlled by the state-owned telephone company, CANTV. Slowly, however, the major private television networks and then the new license holders were allowed to receive their own signals via satellite.

Little serious research exists as to how and why the opening up of satellite transmission and reception happened in such an abrupt manner. Some information is available from interviews and informal conversations with former government officials of Lusinchi's, Pérez's, and Caldera's (second) administrations. There is little tangible evidence or documentation to support any of the possible hypotheses, however, and much remains guesswork and educated speculation.

At the time the opening of satellite transmissions occurred, CANTV had become a center of excellence. Its training and research center, in fact, had become a model for Latin America, with the assistance of the International Telecommunications Union. According to the Herrera authorities (notably CANTV chairman Nerio Neri), however, the company also had become a nest of subversive young engineers coming in from the cold after having been involved in the national guerrilla and subversive movements of the late 1960s and 1970s.

There was no doubt that a group of brilliant and highly qualified engineers and technicians (the Ayacuchos) were working within CANTV. Chairman Neri had no compunction in firing or downgrading all of them because of their political attitudes and affiliations. The end result was the promotion of new, less skilled or experienced technical staff. Their selection was to a great extent based on party affiliation rather than knowledge and skill, a fact that helped reduce the political tension within the large telephone monopoly but contributed little to its reputation for quality and expertise.

At the time, CANTV not only held the monopoly on Venezuelan telephone services but also controlled access to all satellite communication. The latter gave CANTV great leverage over the television broadcasters.

The CANTV firings weakened and disorganized the company. The process that followed, leading to CANTV's eventual privatization, was a result of the continuing decay and disrepair of its services, including the provision of satellite services, which provided a major argument for private sector investors looking for a bargain.

For various reasons, the earlier Luis Herrera Campins administration (1979–83) had ended its mandate embroiled in a nasty fight with the broadcast media. One of the main factors contributing to this confrontation was the official ban on liquor and cigarette advertising on radio and television. Another were the attempts by Alejandro Alfonzo, then director of the Department of Planning and Budget of the Ministry of Information, to set in motion a national communication policy within the framework of the national five-year plan.

Alfonzo left the planning office amid pressures on the government and soon after was appointed chairman of Venezolana de Televisión, the major government-owned TV network. From this position, he clashed with the two major private TV networks regarding their attempts to use the satellite facilities of the state in a questionable manner.

As elections approached, President Herrera finally capitulated to the demands of the private media, and Alfonzo was sacrificed on the altar of realpolitik. Despite this sacrifice, the Christian Democratic candidate lost. For many years to come, however, former president Herrera continued to be banned from the screen of at least one of the major networks.

Lusinchi, a charming pediatrician, rode the popular crest of protest against Herrera to become the president elected with the highest electoral majority ever recorded in Venezuela. Although Lusinchi filled the post of minister of information, his relations with the media basically were dictated through his private secretary, mistress, and later wife, Blanca Ibáñez, a former radio announcer and self-appointed communication expert. During this period there is no doubt that frequent direct and indirect pressures were put on the broadcast media to tow an invisible, nondeclared line of behavior. Most although not all of the media did so gladly or at least with some alacrity.

The broadcast media, both radio and television, felt protected by the 1939 Communications Law. Through various means, this law restricted the award of new broadcast licenses, thereby keeping a virtual monopoly in the nation for those few broadcasters who already were lucky enough to be on the air. By the end of his administration Lusinchi had publicly broken with the media, both in person and on camera. Members of the media, sensing blood, were becoming more aggressive and muckraking in their relations with the government and with the president himself.

The Lusinchi administration set in motion the process of liberalization in the broadcasting industry. As Gustavo Hernández shows, it awarded fifty-two new FM licenses. Until then only four FM commercial stations had been licensed, along with one cultural and one government-owned station. By then there were slightly more than 120 AM stations in the country, all but one privately owned. The Lusinchi administration also granted seven television licenses in the interior and one in Caracas to Televen–Channel 10 in 1988. A decade later, there was one public and eighteen private television stations. In the context of a lack of coherent and organized media policies, public television continued to experience economic troubles. The mission of public television remained undefined, and the medium was subject to continuous government pressures to favor partisan interests (Colina 1996).

As a consequence of liberalization, new industrial groups entered the media sector, including oil and mining interests. A brief analysis of the list of licensees that benefited by Lusinchi's opening of the radio frequency spectrum shows that most of the awards went either to members of his party or to other political cronies, in some cases funneled through third parties, including awards to his private secretary and future wife (Zerpa 1998).

Former president Carlos Andrés Pérez was reelected and followed President Lusinchi. Pérez, though a member of the same party as Lusinchi, was seen as an enemy by the outgoing administration. Pérez attempted to mix his brand of populism and his charisma with neoliberal dogma and a certain amount of pomp and circumstance. A large number of heads of state attended his inauguration, popularly referred to as "the Coronation." Rather early in his term, however, Pérez ran into trouble. In February 1989, barely months after taking office, Pérez faced what were possibly the largest protest riots in Venezuelan history over a half century.

The army and police brutally repressed the riots. The number of dead and disappeared continues to be unknown to this day. Perhaps more importantly, the brutality of the repression sowed the seeds of discontent among the young officers who were charged with carrying out the government's orders. The fruits would become apparent in the not too distant future.

Pérez had an aloof and sometimes conflictive relation with the broadcast media, but he knew how to play the game. Immediately after the election, his first formal visits, widely covered in the press, were to the two major television channels, Radio Caracas (Channel 2) and Venevisión (Channel 4). While Pérez's relation with Channel 2 appeared to have worsened over time, his friendship with the Cisneros brothers, owners of Channel 4 Venevisión, seemed to grow closer over the years.

During the 1990 attempted coup President Pérez's first act was to flee to the safety of the Venevisión studios. This was a strategic move that allowed him to go on the air nationally and show that he was still alive and in command while the putschists were claiming his death or disappearance. Pérez did not much change the radio or television spectrum from where Lusinchi had left it at the end of his administration. Sheer inertia on the part of the state, however, allowed the media to continue to grow.

Globalization and the Venezuelan Media

With perhaps one exception, globalization of the media appears to have bypassed Venezuela altogether. The exception, of course, is Grupo Cisneros, which apparently decided to restructure its operations in Venezuela around its international communications operations. In the 1990s, the group sold off interests in a number of industries (including automobile, publishing, real estate, food, retail goods, and music) and decided to focus on television businesses such as programming production and export, station ownership (in Chile, Colombia, and the United States), satellite television, and video (Cañizales 1997). It also controls interests in cellular telephony and Internet portals. In 2000, Grupo Cisneros decided to move its headquarters to South Florida to oversee its activity in forty countries and 37,000 employees. According to 1997 reports, its revenue topped $3.7 billion. Grupo Phelps, the other major communications company, remains in control of recording, food, and media interests. Together with Televen, Cisneros and Phelps receive 70 percent of total television advertising revenues, for an estimated 80 percent of total advertising in the media (Hernández Díaz 1993).

While other media operations have based themselves in Venezuela, this appears simply to be the result of a strategic business decision and not a policy to either use or strengthen the Venezuelan communications infrastructure. Since operational costs in the country are favorable and there is enough professional expertise, particularly young professionals, operators such as HBO and Sony have established offices in Caracas but appear to be working without any particular relations to local media. Overall, in the past years it is possible to detect a significant lowering of quality both of programming and of technical broadcasting in all of the local media, including the two major networks: Radio Caracas and Venevisión.

The Media and Foreign Investment

As far as can be detected, and not counting Grupo Cisneros as "foreign capital," there seems to be no foreign investment at present in the Venezuelan media. Some gambling groups from the United States appear to have attempted to buy into regional stations to promote lotteries, but there is no hard evidence on whether they have succeeded or not. There also were strong rumors regarding the possibility of Colombian venture capitalists investing in the Radio Caracas (Phelps) Group, but here too no hard evidence exists.

The Catholic Church is a strong television presence in Venezuela, owning and operating TV channels such as Amavisión, Televisora Andina de Mérida, and Niños Cantores Television, all based in the provinces, and more recently Vale TV. This last operates in the frequency of Channel 5, formerly reserved for the government. Former president Caldera assigned Channel 5 to the Caracas Dioceses in a rather sudden and perhaps even illegal manner shortly before the end of his administration. His decision bypassed Article 1 of the 1940 Telecommunications Law according to which the state, not the president unilaterally, decides communications matters. A local group, the Committee for Public Service Radio and Television, publicly protested the assignment of Channel 5 to the Church and the manner in which it was done, but to no effect. Vale TV is run by Venevision government employees and receives some backing from Radio Caracas. Channel 5 broadcasts the educational and documentary programs that the commercial stations consider to have no ratings possibilities, but which they are forced to buy as part of their programming packages. In radio, particularly in the provinces, the evangelical churches have made some inroads. This phenomenon still appears to be small in terms of audiences and transmission power.

The Media and Political Power

Without doubt, prior to the Caldera government the broadcast media, in particular Radio Caracas and Venevision in the television field, were very influential media. Radio, on the other hand, traditionally had been less influential nationally but a growing power at the regional level. At least two state governors and several senators and representatives were elected to their posts on the strength of their popularity as hosts of influential radio shows in their regions.

The power of the media appears to have changed with the Chávez administration. With one exception—the owner of a regional radio station elected as an independent—no member of the National Constituent Assembly seems to be directly linked to any media.

During the past elections, all media adopted anti-Chávez positions. To greater or lesser degree, all major broadcast media were against Chávez's candidacy until the very last moment, giving abundant space to the final opposition candidate, Henrique Salas Romer, and to opinion poll results that proved to be quite mistaken. Since the elections, the media have taken a low profile. They seldom refer to the government and voice few opposing views in their political commentary shows and newscasts. Overall the media are much less aggressive or even active in local politics when compared to their role during previous administrations.

It is no exaggeration to state that the media, as well as most of the members of the traditional established political parties and organizations, were in denial regarding the possibility of a victory by Chávez. When the "unthinkable" happened they went into shock, a shock from which they have been slow to recover. On the other hand, the new president proved to be a wily communicator and user of the media. Chávez's constant appearances on television—whether on his own programs (Con el Presidente and Adelante con El Presidente) or through his frequent use of national network chains (where all television and radio stations must link to a central program generated by the Central Office of Information (OCI) to broadcast presidential speeches, military parades, or other "official" ceremonies—have the private broadcasters reeling.

Chávez's domination of the airwaves, while potentially damaging to democracy, has not resulted in any backlash on the part of the public. Even among those who oppose Chávez, the general feeling is that the broadcast media are one of the main parties guilty of bringing about the arrival of the Chávez regime. Over the past years (during the Pérez and Caldera regimes) radio and television in Venezuela, in particular the latter, had dropped any pretensions of quality or of a minimal sense of social responsibility.

The new Venezuelan Constitution, ratified in December 1999 by an overwhelming margin, contains an amendment guaranteeing the public's "right to timely, truthful, and impartial information."[3] The Venezuelan media are concerned that this "right" could be used as justification to censor critical stories. Venezuelan journalists have a long history of opposition to such an amendment. In 1992 they successfully blocked an effort by former president Rafael Caldera to include it in the amended constitution that he proposed.

The CPJ (see http://www.cpj.org/attacks99/americas99/Venezuela.html) documented two of Chávez's efforts to pass the new constitution and his criticism of the press.

First, speaking on his radio program on 28 November 1998, Chávez accused the publisher of the leading national daily *El Universal*, Andrés Mata, of orchestrating a campaign "against the approval of the constitution, against the Bolivarian revolution, against the majority of Venezuelans, against social justice and progress." Subsequently, Chávez proceeded to attack the Bloque de Armas, the publishing company that owns *El Universal*, along with 2001, Meridiano, and Meridiano Televisión. Also on 28 November, *El Universal* quoted the president of the Coro-based religious station Radio Guadalupana, who is also archbishop of Coro, as saying that it was dangerous to give Chávez so much power. The next day, two members of the Department of Military Intelligence (DIM) visited the station and asked a technician to clarify the president's statement.

Second, on 30 November Radio Guadalupana received intimidating phone calls while an announcer was reading a Venezuelan Episcopal Conference document that called on the population to vote "responsibly" on 15 December. Someone who identified himself as a DIM member ordered the presenter to stop reading the document (the order was not heeded).

According to the Committee to Protect Journalists, Chávez has displayed an equally thin skin with regard to international news coverage of his presidency. In August, Chávez had used his radio program to accuse the *New York Times* of publishing "gigantic lies" in a 21 August editorial that called him a "potentate" who sought to concentrate power in the presidency.

Clearly there was a new paradigm in the relations between media and politics in Venezuela. Continually buoyed by high oil prices, Chávez's history with the Venezuelan and world media is not finished. Several more chapters will be written in the years to come. (José Antonio Mayobre died on 17 December 2000 soon after revising this chapter.)

Notes

1. The two main "traditional" parties are Acción Democratica (AD), a social democratic party, and COPEI, a Christian democratic party. In the beginning of the 1960s, the two parties had cooperated in creating the nation's present democratic structure and institutions, includ-

ing the Constitution, and since then had alternated in governing the country and guiding it through oil "booms" and crisis. AD was founded in the 1930s and COPEI in the 1940s. Another "traditional" party, URD, also social democratic, virtually disappeared in the 1970s, and the oldest national party, the Communist Party (PCV), had become increasingly irrelevant after undergoing several divisions affiliating with a disastrous guerrilla effort. Paradoxically, the major and most influential new political leaders in the country, Chávez and his contingent, are previous leaders of either the PCV, the URD, or both.

2. Hernández is head of the Institute for Communication Research (ININCO) of the Universidad Central de Venezuela and head of its long-term broadcast media research project.

3. The new constitution also extends the presidential term from five to six years, allows the president to run for a second term, abolishes the Senate, gives additional powers to the military, and changes the official name of the country to the Bolivarian Republic of Venezuela.

REFERENCES

Acosta, Carlos. 1991. "Televisa, gigante en crisis de liquidez por tres años de pérdidas y por la salida de socios." *Proceso*, 23 December, 14–19.

Alamilla, Ileana Joáquin Pérez, and Ruth Taylor, eds. 1996. *The Guatemalan Media: The Challenge of Democracy.* Guatemala City: Cerigua.

Albornoz, Luis, P. Hernández, and G. Postolski. 1999. "La televisión digital en la Argentina: Aproximaciones a un proceso incipiente." Typescript. Universidad de Buenos Aires.

Albornoz, Luis, Guillermo Mastrini, and M. Mestman. 1996. "Radiodifusión: Los caminos de la regulación." *Causas y Azares* 4:25–33.

Allyn, Rob. 2000. "Mexico's Big Change." *Campaigns & Elections*, September, 29.

Anderson, John Ward. 2000. "Mexican Papers Use Impartiality to Influence Change: Reforma Group Sets Standard for Election News." *Washington Post*, 22 June, A20.

"Avanza TV Azteca." 1997. *La Jornada*, 16 May, 16.

"Azteca into El Salvador." 1997. *Broadcasting & Cable International*, June, 8.

Baer, Dalel. 2000. Public statements as panelist at "Mexican Politics and Journalism: What Happens Now?" National Press Club, Washington, D.C., 14 September.

Bahiana, Ana Maria. 1994. "Brazil." *Television Business International*, February, 21–22.

Bejarano, M. 1963. *Vias y medios de comunicaciones del Paraguay (1811–1961).* Asunción: Toledo.

Biernazki, Williams. 2000. "Globalização da comunicação." *Comunicação & Educação* 7.

"Big Shuffle in Mexican TV Ownership." 1991. *Variety*, 25 March, 66.

Blume, Klaus. 2000. "Winds of Change Ruffle the Pages of Mexico's Newspaper World." *Deutsche Presse-Agentur*, 27 October.

Bobbio, Norberto, N. Matteucci, and G. Pasquino. 1988. *Diccionario de política.* Mexico: Siglo XXI.

Bodán, Oliver. 1998. "Publicistas deben reevaluar sus estrategias." *Confidencial*, 5 July, 16.

Brecha. 1993. "The Ousting of Arellano." 4 June, 32.

Brewster, Deborah. 1995. "News Links Up with Latin America." *Australian*, 22 November, 37.

Bulloch, Chris. 1997. "DTH in Latin America." *International Cable*, July, 18–22.

Burgelman, Jean-Claude. 1997. "Issues and Assumptions in Communications Policy and Research in Western Europe: A Critical Analysis." In *International Media Research: A Critical Survey*, edited by James Corner, Philip Schlesinger, and Roger Silverstone. New York: Routledge.

Búsqueda. 1990. "Interview with Carlos Maggi." 17 October, 38, 39.

Bustamante, Enrique. 1999. *La televisión económica*. Barcelona: GEDISA.

Cajueiro, Marcelo. 1997. "Brazilian Investors Play Waiting Game." *Variety*, 21–27 July, 28.

Cañizales, Andrés. 1997. "El grupo Cisneros o una recomposición telecomunicacional." *Comunicación*, 98.

Cardoso, Victor. 1997. "Pagan 650 mdd a Televisa por su parte de la empresa PanAmSat." *La Jornada*, 17 May, 16.

Carreño, José. 2000. Public statements as panelist at "Mexican Politics and Journalism: What Happens Now?" at the National Press Club, Washington, D.C., 14 September.

Castells, Manuel. 1996. *The Information Age: Economy, Society, and Culture*. Oxford: Blackwell.

Celis Estrada, Dario. 1997. "Corporativo." *El Financiero*, 26 June, 12.

Chacón, S. 2000. "La televisión del congreso brasileño." In *Los medios públicos de comunicación en el marco de la reforma del Estado de México*, edited by Comisión de Radio, TV y Cine. Mexico: Cámara de Diputados.

Chasan, Alice ed. 1998. *Attacks on the Press in 1997*. New York: Committee to Protect Journalists.

CIIDU. 1986. *SERCOM* 8, 7.

Colina, Carlos Eduardo. 1996. "Venezuela: Hacia un canal de servicio público." *Chasqui* 54 (June): 46–55.

Collins, Richard. 1994. "Trade in Culture: The Role of Language." *Canadian Journal of Communication* 19:377–99.

Committee to Protect Journalists (CPJ). 2000a. "Radio Reporter Stabbed to Death." From CPJ website at: <http://www.cpj.org/news/2000/Mexico 01mayoona.html>.

———. 2000b. "Reporter's Body Dumped over Texas Border." From CPJ website at: <http://www.cpj.org/news/2000/Mexico14apriloona.html>.

Cooper, Ann. 2000. "Letter to Pres. Ernesto Zedillo Ponce de León," 29 June. From CPJ website at: <http://www.cpj.org/protests/00ltrs/Mexico29june 00pl.html>.

Corral, J. 2000. "Canal legislativo: Un reto para la TV pública." In *Los medios públicos de comunicación en el marco de la reforma del Estado de Mexico*, edited by Comisión de Radio, TV y Cine. Mexico: Cámara de Diputados.

Correa Jolly, Fernando. 1992. "La necesidad de un sistema de mercadeo para la radio en Panamá." Typescript. Panama City: University of St. María La Antigua.

"Country profile: Mexico." 1996. *TV International*, 6 May, 5–8.

Crovi Druetta, Delia. 1995. "La industria de la TV por cable en Mexico, antecedentes y perspectives." In *Desarrollo de las industrias audiovisuales en México y Canadá*, edited by Delia Crovi Druetta. Mexico City: UNAM.

Day, James. 1995. *The Vanishing Vision: The Inside Story of Public Television*. Berkeley and Los Angeles: University of California Press.

Dillon, Sam. 2000. "TV Debate Energizes Challenger in Mexico." *New York Times*, 26 April, A9.

Dillon, Sam, and Julie Preston. 2000. "Old Ways Die Hard in Mexican Election despite the Pledges." *New York Times*, 8 May, A1.

Domínguez, R. 1966. *El valle y la loma*. Asunción: Emasa.

Enríquez, Alfredo. 1995. "Television Azteca: Estrategia de un esquema oculto?" In *Desarrollo de las industrias audiovisuales en Mexico y Canadá*, edited by Delia Crovi Druetta. Mexico City: UNAM.

Falkenheim, Jacqueline. 1998. "The Flows of Television Programming in South America." Typescript.

Faraone, Roque. 1989. *Estado y TV en el Uruguay*. Montevideo: FCU.

Folha de São Paulo. 2000. 15 October, 6.

Fox, Elizabeth. 1988a. "Las políticas de los mass media en Latinoamérica." In *Medios de comunicación y política en América Latina*, edited by Elizabeth Fox. Mexico City: Gustavo Gili.

———. 1988b. *Media and Politics in Latin America: The Struggle for Democracy*. London: Sage.

———. 1990. *Dias de baile: El fracaso de la reforma en la televisión de América Latina*. Mexico City: FELAFACS-WACC.

———. 1997. *Latin American Broadcasting: From Tango to Telenovela*. Luton, United Kingdom: University of Luton Press.

Francis, Greg, and Robustiano Fernández. 1997. "Satellites South of the Border." *Via Satellite*, February, 28–42.

Fromson, Murray. 1996. "Mexico's Struggle for a Free Press." In *Communication in Latin America: Journalism, Mass Media, and Society*, edited by Richard R. Cole. Wilmington, Del.: Scholarly Resources.

"FT: La batalla por el control en Televisa parece 'una telenovela.'" 1997. *La Jornada*, 18 June, 24.

Fuenzalida, Valerio. 1997. *Televisión y cultura cotidiana*. Santiago: CPU.

———. 2000. *La televisión pública en América Latina: Reforma o privatización*. Santiago: FCE.

Gaddis Smith, David. 2000. "Journalists Concerned Their Papers Will Fold." *San Diego Union-Tribune*, 8 September, A3.

Galperín, Hernán. 1999. "Cultural Industries in the Age of Free-Trade Agreements." *Canadian Journal of Communication* 24 (1): 49–77.

García Canclini, Néstor. 1990. *Culturas híbridas*. Mexico City: Grijalbo.

García Rubio, Carlos. 1994. *Lo que el cable nos dejó*. Montevideo: Ediciones de la Pluma.

Garnham, Nicholas. 1990. *Capitalism and Communication*. London: Sage.

Gerchunoff, Pablo, and Juan Carlos Torre. 1996. "Argentina: La política de liberalización económica bajo un gobierno de base popular." *Desarrollo Económico* 36:733–68.

Gershon, R. A. 1997. *The Trasnational Media Corporation: Global Messages and Free Market Competition*. Mahwah, N.J.: LEA.

Getino, Octavio. 1998. *La tercera mirada: Panorama del audiovisual Latinoamericano*. Buenos Aires: Paidos.

Glasberg, Rubens. 1995. "Bringing Up Brazil." *Multichannel News International*, April, supplement, 6B, 34–36B.

Godard, François. 1997. "TV Azteca Is Building an Empire." *Broadcasting & Cable International*, October, 48.

González Amador, Roberto. 1997. "Plan Televisa 2000: Disminuir costos de operación por 270 mdd." *La Jornada*, 22 May, 15.

Grupo Televisa. 1997. *Annual Report 1996*. Mexico City: Televisa.

Gruzinski, S. 1994. *La guerra de las imágenes*. Mexico City: FCE.

Guggenheim, Ken. 2000. "Brazen Newcomer's Charisma, Audacity Engineered Victory." *News* (Mexico City), 3 July, 2.

Guia de Programação Net. 2000. October, 8.

Guzmán, Armando. 2000. Public statements as panelist at "Mexican Politics and Journalism: What Happens Now?" at the National Press Club, Washington, D.C., 14 September.

Hall Jamieson, Kathleen. 1988. *Packaging the Presidency*. New York: Oxford University Press.

Herman, Edward, and Robert McChesney. 1997. *The Global Media: The New Missionaries of Corporate Capitalism*. London: Cassell Academic.

Hernández Díaz, Gustavo 1993. "Tendencias de la radiodifusión en Venezuela." *Anuario Ininco* 5:107–29.

Hobsbawn, Eric. 1995. *The Age of Extremes*. London: Abacus.

Hoineff, Nelson. 1993. "Globo Dominates Brazil's $1.3B TV Scene." *Variety*. 29 March. 50. 62.

Hoskins, Colin, Stuart McFayden, and Adam Finn. 1997. *Global Television and Film*. Oxford: Oxford University Press.

Hudson, P. 1998. "Satcaster Galaxy Faces Tough Battle in the Sky." *Variety*, 30 November.

Ícaro Brasil. 2000. "Orelhão.com." October, 22.

Inforpress CentroAmericana. 1998. "Principales medios de comunicación (Honduras, El Salvador y Guatemala)." April.

Instituto Brasileiro de Opinião Pública e Estatística Ltda. (IBOPE). 2000. <www.ibope.com.br/digital/produtos/internet>.

International Telecommunication Union. 1999. *Annual Report.* Geneva: ITU.

Jordan, Mary. 2000. "Mexicans Seek to Lift Government's Veil." *Washington Post,* 16 November, A29.

Jornal do Brasil. 1996. "Grupo Abril inaugura TV digital," 21 June, 19.

Kammer, Jerry. 2000. "Mexican Press Becoming Activist." *Arizona Republic,* 18 June, J1.

Landi, Oscar. 1987. "Medios, procesos culturales y sistema político." In *Medios, transformación cultural y política,* edited by Oscar Landi. Buenos Aires: Legasa.

Lloyd, Marion. 2000. "Turning to New Page, Workers Oust Embattled Head of Mexico Paper." *Boston Globe,* 4 November, C1.

Lovino, G. A. 1998. "Impacto y desarrollo de la TV por cable: Caso Salta Argentina." *Revista latinoamericana de comunicación social* 10. From website at: <www.lazarillo.comj/latinaa/24gustavo.htm>.

McChesney, Robert. 1993. *Telecommunications, Mass Media, and Democracy.* New York: Oxford University Press.

———. 1997. "The Global Media Giants: The Nine Firms That Dominate the World." *Extra!* 10 (6): 12–13.

McQuail, Dennis, and Karen Siune, eds. 1991. *European Media Politics.* London: Sage.

Mandel-Campbell, Andrea. 2000. "Balloon Bursts for PRI's Pet Propaganda Paper." *Financial Times* (London), 27 October, 3.

Martín-Barbero, Jesús. 1987. *De los medios a las mediaciones: Comunicación, cultura y hegemonía.* Mexico City: Gustavo Gili.

———. 1993. *Communication, Culture, and Hegemony: From Media to Mediations.* London: Sage.

Martínez Staines, Javier. 1991. "¿Televisa: Adiós a la familia?" *Expansión,* 1 May, 31–37.

Mastrini, Guillermo. 1999. *Globalización y monopolización en América Latina.* Buenos Aires: Biblos.

Mayobre, José Antonio. 1993. *La labor de Sísifo: Los intentos por cambiar la televisión en Venezuela.* Caracas: Monte Avila Editores.

———. 1996. "Politics, Media, and Modern Democracy: The Case of Venezuela." In *Politics, Media, and Democracy: Innovations in Electoral Campaigning and Their Consequences,* edited by David Swanson and Paolo Mancini. Westport, Conn.: Praeger.

Mejía Barquera, Fernando. 1995. "Echoes of Mexican Media in 1993." *Revista Mexicana de Comunicación* 2:71–91.

Miranda, C. R. 1990. *The Stroessner Era.* Boulder, Colo.: Westview.

Moffett, Matt, and Johnnie Roberts. 1992. "Mexican Media Empire, Grupo Televisa, Casts Its Eye on U.S. Market." *Wall Street Journal,* 30 July, 1, 6A.

Morgan Stanley and Company. 1992. *Grupo Televisa: Company Report.*

Mosco, Vicent. 1996. *The Political Economy of Communication.* London: Sage.

Muraro, Heriberto. 1985. "El modelo latinoamericano." *Telos,* no. 13.

———. 1988. "Dictadura y transición a la democracia: Argentina, 1973–1986." In *Medios de Comunicación y Política en América Latina,* edited by Elizabeth Fox. Mexico City: Gustavo Gili.

Murillo, Victoria. 1998. "Institutions, Politics, and Policy-making: The Case of Regulatory Agencies in Electricity and Telecommunications in Argentina." Typescript. Buenos Aires: Universidad de San Andrés.

Murphy, T. S. 2000. "La comunicación parlamentaria en los Estados Unidos." In *Los Medios públicos de comunicación en el marco de la reforma del Estado de México,* edited by Comisión de Radio, TV y Cine. Mexico City: Cámara de Diputados.

Navarrete, J. 1990. "Cuenta pública del director general de televisión nacional de Chile acerca de la situación actual y el futuro de la empresa." 31 March. Santiago: TVN.

Navarro, Mireya. 1999a. "Man in the News: Francisco Guillermo Flores Pérez; New Salvadoran Puzzle." *New York Times,* 9 March, A10.

———. 1999b. "Woman in the News: Mireya Elisa Moscoso; Earnest Icon for Panama." *New York Times,* 4 May, A11.

Neuman, Russell, L. McKnight, and R. Solomon. 1997. *The Gordian Knot: Political Gridlock in the Information Highway.* Cambridge: MIT Press.

Noam, Eli. 1996. "Media Concentration in the United States: Industry Trends and Regulatory Responses." *Communication & Strategies* 24:11–23.

Noguer, J. 1985. *Radiodifusión en la Argentina.* Buenos Aires: Bien Común.

Nordwall, Smita. 1999. "Panama Elects First Female President." *USA Today,* 4 May, A7.

O'Farrill Avila, José Antonio. 2000. "Under-Table Deals Occurred between the PAN and Former President Salinas." *News* (Mexico City), special section Political Profiles, 12 June, 2–3.

O Globo. 1996. "Pesquisa traça perfil de quem assiste à Net." 21 June, 25.

Olivas, Mireya, and Bernardo Lince. 1996. "15 Minutes with Ernesto Vargas." *Business Mexico,* August, 6–7.

Orme, William A., ed. 1996. *A Culture of Collusion: An Inside Look at the Mexican Press.* Miami: North-South Center Press.

Orué Pozzo, Aníbal. 1997. "Cooperación e investigación en comunicación: Paraguay en la perspectiva del Mercosur." In *Politicas regionais de comunicação,* edited by Maria Vassallo de Lopes and Jose Marques de Melo. São Paulo: UEL-Intercom.

Parker, C. 1999. "Nuevos enfoques sobre pobreza e impacto en programas sociales." *Estudios Sociales* 99. Santiago: CPU.

Paxman, Andrew. 1997. "Satcasters Transmit Signs of Success." *Variety*, 21–27 July, 28.

Pickard, Christopher. 1991. "Abril in Rio: I Want My Pay TV." *Rio Life*, October.

Preston, Julia. 2000. "Mexican TV, Unshackled by Reform, Fights for Viewers." *New York Times*, 7 June, A3.

Przeworski, Adam. 1991. *Democracy and the Market: Political and Economic Reforms in Eastern Europe and Latin America.* New York: Cambridge University Press.

Puig, Carlos. 1997a. "Alemán, de regreso a Televisa, al frente de un compacto grupo de jóvenes priistas." *Proceso*, 30 March, 33.

———. 1997b. "El imperio construido por Emilio Azcárraga en Mexico si tuvo reveses . . . en el extranjero." *Proceso*, 20 April, 12–16.

Ramón Huerta, José. 1997. "Noticias de otro imperio." *Expansión*, 4 June, 19–35.

Rebollo Pinal, Herminio. 1997. "Crece el reclamo NBC contra TV Azteca." *El Financiero*, 8 May, 24.

Recondo, Gregorio, ed. 1997. *Mercosur: La dimensión cultural de la integración.* Buenos Aires: La Crujía.

Rede Globo. 1997. "History of the Company." From website at: <www.redeglobo. com.br/inst/english/inst2.html>.

Reforma. 2000. "Concede mas tiempo la radio a Fox." 30 June, A6.

Rey, Germán. 1998. *De balsas y medusas.* Bogotá: Norma.

Richeri, Giusseppe. 1994. *La transición a la televisión.* Barcelona: Bosch.

Riquelme, Marcial Antonio, et al. 1994. *Negotiating Democratic Corridors in Paraguay.* Pittsburgh, Pa.: University of Pittsburgh.

Rockwell, Rick. 1999. "Killing the Messenger: Methods of Media Repression in Mexico." In *Mexico: Facing the Challenges of Human Rights and Crime,* edited by William Cartwright. Ardsley, N.Y.: Transnational Publishers.

Rodríguez, Francisco, and Arturo Sánchez. 2000. "Investigan rastro de narcos en ataque a tellez." *Reforma* (Mexico City), 24 June, A1.

Romanet, Ignacio. 1996. "Medias en danger." *Le Monde Diplomatique*, February.

Ruhl, J. Mark. 1997. "Doubting Democracy in Honduras." *Current History*, February, 81.

Sánchez Ruiz, Enrique. 1991. "Historia mínima de la televisión mexicana." *Revista Mexicana de Comunicación* 18:29–36.

Secretaría General de Gobierno (SGG). 1999. *Reseña de medios 35: Audiencias y evaluación de informativos.* Santiago: SGG.

Sheridan, Mary Beth. 2000. "Its Own Transition Grips Mexico." *Los Angeles Times*, 28 November, A1.

Sinclair, John. 1986. "Dependent Development and Broadcasting: The 'Mexican Formula.'" *Media, Culture, and Society* 8 (1): 81–101.

———. 1999. *Latin American Broadcasting: A Global View.* Oxford: Oxford University Press.

Sinclair, John, Elizabeth Jacka, and Stuart Cunningham. 1996. "Peripheral Vision." In *New Patterns in Global Television: Peripheral Vision,* edited by John Sinclair, Elizabeth Jacka, and Stuart Cunningham. New York: Oxford University Press.

Skidmore, Thomas E., and Peter H. Smith. 1992. *Modern Latin America.* New York: Oxford University Press.

Stephens, Mitchell. 1988. *A History of News.* New York: Penguin.

Straubhaar, Joseph. 1991. "Beyond Media Imperialism: Assymetrical Interdependence and Cultural Proximity." *Critical Studies in Mass Communication* 8 (1): 39–59.

———. 1996. "The Electronic Media in Brazil." In *Communication in Latin America: Journalism, Mass Media, and Society,* edited by Richard Cole. Wilmington, Del.: Scholarly Resources.

Strover, Sharon, Patrick Burkhart, Omar Hernández, Kenton Wilkinson, and Emile McAnany. 1997. "Global Media and Latin America." Paper presented at the annual conference of the International Association for Media and Communication Research, Oaxaca, Mexico.

Sunkel, Guillermo. 1999. "Consumo de periódicos en la transición democrática chilena." In *El consumo cultural en América Latina.* Bogotá: Convenio Andres Bello.

Sutter, Mary. 1999. "Azteca Struggles On." *Variety,* 29 March–4 April, 45.

Symmes, Patrick. 1997. "The Hacker Tourist Maps Brazil." *Wired,* October, S11–15.

"Televisa anunció oficialmente la compra del canal peruano." 1992. *La Epoca,* 11 July, S33.

"Televisa compró 49 por ciento de Megavisión." 1991. *El Mercurio,* 22 December.

Toussaint, Florence. 1996a. "Entre Sky y Galaxy Latin America." *Proceso,* 22 December, 61.

———. 1996b. "Los retos de la TV por cable." *Proceso,* 15 December, 65.

Tracey, Michael. 1998. *The Decline and Fall of Public Service Broadcasting.* New York: Oxford University Press.

Tremblay, Gaetan. 1988. "La noción de servicio público." *Telos,* no. 114.

Tricks, Henry. 2000. "Mexico's Dream Factory Likely to Lose Charmed Existence: Televisa Faces Future without Its Friends in Former Ruling Party." *Financial Times* (London), USA ed., 26 October, 8.

TVA. 2000. July, 107. From website at: <www.tva.com.br>.

TVN. 1993. *Política editorial de TVN.* October. Santiago: TVN.

United Nations. 1999. *Relatorio de Desenvolvimento da Humanidade.*

United Nations Educational, Scientific, and Cultural Organization (UNESCO).

1996. *Public Service Broadcasting: Cultural and Educational Dimensions.* Paris: UNESCO.

———. 1998. *Annual Yearbook.* Paris: UNESCO.

Valverde, Miguel. 1997. "Las elecciones federales de 1997 según TV Azteca y Televisa." *Revista Mexicana de Comunicación,* May, 21–23.

Vanden Heuvel, Jon, and Everette E. Dennis. 1995. *Changing Patterns: Latin America's Vital Media.* New York: The Freedom Forum Media Center.

Varis, Tapio. 1974. "Global Traffic in Television." *Journal of Communication* 24 (1): 102–9.

Villalobos, Enrique. 1997. *El derecho a la información.* San Jose, Costa Rica: La Editorial Universidad Estatal a Distancia.

Virtue, John, ed. 1996. *Latin American Media Directory.* Miami: Florida International University.

Waisbord, Silvio. 1995. "Leviathan Dreams: State and Broadcasting in South America." *Communication Review,* no. 1.

———. 1998. "The Ties That Still Bind: Media and National Culture in Latin America." *Canadian Journal of Communication* 23:381–411.

———. 2000. *Watchdog Journalism in South America: News, Accountability, and Democracy.* New York: Columbia University Press.

Weiner, Tim. 2000. "Mexico Ending Coziness for Press and Powerful." *New York Times,* 29 October, 12.

Whigham, T. L., and B. Potthast. 1999. "The Paraguayan Rosetta Stone." *Latin American Research Review* 34 (1): 174–86.

Zappa, Regina. 1996. "A vez da inteligência na Internet." *Jornal do Brasil,* 15 May, 18.

Zepeda Patterson, Jorge. 1997. "Neotelevisa." *Siglo 21,* 20 April, 3.

Zerpa, Flor. 1998. "Las nuevas plantas de TV en Venezuela." *Comunicación* 84:17–21.

About the Editors

Elizabeth Fox has published extensively on broadcasting and politics in Latin America. In 1988 she edited *Media and Politics in Latin America: The Struggle for Democracy* (Sage and G. Gili), bringing together leading Latin American scholars to examine the relationship between media and the political turmoil that had engulfed the region. In 1990 she chronicled the early political origins of radio and television, the legacies of censorship and repression, the heyday of unfettered economic growth, and the crushed hopes of public service broadcasting in *Días de Baile: El Fracaso de la Reforma de la Televisión en América Latina* (Felafacs-WACC). In 1997 Fox examined the relationship between Latin American broadcasting and the U.S. government and industry in *Latin American Broadcasting: From Tango to Telenovela* (University of Luton Press). She continues to publish extensively on Latin American media and development issues, currently from the Office of Health and Nutrition at USAID where she applies lessons from the changing media environment to health and nutrition programs worldwide.

Silvio Waisbord is an associate professor in the Department of Journalism and Media Studies and director of the Journalism Resources Institute at Rutgers University. He is the author, most recently, of *Watchdog Journalism in South America: News, Accountability and Democracy* (Columbia University Press), and the co-editor of *Media and Globalization: Why the State Matters* (Rowan and Littlefield). Waisbord has published in several academic journals in the United States, Europe, and Latin America. He was a fellow at the Kellogg Institute for International Studies at the University of Notre Dame, the Annenberg School for Communication at the University of Pennsylvania, the Center for Critical Analysis of Contemporary Cultures, and the Freedom Forum's Media Studies Center in New York City.

About the Contributors

Hernán Galperín is an assistant professor at the Annenberg School for Communication, University of Southern California. He holds a social science degree from the University of Buenos Aires, Argentina, and a Ph.D. in Communication from Stanford University. His research and teaching interests include comparative communication policy, international audiovisual trade, and regulatory reform in Latin America. He is currently working on a book about digital TV in the United States and the European Union. His research has been published in article collections and journals such as the *Canadian Jour-*

nal of Communication, Telecommunications Policy, and *Media, Culture, and Society.*

Roberto Amaral is the editor of *Comunicação e Política,* Rio de Janeiro, Brazil. He has written extensively about politics and communication in Brazil.

Rick Rockwell is an assistant professor of journalism at American University in Washington, D.C. He is the coauthor of the forthcoming book *Media Power in Central America.* Previously, Rockwell was a journalist covering Mexico and Central America for the Associated Press, PBS, and other media outlets. In 2000, he covered the historic Mexican elections for the political magazine *In These Times* and also contributed to the book *Mexico: Facing the Challenges of Human Rights and Crime.* A graduate of the Medill School of Journalism at Northwestern University, he also holds a master's degree in international journalism from the University of Southern California.

Noreene Janus recently carried out a major review, with Rick Rockwell, of the Central American media environment for USAID's program of media and democracy. It was an evaluation of a twenty-year program to train journalists in the region. Janus has worked extensively in Latin America, mainly in Mexico with the Latin American Institute of Transnational Studies (ILET). Upon her return to the United States, she wrote two major source books on the Latin American media.

Valerio Fuenzalida Fernández is a Chilean TV producer and media researcher who specializes in audience reception studies. Fuenzalida is a professor in the graduate program in communication at the Diego Portales University in Santiago de Chile. He has been a consultant for UNESCO, UNICEF, CEPAL-FAO, IICA, and CIESPAL, among others. He has published widely on issues of Latin American television and public broadcasting. In 1990 Fuenzalida joined the new administration of the Chilean National Television Channel, TVN, where he worked on the reform process. He is currently the chief of qualitative research at the programming office of TVN.

Fernando Calero Aparicio heads the Office of Planning of the Comisión Nacional de Televisión in Colombia. He is on the faculty of the School of Social Communication at the Universidad del Valle. He has worked in the IberoAmerican Association of Educational Television, Telepacífico, and Inravisión. He has authored several articles and reports on the state of television in Colombia and Latin America.

John Sinclair is a professor in the Department of Communication, Language, and Cultural Studies at Victoria University of Technology, Australia. He is the author of *Latin American Broadcasting* (Oxford University Press) and coauthor of *Floating Lives: The Media and Asian Diasporas.* He has written extensively about media industries in Latin America, technology, and media and culture.

Aníbal Orué Pozzo is chair of the Department of Communication in the Universidad Católica in Asunción, Paraguay. He is the author of numerous articles about media and politics in Paraguay and in the MERCOSUR.

Luis Peirano is the author of a book about the contradictions in the Peruvian military's reform of the Peruvian press. He followed this book with an insightful publication on the overall impact of the Peruvian military's almost two-decade rule on the media. For the five years, Peirano was the director of DESCO, Peru's largest private research and action group working in the area of popular movements and social change. Peirano left DESCO to become the dean of the school of communication of the Catholic University of Peru. In addition to his academic career, Peirano is one of Peru's leading theater directors.

Roque Faraone is a Uruguayan lawyer, who, before going into exile in 1974, wrote the first book on the Uruguayan media. He spent the next fifteen years in Paris as a correspondent for Agence France Press and consultant to UNESCO. He returned to his country, now a democracy, in 1990, and was reinstated as dean of the school of communication of the Federal University of Uruguay, where he continues to teach. He has just published *Televisión y Estado,* a book that analyzes the new television environment in Uruguay.

José Antonio Mayobre worked in the Venezuelan government during the period of media reform in the early 1970s. He then worked in Paris as the UNESCO Latin American desk officer for communications. Upon his return to Venezuela he established CIEDESCO, an independent research center dedicated to the analysis of media and development. He has owned and operated radio stations in Caracas and published widely in the field. José Antonio died in Caracas on December 17, 2000, after a long illness.

I N D E X